ABORTION DECISIONS
OF THE UNITED STATES
SUPREME COURT

THE 1990'S

MAUREEN HARRISON & STEVE GILBERT
EDITORS

ABORTION DECISIONS SERIES

EXCELLENT BOOKS
BEVERLY HILLS, CALIFORNIA

EXCELLENT BOOKS
Post Office Box 7121
Beverly Hills, CA 90212-7121

Publisher's Cataloging in Publication Data

Abortion Decisions of the United States Supreme Court: The 1990's/
  Maureen Harrison, Steve Gilbert, editors.
  p. cm. - (Abortion Decisions Series)
  Bibliography: p.
  Includes Index.
  1. Abortion - United States, 2. Abortion - Political Aspects -
  United States, 3. Abortion - Government Policy, 4. Abortion -
  Law and Legislation, 5. United States Supreme Court
  I. Title. II. Harrison, Maureen. III. Gilbert, Steve.
  IV. Series: Abortion Decisions.
  HQ767.5.U5 H24 1993 LC 92-75836
  363.4'6 - dc20

ISBN 0-9628014-6-1

Introduction

"The right of privacy [founded] in the Fourteenth Amendment's concept of personal liberty and restrictions upon state action . . . is broad enough to encompass a woman's decision whether or not to terminate her pregnancy."

Justice Harry Blackmun
Roe v. Wade (1973)

"For today, at least, the law of abortion stands undisturbed. For today, the women of this Nation still retain the liberty to control their destinies. But the signs are evident and very ominous, and a chill wind blows."

Justice Harry Blackmun
Webster v. Reproductive Health (1989)

"I am 83 years old. I cannot remain on this Court forever, and when I do step down, the confirmation process for my successor well may focus on the issue before us today. That, I regret, may be exactly where the choice between the two worlds will be made."

Justice Harry Blackmun
Planned Parenthood v. Casey (1992)

Twenty-one times in the twenty years since the *Roe* decision, the United States Supreme Court has issued major abortion decisions. The legal war of words that has resulted in challenges to and defenses of the right of women to choose abortion is the reason for the Abortion Decisions Series. This book, the third in the Abortions Decisions Series, covers the Supreme Court's five major abortion decisions issued to date in the decade of the 1990's.

In 1973 the *Roe* Court divided 7-2 on the question of the constitutionality of the Texas abortion law. The majority and minority of that court were:

Warren Burger

William O. Douglas

William Brennan, Jr.

Potter Stewart

Thurgood Marshall

Harry A. Blackmun

Lewis Powell, Jr.

Byron R. White

William H. Rehnquist

In 1992 the *Casey* Court divided 5-4 on the question of the constitutionality of the Pennsylvania abortion law. The majority and minority of that court were:

Harry Blackmun

John Paul Stevens

Sandra Day O'Connor

Anthony Kennedy

David Souter

William Rehnquist

Byron White

Antonin Scalia

Clarence Thomas

The evolution of the Court from *Roe* to *Casey* can be traced as follows: In 1975 Justice Douglas resigned from the Court and was replaced by President Ford's only appointee, John Paul Stevens. In 1981 Justice Stewart resigned and was replaced by President Reagan's first appointee, Sandra Day O'Connor. In 1986 Chief Justice Burger resigned from the Court and was replaced by President Reagan's second appointee, Associate Justice William Rehnquist. The Associate Justice seat on the Court vacated by William Rehnquist was filled in that same year by President Reagan's third appointee, Antonin Scalia. In 1988 Justice Powell resigned from the Court and was replaced by President Reagan's fourth, and last, appointee, Anthony Kennedy. In 1991 Justice Brennan resigned from the Court and was replaced by President Bush's first appointee, David Souter. In 1992 Justice Marshall resigned from the Court and was replaced by President Bush's second appointee, Clarence Thomas.

The first book in the Abortion Decisions Series details the eight major abortion decisions issued by the U.S. Supreme Court in the 1970's. The second book details the eight major abortion decisions issued in the 1980's. This book, the third in the Abortion Decisions Series, details the five major abortion decisions issued in the first years of the 1990's.

For the first time, these five decisions are presented in plain English for the general reader. In each of these carefully edited versions of the official texts issued by the Supreme Court, the editors have tried to decipher the Court's legalese without damaging or diminishing the original decision. Edited out are alpha-numeric legal citations, micro print footnotes, and wordy wrangles over points of procedure. Edited in [in brackets] are definitions [*stare decisis* = leave past decisions undisturbed], translations [*certiorari* = the decision of the Court to review a case], identifications [Appellant = Roe, Appellee = Wade], and explanations [where the case originated, how it got before the court, and who the major parties were]. You will find in this book the majority opinion of the Court as expressed by the Justice chosen to speak for the Court. All concurring and dissenting opinions of the Justices are included. A complete copy of the United States Constitution, to which all the decisions refer, follows the abortion decisions.

The Supreme Court of the United States is the court of final appeal for all legal controversies arising in the federal courts and all federal issues arising in the state courts.

Only the Court has the authority to construct and interpret the meaning of the Constitution. "We are not final," wrote Justice Robert Jackson, "because we are infallible, but we are infallible because we are final." From 1857's Slavery Decision in *Dred Scott* to 1973's Abortion Decision in *Roe v. Wade*, controversy and the Court have been longtime companions.

Justice Oliver Wendell Holmes wrote: "[The Constitution] is made for people of fundamentally differing views, and the accident of our finding certain opinions natural and familiar or novel and even shocking ought not to conclude our judgment upon the question whether statutes embodying them conflict with the United States Constitution."

Those "fundamentally differing opinions" are evident in the five major abortion decisions issued in the 1990's:

In 1990's *Hodgson v. Minnesota*, at issue is the constitutionality of Minnesota's two-parent notification for a minor's abortion. The parties are Jane Hodgson and the State of Minnesota. The majority decision of the Court is by Justice John Paul Stevens.

In 1990's *Arkon v. Ohio*, called *Akron II*, at issue is the constitutionality Ohio's abortion law for minors. The parties are the State of Ohio and the Akron Center for Reproductive Health. The majority decision of the Court is by Justice Anthony Kennedy.

In 1991's *Rust v. Sullivan*, at issue is the constitutionality of the "gag rule" imposed on federally funded family planning clinics by the U.S. Government. The parties are Irving Rust, representing providers of family planning services, and Louis Sullivan, Secretary, U.S. Department of

Health and Human Services. The majority decision of the Court is by Chief Justice William Rehnquist.

In 1992's *Casey v. Planned Parenthood*, at issue is the constitutionality of Pennsylvania's abortion laws. The parties are Robert Casey, Governor, Pennsylvania, and Planned Parenthood of Southeastern Pennsylvania. The majority decision of the Court is by Justices Sandra Day O'Connor, Anthony Kennedy and David Souter.

In 1993's *Bray v. Alexandria Women's Health Clinic*, at issue is the applicability of the Civil Rights [Ku Klux] Act of 1871 to abortion blockade cases. While strictly speaking a civil rights case, we include it here for its impact on access to abortion. The parties are Jayne Bray, a member of Operation Rescue, and Alexandria Women's Health Clinic. The majority decision of the Court is by Justice Antonin Scalia.

Nowhere in the twenty-one abortion decisions in this three book series have we found a clearer example of the divisions within the Court than in the 1992 *Casey* decision wherein Justices O'Connor, Kennedy, and Souter write: "Liberty finds no refuge in a jurisprudence of doubt," to which Chief Justice Rehnquist answers: "Reason finds no refuge in this jurisprudence of confusion."

Judge Learned Hand wrote: "The language of the law must not be foreign to the ears of those who are to obey it." This is the last of three volumes that will reproduce in readable form the abortion decisions of the United States Supreme Court. We have tried as hard as we could, as Judge Hand urged us, to make these decisions less foreign to your ears.

M.H. & S.G.

ABOUT THE EDITORS
OF THE ABORTION DECISIONS SERIES

MAUREEN HARRISON is a textbook editor and a
member of the Supreme Court Historical Society

STEVE GILBERT is a law librarian and a member of the
American Association of Law Libraries and the
American Bar Association

Harrison & Gilbert are also the editors of:

THE LANDMARK DECISIONS SERIES

THE AMERICANS WITH DISABILITIES ACT
HANDBOOK

THE ABORTION LAW SOURCEBOOK

TABLE OF CONTENTS

HODGSON v. MINNESOTA

EXCERPTS

"The constitutional protection against unjustified state intrusion into the process of deciding whether or not to bear a child extends to pregnant minors as well as adult women."

Justice John Paul Stevens

"Parental authority is not limitless. Certainly where parental involvement threatens to harm the child, the parent's authority must yield."

Justice Thurgood Marshall

"[T]he tools for this job are not to be found in the lawyer's - and hence not in the judge's - workbox. I continue to dissent from this enterprise of devising an Abortion Code, and from the illusion that we have authority to do so."

Justice Antonin Scalia

In Brief

Question: Is Minnesota's two-parent notification for a
minor's abortion unconstitutional?

Lower Court: U.S. District Court, Minnesota
U.S. Court of Appeals, Eighth Circuit

Law: Minnesota Statutes, Sections 144.343(2)-(7) (1988)

Parties: Jane Hodgson
The State of Minnesota

Counsel: For Hodgson: Janet Benshoof
For Minnesota: John Tunheim

Arguments: November 29, 1989

Decision: June 25, 1990

Majority: Justice Stevens, Brennan, Marshall, Blackmun,
O'Connor

Minority: Chief Justice Rehnquist, Justices White, Scalia,
Kennedy

Decision by: Justice Stevens (p. 5)

Concurrences: Justice O'Connor (p. 20)

Concurring in part/Dissenting in part:

         Justice Marshall (p. 21)
Justice Scalia (p. 30)
Justice Kennedy (p. 31)

Offical Text: U.S. Reports, Vol. 497
Lower Court: Federal Supplement, Vol. 648, p. 756
Federal Reporter 2d, Vol. 853, p. 1452

THE HODGSON COURT

Chief Justice William Rehnquist
Appointed Associate Justice 1971 by Richard M. Nixon
Appointed Chief Justice 1986 by Ronald W. Reagan

Associate Justice William Brennan
Appointed 1956 by Dwight D. Eisenhower

Associate Justice Byron White
Appointed 1962 by John F. Kennedy

Associate Justice Thurgood Marshall
Appointed 1967 by Lyndon B. Johnson

Associate Justice Harry Blackmun
Appointed 1970 by Richard M. Nixon

Associate Justice John Paul Stevens
Appointed 1975 by Gerald R. Ford

Associate Justice Sandra Day O'Connor
Appointed 1981 by Ronald W. Reagan

Associate Justice Antonin Scalia
Appointed 1986 by Ronald W. Reagan

Associate Justice Anthony Kennedy
Appointed 1988 by Ronald W. Reagan

HODGSON v. MINNESOTA

June 25, 1990

JUSTICE STEVENS: A Minnesota statute, Section 144.343(2)-(7), provides, with certain exceptions, that no abortion shall be performed on a woman under 18 years of age until at least 48 hours after both of her parents have been notified. In subdivisions 2-4 of the statute the notice is mandatory unless (1) the attending physician certifies that an immediate abortion is necessary to prevent the woman's death and there is insufficient time to provide the required notice; (2) both of her parents have consented in writing; or (3) the woman declares that she is a victim of parental abuse or neglect, in which event notice of her declaration must be given to the proper authorities. The United States Court of Appeals for the Eighth Circuit . . . unanimously held this provision unconstitutional. [We agreed] to review that holding. Subdivision 6 of the same statute provides that if a court enjoins [stops] the enforcement of subdivision 2, the same notice requirement shall be effective unless the pregnant woman obtains a court order permitting the abortion to proceed. By a vote of 7-3, the Court of Appeals upheld the constitutionality of subdivision 6. [We also agreed] to review that holding.

For reasons that follow, we now conclude that the requirement of notice to both of the pregnant minor's parents is not reasonably related to legitimate state interests and that subdivision 2 is unconstitutional. A different majority of the Court, for reasons stated in separate opinions, concludes that subdivision 6 is constitutional. Accordingly, the judgment of the Court of Appeals in its entirety is affirmed [confirmed].

The parental notice statute was enacted in 1981 as an amendment to the Minor's Consent to Health Services Act. The earlier statute ... had modified the common law [judicial rather than legislative law] requirement of parental consent for any medical procedure performed on minors. It authorized "any minor" to give effective consent without any parental involvement for the treatment of "pregnancy and conditions associated therewith, venereal disease, alcohol and other drug abuse." The statute, unlike others of its age, applied to abortion *services.*

The 1981 amendment qualified the authority of an "unemancipated minor" to give effective consent to an abortion by requiring that either her physician or an agent notify "the parent" personally or by certified mail at least 48 hours before the procedure is performed. The term "parent" is defined in subdivision 3 to mean "both parents of the pregnant woman if they are both living." No exception is made for a divorced parent, a noncustodial parent, or a biological parent who never married or lived with the pregnant woman's mother. The statute does provide, however, that if only one parent is living, or "if the second one cannot be located through reasonably diligent effort," notice to one parent is sufficient. It also makes exceptions for cases in which emergency treatment prior to notice "is necessary to prevent the woman's death," both parents have already given their consent in writing, or the proper authorities are advised that the minor is a victim of sexual or physical abuse. The statute subjects a person performing an abortion in violation of its terms to criminal sanctions and to civil liability in an action brought by any person "wrongfully denied notification."

Subdivision 6 authorizes a judicial bypass of the two-parent notice requirement if subdivision 2 is ever "temporarily or permanently" [stopped] by judicial order. If the pregnant minor can convince "any judge of a court of competent jurisdiction" that she is "mature and capable of giving informed consent to the proposed abortion," or that an abortion without notice to both parents would be in her best interest, the court can authorize the physician to proceed without notice. The statute provides that the bypass procedure shall be confidential, that it shall be expedited, that the minor has a right to court-appointed counsel, and that she shall be afforded free access to the court "24 hours a day, seven days a week." An order denying an abortion can be appealed on an expedited basis, but an order authorizing an abortion without notification is not subject to appeal.

. . . . The District Court found that the primary purpose of the legislation was to protect the well-being of minors by encouraging them to discuss with their parents the decision whether to terminate their pregnancies. It also found that the legislature was motivated by a desire to deter and dissuade minors from choosing to terminate their pregnancies. . . .

This litigation was commenced on July 30, 1981, two days before the effective date of the parental notification statute. The plaintiffs include two Minnesota doctors who specialize in obstetrics and gynecology, four clinics providing abortion and contraceptive services in metropolitan areas in Minnesota, six pregnant minors representing a class [a group with similar characteristics] of pregnant minors, and the mother of a pregnant minor. [Hodgson] alleged that the statute violated the Due Process and

Equal Protection Clauses of the Fourteenth Amendment and various provisions of the Minnesota Constitution.

.... [T]he District Court entered a temporary restraining order [stopping] the enforcement of subdivision 2 of the statute. After a hearing, the court entered a preliminary injunction [court order stopping an action] which still remains in effect. ...

In 1986, after a 5-week trial, the District Court concluded that both the two-parent notification requirement and the 48-hour waiting period were invalid. It further concluded that the definition of the term "parent," which is carried over into the notification requirement, was not severable from the remainder of the statute. The court declared the entire statute unconstitutional and [stopped Minnesota] from enforcing it.

A three-judge panel of the Court of Appeals affirmed. The court first held that a compulsory notification requirement is invalid if it does not provide the pregnant minor with the option of an alternative court procedure in which she can demonstrate either her maturity or that performance of an abortion without notification would be in her best interests. Second, relying heavily on the findings of the District Court concerning the impact of a two-parent notice requirement on families in which the parents are divorced, separated, or unmarried, the panel also concluded that the unconstitutional notification requirement could not be saved by the judicial bypass. ...

The panel opinion was vacated [annulled] and the Court of Appeals reheard the case. ... The court unanimously and summarily rejected the State's submission that the two-parent notice requirement was constitutional without any bypass procedure. The majority concluded, however, that subdivision 6 of the statute was valid. . . .

After noting that the State did not challenge the District Court's findings, the court concluded that these findings placed undue emphasis on one-parent and no-parent households. For even though the two-parent notice requirement may not further the interests of the pregnant minor in such cases, the rights of "best-interest" and mature minors were nevertheless protected by the bypass procedure. More importantly, "as applied to all pregnant minors, regardless of their family circumstances, the district court did not consider whether parental and family interests (as distinguished from the interests of the minor alone) justified the two-parent notice requirement." . . .

The Court of Appeals also rejected the argument that the 48-hour waiting period imposed a significant burden on the minor's abortion right, finding that the waiting period could run concurrently with the scheduling of an appointment for the procedure. Accordingly, the court reversed the judgment of the District Court. . . .

We granted certiorari [agreed to hear the case].

There is a natural difference between men and women: only women have the capacity to bear children. A woman's decision to conceive or to bear a child is a component of her liberty that is protected by the Due Process Clause of the Fourteenth Amendment to the Constitution. That Clause . . . protects the woman's right to make such decisions independently and privately, free of unwarranted governmental intrusion.

. . . . [T]he constitutional protection against unjustified state intrusion into the process of deciding whether or not to bear a child extends to pregnant minors as well as adult women.

In cases involving abortion, as in cases involving the right to travel or the right to marry, the identification of the constitutionally protected interest is merely the beginning of the analysis. State regulation of travel and of marriage is obviously permissible even though a State may not categorically exclude nonresidents from its borders, or deny prisoners the right to marry. But the regulation of constitutionally protected decisions, such as where a person shall reside or whom he or she shall marry, must be predicated on legitimate state concerns other than disagreement with the choice the individual has made. In the abortion area, a State may have no obligation to spend its own money, or use its own facilities, to subsidize nontherapeutic abortions for minors or adults. A State's value judgment favoring childbirth over abortion may provide adequate support for decisions involving such allocation of public funds, but not for simply substituting a state decision for an individual decision that a woman has a right to make for herself. Otherwise, the interest in liberty protected by the Due Process Clause would be a nullity. A state policy favoring childbirth over abortion is not in itself a sufficient justification for overriding the woman's decision or for placing "obstacles - absolute or otherwise - in the pregnant woman's path to an abortion."

. . . . Because the Minnesota statute unquestionably places obstacles in the pregnant minor's path to an abortion, the State has the burden of establishing its constitutionality. Under any analysis, the Minnesota statute cannot be sustained [granted] if the obstacles it imposes are not reasonably related to legitimate state interests.

The Court has considered the constitutionality of statutes providing for parental consent or parental notification in six abortion cases decided during the last 14 years. Although the Massachusetts statute reviewed in *Belotti v. Baird* and *Belotti II* required the consent of both parents, and the Utah statute reviewed in *H.L. v. Matheson* required notice to "the parents," none of the opinions in any of those cases focused on the possible significance of making the consent or the notice requirement applicable to both parents instead of just one. In contrast, the arguments in these cases, as well as the extensive findings of the District Court, are directed primarily at that distinction. . . .

Approximately one out of every two marriages ends in divorce. Unrebutted evidence indicates that only 50% of minors in the State of Minnesota reside with both biological parents. This conclusion is substantially corroborated by a study indicating that 9% of the minors in Minnesota live with neither parent and 33% live with only one parent.

The District Court found - on the basis of extensive testimony at trial - that the two-parent notification requirement had particularly harmful effects on both the minor and the custodial parent when the parents were divorced or separated. . . .

The District Court also found that the two-parent notification requirement had adverse effects in families in which the minor lives with both parents. These effects were particularly pronounced in the distressingly large number of cases in which family violence is a serious problem. . . . The District Court found that few minors can take advantage of the exception for a minor who declares that she is a victim of sexual or physical abuse because of the obligation to report the information to the authorities and the attendant loss of privacy. This concern about family violence helps to explain why the District Court found that in many instances the requirement that both parents be notified actually impairs family communication. Minors who otherwise would inform one parent were unwilling to do so when such notification likely would also involve the parent in the torturous ordeal of explaining to a court why the second parent should not be notified. . . .

The great majority of bypass petitions are filed in the three metropolitan counties in Minnesota, where courts schedule bypass hearings on a regular basis and have in place procedures for hearing emergency petitions. Courts in the non-metropolitan areas are acquainted with the statute and, for the most part, apply it conscientiously, but a number of counties are served by judges who are unwilling to hear bypass petitions. Aside from the unavoidable notification of court officials, the confidentiality of minors has been maintained.

During the period between August 1, 1981, and March 1, 1986, 3,573 judicial bypass petitions were filed in Minnesota courts. All but 15 were granted. The judges who adjudicated over 90% of these petitions testified; none of them identified any positive effects of the law. The court experience produced fear, tension, anxiety, and shame among minors, causing some who were mature, and some whose best interests would have been served by an abortion, to "forgo the bypass option and either notify their

parents or carry to term." Among parents who supported
their daughters in the bypass proceedings, the court experience evoked similar reactions.

Scheduling petitions in the Minnesota court typically required minors to wait only two or three days for hearings.
The District Court found, however, that the statutory
waiting period of 48 hours was frequently compounded
by a number of other factors that "commonly" created a
delay of 72 hours, and, "in many cases" a delay of a week
or more in effecting a decision to terminate a pregnancy.
A delay of that magnitude increased the medical risk associated with the abortion procedure to "a statistically significant degree." While recognizing that a mandatory delay following the notice to a minor's parent served the
State's interest in protecting pregnant minors, the court
found that that interest could be served by a shorter waiting period.

. . . . Three separate but related interests - the interest in
the welfare of the pregnant minor, the interest of the parents, and the interest of the family unit - are relevant to
our consideration of the constitutionality of the 48-hour
waiting period and the two-parent notification requirement.

The State has a strong and legitimate interest in the welfare of its young citizens, whose immaturity, inexperience,
and lack of judgment may sometimes impair their ability
to exercise their rights wisely. That interest, which justifies state-imposed requirements that a minor obtain his or
her parent's consent before undergoing an operation, mar-
rying, or entering military service, extends also to the
minor's decision to terminate her pregnancy. Although
the Court has held that parents may not exercise "an abso-

lute, and possibly arbitrary, veto" over that decision, it has never challenged a State's reasonable judgment that the decision should be made after notification to and consultation with a parent. . . .

Parents have an interest in controlling the education and upbringing of their children but that interest is "a counterpart of the responsibilities they have assumed." The fact of biological parentage generally offers a person only "an opportunity . . . to develop a relationship with his offspring." But the demonstration of commitment to the child through the assumption of personal, financial, or custodial responsibility may give the natural parent a stake in the relationship with the child rising to the level of a liberty interest.

While the State has a legitimate interest in the creation and dissolution of the marriage contract, the family has a privacy interest in the upbringing and education of children and the intimacies of the marital relationship which is protected by the Constitution against undue state interference. . . .

A natural parent who has demonstrated sufficient commitment to his or her children is thereafter entitled to raise the children free from undue state interference. As Justice White explained in his opinion for the Court in *Stanley v. Illinois*:

" . . . . The integrity of the family unit has found protection in the Due Process Clause of the Fourteenth Amendment, the Equal Protection Clause of the Fourteenth Amendment, and the Ninth Amendment."

We think it is clear that a requirement that a minor wait 48 hours after notifying a single parent of her intention to get an abortion would reasonably further the legitimate state interest in ensuring that the minor's decision is knowing and intelligent. We have held that when a parent or another person has assumed "primary responsibility" for a minor's well-being, the State may properly enact "laws designed to aid discharge of that responsibility." To the extent that subdivision 2 of the Minnesota statute requires notification of only one parent, it does just that. The brief waiting period provides the parent the opportunity to consult with his or her spouse and a family physician, and it permits the parent to inquire into the competency of the doctor performing the abortion, discuss the religious or moral implications of the abortion decision, and provide the daughter needed guidance and counsel in evaluating the impact of the decision on her future.

The 48-hour delay imposes only a minimal burden on the right of the minor to decide whether or not to terminate her pregnancy. Although the District Court found that scheduling factors, weather, and the minor's school and work commitments may combine, in many cases, to create a delay of a week or longer between the initiation of notification and the abortion, there is no evidence that the 48-hour period itself is unreasonable or longer than appropriate for adequate consultation between parent and child. The statute does not impose any period of delay once the parents or a court, acting in loco parentis [in place of the parent], express their agreement that the minor is mature or that the procedure would be in her best interest. Indeed, as the Court of Appeals noted and the record reveals, the 48-hour waiting period may run concurrently with the time necessary to make an appointment for the procedure, thus resulting in little or no delay.

It is equally clear that the requirement that *both* parents
be notified, whether or not both wish to be notified or
have assumed responsibility for the upbringing of the
child, does not reasonably further any legitimate state interest. The usual justification for a parental consent or
notification provision is that it supports the authority of a
parent who is presumed to act in the minor's best interest
and thereby assures that the minor's decision to terminate
her pregnancy is knowing, intelligent, and deliberate. To
the extent that such an interest is legitimate, it would be
fully served by a requirement that the minor notify one
parent who can then seek the counsel of his or her mate
or any other party, when such advice and support is
deemed necessary to help the child make a difficult decision. . . .

Not only does two-parent notification fail to serve any
state interest with respect to functioning families, it dis-
serves the state interest in protecting and assisting the
minor with respect to dysfunctional families. The record
reveals that in the thousands of dysfunctional families
affected by this statute, the two-parent notice requirement proved positively harmful to the minor and her
family. . . .

[A] state interest in standardizing its children and adults,
making the "private realm of family life" conform to
some state-designed ideal, is not a legitimate state interest
at all.

Nor can any state interest in protecting a parent's interest
in shaping a child's values and lifestyle overcome the liberty interests of a minor acting with the consent of a single parent or court. . . . It follows that the combined force
of the separate interest of one parent and the minor's

privacy interest must outweigh the separate interest of the second parent.

. . . . Unsurprisingly, the Minnesota two-parent notification requirement is an oddity among state and federal consent provisions governing the health, welfare, and education of children. A minor desiring to enlist in the armed services or the Reserve Officers' Training Corps (ROTC) need only obtain the consent of "his parent or guardian." The consent of "*a* parent or guardian" is also sufficient to obtain a passport for foreign travel from the United States Department of State, and to participate as a subject in most forms of medical research. In virtually every State, the consent of one parent is enough to obtain a driver's license or operator's permit. The same may be said with respect to the decision to submit to any medical or surgical procedure other than an abortion. Indeed, the only other Minnesota statute that the State has identified which requires two-parent consent is that authorizing the minor to change his name. These statutes provide testimony to the unreasonableness of the Minnesota two-parent notification requirement and to the ease with which the State can adopt less burdensome means to protect the minor's welfare. We therefore hold that this requirement violates the Constitution.

The Court holds that the constitutional objection to the two-parent notice requirement is removed by the judicial bypass option provided in subdivision 6 of the Minnesota statute. I respectfully dissent from that holding.

A majority of the Court has previously held that a statute requiring one's parent's consent to a minor's abortion will be upheld if the State provides an '"alternate procedure whereby a pregnant minor may demonstrate that she is

sufficiently mature to make the abortion decision herself
or that, despite her immaturity, an abortion would be in
her best interests.'" Indeed, in *Belotti II,* four Members of
the Court expressed the same opinion about a statute requiring the consent of both parents. Neither of those
precedents [past decisions] should control our decision today.

. . . . The significance of the distinction between a statute
requiring the consent of one parent and a statute requiring notice to both parents must be tested by the relationship of the respective requirements to legitimate state interests. We have concluded that the State has a strong and
legitimate interest in providing a pregnant minor with the
advice and support of a parent during the decisional period. A general rule requiring the minor to obtain the consent of one parent reasonably furthers that interest. An
exception from the general rule is necessary to protect the
minor from an arbitrary veto that is motivated by the
separate concerns of the parent rather than the best interest of the child. But the need for an exception does not
undermine the conclusion that the general rule is perfectly reasonable - just as a rule requiring the consent of either parent for any other medical procedure would surely
be reasonable if an exception were made for those emergencies in which, for example, a parent might deny life
saving treatment to a child on religious grounds.

. . . . [A] rule requiring consent or notification of both
parents is not reasonably related to the state interest in
giving the pregnant minor the benefit of parental advice.
The State has not called our attention to, nor am I aware
of, any other medical situation in Minnesota or elsewhere
in which the provision of treatment for a child has been
conditioned on notice to, or consent by, both parents rath-

er than just one. Indeed, the fact that one-parent consent is the virtually uniform rule for any other activity which affects the minor's health, safety or welfare emphasizes the aberrant quality of the two-parent notice requirement.

A judicial bypass that is designed to handle exceptions from a reasonable general rule, and thereby preserve the constitutionality of that rule, is quite different from a requirement that a minor - or a minor and one of her parents - must apply to a court for permission to avoid the application of a rule that is not reasonably related to legitimate state goals. A requirement that a minor acting with the consent of *both* parents apply to a court for permission to effectuate her decision clearly would constitute an unjustified official interference with the privacy of the minor and her family. The requirement that the bypass procedure must be invoked when the minor and one parent agree that the other parent should not be notified represents an equally unjustified governmental intrusion into the family's decisional process. When the parents are living together and have joint custody over the child, the State has no legitimate interest in the communication between father and mother about the child. "[W]here the parents are divorced, the minor and/or custodial parent, and not a court, is in the best position to determine whether notifying the non-custodial parent would be in the child's best interests." As the Court of Appeals panel originally concluded, the "minor and custodial parent, . . . by virtue of their major interest and superior position, should alone have the opportunity to decide to whom, if anyone, notice of the minor's abortion decision should be given." I agree with that conclusion.

The judgment of the Court of Appeals in its entirety is affirmed.

It is so ordered.

JUSTICE O'CONNOR, concurring in part and concurring in the judgment in part: . . . . I agree that the Court has characterized "[a] woman's decision to conceive or to bear a child [as] a component of her liberty that is protected by the Due Process Clause of the Fourteenth Amendment to the Constitution." This Court extended that liberty interest to minors in *Belotti v. Baird* and *Planned Parenthood of Central Missouri v. Danforth*, albeit with some important limitations. . . .

It has been my understanding in this area that "[i]f the particular regulation does not 'unduly burde[n]' the fundamental right, . . . then our evaluation of that regulation is limited to our determination that the regulation rationally relates to a legitimate state purpose." It is with that understanding that I agree with Justice Stevens' statement that the "statute cannot be sustained [granted] if the obstacles it imposes are not reasonably related to legitimate state interests."

I agree with Justice Stevens that Minnesota has offered no sufficient justification for its interference with the family's decisionmaking processes created by subdivision 2 - two-parent notification. Subdivision 2 is the most stringent notification statute in the country. The only other state that defines the generic term "parents" as "both parents" is Arkansas, and that statute provides for numerous exceptions to the two-parent notification requirement and permits bypassing notification where notification would not be in the best interests of the minor.

The Minnesota exception to notification for minors who are victims of neglect or abuse is, in reality, a means of notifying the parents. . . . The combination of the abused minor's reluctance to report sexual or physical abuse, with the likelihood that invoking the abuse exception for the purpose of avoiding notice will result in notice, makes the abuse exception less than effectual.

Minnesota's two-parent notice requirement is all the more unreasonable when one considers that only half of the minors in the State of Minnesota reside with both biological parents. A third live with only one parent. Given its broad sweep and its failure to serve the purposes asserted by the State in too many cases, I join the Court's striking of subdivision 2.

In a series of cases, this Court has explicitly approved judicial bypass as a means of tailoring a parental consent provision so as to avoid unduly burdening the minor's limited right to obtain an abortion. . . .

Subdivision 6 passes constitutional muster because the interference with the internal operation of the family required by subdivision 2 simply does not exist where the minor can avoid notifying one or both parents by use of the bypass procedure.

JUSTICE MARSHALL (joined by Justices Brennan and Blackmun), concurring in part, concurring in the judgment in part, and dissenting in part: . . . . Minnesota's two-parent notification requirement is not even reasonably related to a legitimate state interest. Therefore, that requirement surely would not pass the strict scrutiny applicable to restrictions on a woman's fundamental right to have an abortion.

I dissent from the judgment of the Court . . . , however, that the judicial bypass option renders the parental notification and 48-hour delay requirements constitutional. The bypass procedure cannot save those requirements because the bypass itself is unconstitutional. . . . At the very least, this scheme substantially burdens a woman's right to privacy without advancing a compelling state interest. More significantly, in some instances it usurps a young woman's control over her own body by giving either a parent or a court the power effectively to veto her decision to have an abortion.

This Court has consistently held since *Roe v. Wade* that the constitutional right of privacy "is broad enough to encompass a woman's decision whether or not to terminate her pregnancy." We have also repeatedly stated that "[a] woman's right to make that choice freely is fundamental." . . . [W]e have subjected state laws limiting that right to the most exacting scrutiny, requiring a State to show that such a law is narrowly drawn to serve a compelling interest. Only such strict judicial scrutiny is sufficiently protective of a woman's right to make the intensely personal decision whether to terminate her pregnancy.

Roe remains the law of the land. Indeed, today's decision reaffirms the vitality of *Roe*, as five Justices have voted to strike down a state law restricting a woman's right to have an abortion. . . .

I strongly disagree with the Court's conclusion that the State may constitutionally force a minor woman either to notify both parents (or in some cases only one parent) and then wait 48 hours before proceeding with an abortion, or disclose her intimate affairs to a judge and ask that he grant her permission to have an abortion. First, the parental notification and delay requirements significantly restrict a young woman's right to reproductive choice. I base my conclusion not on my intuition about the needs and attitudes of young women, but on a sizable and impressive collection of empirical data documenting the effects of parental notification statutes and of delaying an abortion. Second, the burdensome restrictions are not narrowly tailored to serve any compelling state interest. Finally . . . the judicial bypass procedure does not save the notice and delay requirements.

Neither the scope of a woman's privacy right nor the magnitude of a law's burden is diminished because a woman is a minor. Rather, a woman's minority status affects only the nature of the State's interests. Although the Court considers the burdens that the two-parent notification requirement imposes on a minor woman's exercise of her right to privacy, it fails to recognize that forced notification of only one parent also significantly burdens a young woman's right to have an abortion.

A substantial proportion of pregnant minors voluntarily consult with a parent regardless of the existence of a notification requirement. Minors 15 years old or younger are even more likely voluntarily to discuss the abortion decision with their parents. For these women, the notification requirement by itself does not impose a significant burden. But for those young women who would choose not to inform their parents, the burden is evident: the notification requirement destroys their right to avoid disclosure of a deeply personal matter.

A notification requirement can also have severe physical and psychological effects on a young woman. First, forced notification of one parent, like forced notification of both parents, can be extremely traumatic for a young woman, depending on the nature of her relationship with her parents. . . .

Second, the prospect of having to notify a parent causes many young women to delay their abortions, thereby increasing the health risks of the procedure. The risks posed by this delay are especially significant because adolescents already delay seeking medical care until relatively late in their pregnancies, when risks are higher.

In addition, a notification requirement compels many minors seeking an abortion to travel to a State without such a requirement to avoid notifying a parent. Other women may resort to the horrors of self-abortion or illegal abortion rather than tell a parent. Still others would forgo an abortion entirely and carry the fetus to term, subjecting themselves to the much greater health risks of pregnancy and childbirth and to the physical, psychological, and financial hardships of unwanted motherhood. Clearly, then, requiring notification of one parent significantly burdens a young woman's right to terminate her pregnancy.

The 48-hour delay *after* notification further aggravates the harm caused by the *pre*-notification delay that may flow from a minor's fear of notifying a parent. Moreover, the 48-hour delay burdens the rights of all minors, including those who would voluntarily consult with one or both parents. Justice Stevens' assertion that the 48-hour delay "imposes only a minimal burden" ignores the increased health risks and costs that this delay entails. . . . Even a brief delay can have a particularly detrimental impact if it pushes the abortion into the second trimester, when the operation is substantially more risky and costly. . . .

Because the parental notification and delay requirements burden a young woman's right freely to decide whether to terminate her pregnancy, the State must show that these requirements are justified by a compelling state interest and are closely tailored to further that interest. The main purpose of the notification requirement is to "protect the well-being of minors by encouraging minors to discuss with their parents the decision whether to terminate their pregnancies." The 48-hour delay, in turn, is designed to provide parents with adequate time to consult with their daughters. As Justice Stevens states, such consultation is intended to ensure that the minor's decision is "knowing and intelligent." I need not determine whether the State's interest ultimately outweighs young women's privacy interests, however, because the strictures here are not closely tailored to further the State's asserted goal.

.... [C]ompelled notification is unlikely to result in productive consultation in families in which a daughter does not feel comfortable consulting her parents about intimate or sexual matters. Moreover, in those families with a history of child abuse, a pregnant minor forced to notify a parent is more likely to be greeted by physical assault or psychological harassment than open and caring conversation about her predicament. Forced notification in such situations would amount to punishing the daughter for the lack of a stable and communicative family environment, when the blame for that situation lies principally, if not entirely, with the parents. Parental notification in the less-than-ideal family, therefore, would not lead to an informed decision by the minor.

The State also claims that the statute serves the interest of protecting parents' independent right "to shape the[ir] child[ren]'s values and life style[s]" and "to determine and

strive for what they believe to be best for their children."
If this is so, the statute is surely underinclusive, as it does
not require parental notification where the minor seeks
medical treatment for pregnancy, venereal disease, or alcohol and other drug abuse. Are we to believe that Minnesota parents have no interest in their children's well-being
in these other contexts?

In any event, parents' right to direct their children's upbringing is a right against state interference with family
matters. Yet, ironically, the State's requirements here af-
firmatively interfere in family life by trying to force
families to conform to the State's archetype of the ideal
family. It is a strange constitutional alchemy that would
transform a limitation on state power into a justification
for governmental intrusion into family interactions.
Moreover, as a practical matter, "state intervention is
hardly likely to resurrect parental authority that the parents themselves are unable to preserve."

Even if the State's interest is construed as merely the *fa-
cilitation* of the exercise of parental authority, the notification and delay requirements are not narrowly drawn.
Parental authority is not limitless. Certainly where parental involvement threatens to harm the child, the parent's
authority must yield. . . .

Furthermore, the exercise of parental authority in some
instances will take the form of obstructing the minor's decision to have an abortion. A parent who objects to the
abortion, once notified, can exert strong pressure on the
minor - in the form of stern disapproval, withdrawal of
financial support, or physical or emotional abuse - to
block her from getting an abortion. In such circumstances, the notification requirement becomes, in effect, a

consent requirement. . . . [T]he State may not permit any person, including a parent, to veto a woman's decision to terminate her pregnancy. Because the notification and delay requirements effectively give parents the opportunity to exercise an unconstitutional veto in some situations, those requirements are not narrowly tailored to the State's interest in facilitating *legitimate* exercises of parental authority.

The parental notification and 48-hour delay requirements, then, do not satisfy the strict scrutiny applicable to laws restricting a woman's constitutional right to have an abortion. The judicial bypass procedure cannot salvage those requirements because that procedure itself is unconstitutional.

The State argues that the bypass procedure saves the notification and delay requirements because it provides an alternative way to obtain a legal abortion for minors who would be harmed by those requirements. This Court has upheld a one-parent consent requirement where the State provided an alternative judicial procedure "'whereby a pregnant minor [could] demonstrate that she [was] sufficiently mature to make the abortion decision herself or that, despite her immaturity, an abortion would be in her best interests.'"

I continue to believe, however, that a judicial bypass procedure of this sort is itself unconstitutional because it effectively gives a judge "an absolute veto over the decision of the physician and his patient." No person may veto *any* minor's decision, made in consultation with her physician, to terminate her pregnancy. An "immature" minor has no less right to make decisions regarding her own body than a mature adult.

Minnesota's bypass provision allows a judge to authorize an abortion if he determines either that a woman is sufficiently mature to make the decision on her own or, if she is not sufficiently mature, that an abortion without parental notification would serve her best interests. Of course, if a judge refuses to authorize an abortion, a young woman can then reevaluate whether she wants to notify a parent. But many women will carry the fetus to term rather than notify a parent. Other women may decide to inform a parent but then confront parental pressure or abuse so severe as to obstruct the abortion. For these women, the judge's refusal to authorize an abortion effectively constitutes an absolute veto.

The constitutional defects in any provision allowing someone to veto a woman's abortion decision are exacerbated by the vagueness of the standards contained in this statute. The statute gives no guidance on how a judge is to determine whether a minor is sufficiently "mature" and "capable" to make the decision on her own. The statute similarly is silent as to how a judge is to determine whether an abortion without parental notification would serve an immature minor's "best interests." . . . It is difficult to conceive of any reason, aside from a judge's personal opposition to abortion, that would justify a finding that an immature woman's best interests would be served by forcing her to endure pregnancy and childbirth against her will.

. . . . The Court has never considered the actual burdens a particular bypass provision imposes on a woman's right to choose an abortion. Such consideration establishes that, even if judges authorized every abortion sought by petitioning minors, Minnesota's judicial bypass is far too burdensome to remedy an otherwise unconstitutional statute.

The District Court found that the bypass procedure imposed significant burdens on minors. . . . [A] delay of only a few days can significantly increase the health risks to the minor; a week-long delay inevitably does. Furthermore, in several counties in Minnesota, no judge is willing to hear bypass petitions, forcing women in those areas to travel long distances to obtain a hearing. The burden of such travel, often requiring an overnight stay in a distant city, is particularly heavy for poor women from rural areas. Furthermore, a young woman's absence from home, school, or work during the time required for such travel and for the hearing itself can jeopardize the woman's confidentiality.

The District Court also found that the bypass procedure can be extremely traumatic for young women. . . .

Yet, despite the substantial burdens imposed by these proceedings, the bypass is, in effect, a "rubber stamp." Only an extremely small number of petitions are denied. The judges who have adjudicated over 90% of the bypass petitions between 1981 and 1986 could not identify any positive effects of the bypass procedure. The large number of women who undergo the bypass process do not receive any sort of counseling from the court - which is not surprising, given the court's limited role and lack of expertise in that area. The bypass process itself thus cannot serve the state interest of promoting informed decision-making by all minors. If the State truly were concerned about ensuring that all minors consult with a knowledgeable and caring adult, it would provide for some form of counseling rather than for a judicial procedure in which a judge merely gives or withholds his consent.

. . . . Minnesota's procedure in practice imposes an excessive burden on young women's right to choose an abortion. Furthermore, the process does not serve the State's interest of ensuring that minors' decisions are informed. Surely, then, a State could not require that *all* minor women seeking an abortion obtain judicial approval. The Court's holding that the burdensome bypass procedure saves the State's burdensome notification and delay requirements thus strikes me as the equivalent of saying that two wrongs make a right. I cannot accept such a novel judicial calculus.

A majority of the Court today strikes down an unreasonable and vastly overbroad requirement that a pregnant minor notify both her parents of her decision to obtain an abortion. With that decision I agree. At the same time, though, a different majority holds that a State may require a young woman to notify one or even both parents and then wait 48 hours before having an abortion, as long as the State provides a judicial bypass procedure. From that decision I vehemently dissent. This scheme forces a young woman in an already dire situation to choose between two fundamentally unacceptable alternatives: notifying a possibly dictatorial or even abusive parent and justifying her profoundly personal decision in an intimidating judicial proceeding to a blackrobed stranger. For such a woman, this dilemma is more likely to result in trauma and pain than in an informed and voluntary decision.

JUSTICE SCALIA, concurring in the judgment in part and dissenting in part: As I understand the various opinions today: One Justice holds that two-parent notification is unconstitutional (at least in the present circumstances) without judicial bypass, but constitutional with bypass;

four Justices would hold that two-parent notification is
constitutional with or without bypass; four Justices would
hold that two-parent notification is unconstitutional with
or without bypass, though the four apply two different
standards; six Justices hold that one-parent notification
with bypass is constitutional, though for two different sets
of reasons; and three Justices would hold that one-parent
notification with bypass is unconstitutional.   One will
search in vain the document we are supposed to be construing for text that provides the basis for the argument
over these distinctions; and will find in our society's tradition regarding abortion no hint that the distinctions are
constitutionally relevant, much less any indication how a
constitutional argument about them ought to be resolved.
The random and unpredictable results of our consequently
unchanneled individual views make it increasingly evident, Term after Term, that the tools for this job are not
to be found in the lawyer's - and hence not in the judge's
- workbox. I continue to dissent from this enterprise of
devising an Abortion Code, and from the illusion that we
have authority to do so.

JUSTICE KENNEDY (joined by Chief Justice Rehnquist,
and Justices White and Scalia), concurring in the judgment in part and dissenting in part: "'There can be little
doubt that the State furthers a constitutionally permissible
end by encouraging an unmarried pregnant minor to seek
the help and advice of her parents in making the very important decision whether or not to bear a child. That is a
grave decision, and a girl of tender years, under emotional
stress, may be ill-equipped to make it without mature advice and emotional support.'" Today, the Court holds that
a statute requiring a minor to notify both parents that she
plans to have an abortion is not a permissible means of
furthering the interest described with such specificity in

Belotti II. This conclusion, which no doubt will come as a surprise to most parents, is incompatible with our constitutional tradition and any acceptable notion of judicial review of legislative enactments. I dissent from the portion of the Court's judgment affirming the Court of Appeals' conclusion that Minnesota's two-parent notice statute is unconstitutional.

. . . . The provisions of the statute before us are straightforward. In essence, the statute provides that before a physician in Minnesota may perform an abortion on an unemancipated minor, the physician or the physician's agent must notify both of the minor's parents, if each one can be located through reasonable effort, either personally or by certified mail at least 48 hours before the abortion is performed. Notification is not required if the abortion is necessary to prevent the minor's death; or if both parents have consented to the abortion; or if the minor declares that she is the victim of sexual abuse, neglect, or physical abuse. Failure to comply with these requirements is a misdemeanor, and the statute authorizes a civil action against the non-complying physician by the minor's parents.

The statute also provides that, if a court enjoins [stops] the notice requirement of subdivision 2, parental notice under the subdivision shall still be required, unless the minor obtains a court order dispensing with it. Under the statute, the court is required to authorize the physician to perform the abortion without parental notice if the court determines that the minor is "mature and capable of giving informed consent to the proposed abortion" or that "the performance of an abortion upon her without notification of her parents, guardian, or conservator would be in her best interests."

The State identifies two interests served by the law. The first is the State's interest in the welfare of pregnant minors. The second is the State's interest in acknowledging and promoting the role of parents in the care and upbringing of their children. . . . I cannot agree that the Constitution prevents a State from keeping both parents informed of the medical condition or medical treatment of their child under the terms and conditions of this statute.

The welfare of the child has always been the central concern of laws with regard to minors. The law does not give to children many rights given to adults, and provides, in general, that children can exercise the rights they do have only through and with parental consent. Legislatures historically have acted on the basis of the qualitative differences in maturity between children and adults, and not without reason. Age is a rough but fair approximation of maturity and judgment, and a State has an interest in seeing that a child, when confronted with serious decisions such as whether or not to abort a pregnancy, has the assistance of her parents in making the choice. If anything is settled by our previous cases dealing with parental notification and consent laws, it is this point.

Protection of the right of each parent to participate in the upbringing of her or his own children is a further discrete interest that the State recognizes by the statute. . . . Limitations have emerged on the prerogatives of parents to act contrary to the best interests of the child with respect to matters such as compulsory schooling and child labor. As a general matter, however, it remains "cardinal with us that the custody, care and nurture of the child reside first in the parents, whose primary function and freedom include preparation for obligations the state can neither supply nor hinder."

A State pursues a legitimate end under the Constitution when it attempts to foster and preserve the parent-child relation by giving all parents the opportunity to participate in the care and nurture of their children. We have held that parents have a liberty interest, protected by the Constitution, in having a reasonable opportunity to develop close relations with their children. We have recognized, of course, that there are limits to the constitutional right of parents to have custody of or to participate in decisions affecting their children. If a parent has relinquished the opportunity to develop a relation with the child, and his or her only link to the child is biological, the Constitution does not require a State to allow parental participation. But the fact that the Constitution does not protect the parent-child relationship in all circumstances does not mean that the State cannot attempt to foster parental participation where the Constitution does not demand that it do so. A State may seek to protect and facilitate the parent-child bond on the assumption that parents will act in their child's best interests. . . .

Minnesota asserts no such purpose, by explicit statement or by any permissible inference. All that Minnesota asserts is an interest in seeing that parents know about a vital decision facing their child. That interest is a valid one without regard to whether the child is living with either one or both parents, or to the attachment between the minor's parents. How the family unit responds to such notice is, for the most part, beyond the State's control. The State would no doubt prefer that all parents, after being notified under the statute, would contact their daughters and assist them in making their decisions with the child's best interests at heart; but it has not, contrary to the Court's intimation, "decreed" communication, nor could it. What the State can do is make the communication possible by at least informing parents of their daughter's intentions.

. . . . Given the societal interest that underlies parental notice and consent laws, it comes as no surprise that most States have enacted statutes requiring that, in general, a physician must notify or obtain the consent of at least one of her parents or legal guardian before performing an abortion on a minor. Whether these statutes are more or less restrictive than the Minnesota statute is not the issue, although I pause to note that because the Court's decision today turns upon its perception that the law's requirements, despite its exceptions, are the most "stringent" in the country, the Court's decision has no import for the validity of these other statutes. What is important is that Minnesota is not alone in acknowledging the vitality of these governmental interests and adopting laws that, in the legislature's judgment, are best suited to serving them while protecting the minor's welfare.

. . . . With all respect, I submit the Court today errs when it states that Minnesota's two-parent notice law is an "oddity among state and federal consent provisions."

. . . . Given the substantial protection that minors have under Minnesota law generally, and under the statute in question, the judicial bypass provisions of the law are not necessary to its validity. The two-parent notification law enacted by Minnesota is, in my view, valid without the judicial bypass provision of subdivision 6.

We have been over much of this ground before. It is beyond dispute that in many families, whether the parents
are living together or apart, notice to both parents serves
the interests of the parents and the minor, and that the
State can legislate with this fact in mind. . . .

The Court today . . . suggests that a general requirement
that both parents be notified is unconstitutional because
of its own conclusion that the law is unnecessary when
notice produces favorable results, and irrational in all of
the instances when it produces unfavorable results. . . .

In applying the standards established in our prior decisions to the case at hand, "we must keep in mind that
when we are concerned with extremely sensitive issues,
such as the one involved here, 'the appropriate forum for
their resolution in a democracy is the legislature. We
should not forget that "legislatures are ultimate guardians
of the liberties and welfare of the people in quite as great
a degree as the courts." The Minnesota Legislature, like
the legislatures of many States, has found it necessary to
address the issue of parental notice in its statutory laws.
In my view it has acted in a permissible manner.

All must acknowledge that it was reasonable for the legislature to conclude that in most cases notice to both parents will work to the minor's benefit. . . .

I acknowledge that in some cases notifying both parents
will not produce desirable results despite the fact that no
actual instance is in the record before us, as the two-
parent notification requirement was [stopped] before it
went into effect. We need not decide today, however,
whether the Constitution permits a State to require that a
physician notify both biological parents before perform-

ing an abortion on any minor, for the simple reason that Minnesota has not enacted such a law.

The Minnesota statute in fact contains exceptions to ensure that the statutory notice requirement does not apply if it proves a serious threat to the minor's health or safety. First, the statute does not require notice at all costs; to comply with the law, a physician need only use "reasonably diligent effort" to locate and notify both of the minor's parents. If the second parent cannot be located, as may be the case if the parent has deserted the family or ceased to maintain contact with the minor or the other parent, the only notice required is to the first parent.

Second, even where both parents can be located, notice is not required if the physician certifies that the abortion is necessary to prevent the woman's death and there is insufficient time to provide the required notice, if the minor's parents have authorized the abortion in writing, or if the minor declares that she is the victim of sexual abuse, neglect, or physical abuse. Under Minnesota law, "neglect" of a minor means the failure of a parent "to supply a child with necessary food, clothing, shelter or medical care when reasonably able to do so or failure to protect a child from conditions or actions which imminently and seriously endanger the child's physical or mental health when reasonably able to do so," physical abuse is defined as "any physical injury inflicted by a person responsible for the child's care on a child other than by accidental means," and sexual abuse includes any sexual contact by a parent or other person responsible for the child's care or in a position of authority with respect to the child. I cannot believe that these exceptions are too narrow to eliminate from the statute's coverage those instances in which no-

tice would place the minor in danger of parental violence
or other conduct that is a real threat to the physical or
mental health of the child.

The Court challenges the efficacy of this last exception
because it believes that the statutory requirement that a
physician report a minor's declaration of abuse to appropriate authorities, will deter minors from using the exception. This is not a proper basis for declaring the law invalid. Laws are not declared unconstitutional because of
some general reluctance to follow a statutory scheme the
legislature finds necessary to accomplish a legitimate state
objective. . . .

No one can contend that a minor who is pregnant is somehow less deserving of the State's protection. It is reasonable to provide that any minor who contends that she cannot notify her parent or parents because she is the victim
of neglect or abuse allow the State to use its power to in-
vestigate her declaration and protect her from harm. Any
parent, moreover, who responds to notice by threatening
or harming the minor or the other parent may be prosecuted by the State to the full extent of its laws. Just as it
relies upon such laws as its first line of defense for dealing with all other instances of abuse in family situations,
so too is the State entitled to rely upon them here.

Notwithstanding the exceptions and protections we have
discussed, it does remain possible, of course, that in some
instances notifying one or both parents will not be in the
minor's best interests. . . .

The only cases in which a majority of the Court has devi-
ated from this principle are those in which a State sought
to condition a minor's access to abortion services upon re-

ceipt of her parent's consent to do so. In *Planned Parenthood of Central Missouri v. Danforth*, the Court invalidated a Missouri law requiring that a physician obtain the consent of one parent before performing an abortion. The Court's reasoning was unmistakable: "[T]he State does not have the constitutional authority to give a third party an absolute, and possibly arbitrary, veto over the decision of the physician and his patient to terminate the patient's pregnancy, regardless of the reason for withholding the consent." The Court today, ignoring this statement, relies heavily upon isolated passages from *Danforth*, and other cases involving parental consent laws. . . .

The difference between notice and consent was apparent to us before, and is apparent now. Unlike parental consent laws, a law requiring parental notice does not give any third party the legal right to make the minor's decision for her, or to prevent her from obtaining an abortion should she choose to have one performed. We have acknowledged this distinction as "fundamental," and as one "substantially modify[ing] the federal constitutional challenge." The law before us does not place an absolute obstacle before any minor seeking to obtain an abortion, and it represents a considered weighing of the competing interests of minors and their parents.

 . . . . Like all laws of general application, the Minnesota statute cannot produce perfect results in every situation to which it applies; but the State is under no obligation to enact perfect laws. The statute before us, including the 48-hour waiting period, which is necessary to enable notified parents to consult with their daughter or their daughter's physician, if they so wish, and results in little or no delay, represents a permissible, reasoned attempt to preserve the parents' role in a minor's decision to have an

abortion without placing any absolute obstacles before a
minor who is determined to elect an abortion for her own
interest as she sees it. Section 144.343, without the judicial bypass provision of subdivision 6, is constitutional. I
would reverse the contrary judgment of the Court of Appeals.

Because a majority of the Court holds that the two-parent
notice requirement contained in subdivision 2 is unconstitutional, it is necessary for the Court to consider whether
the same notice requirement is constitutional if the minor
has the option of obtaining a court order permitting the
abortion to proceed in lieu of the required notice. Assuming, as I am bound to do for this part of the analysis, that
the notice provisions standing alone are invalid, I conclude
that the two-parent notice requirement with the judicial
bypass alternative is constitutional.

The Court concludes that Minnesota's two-parent notice
law without a judicial bypass is unconstitutional because
of the possibility that, in some cases, the rule would not
work to the benefit of minors or their parents. If one
were to attempt to design a statute that would address the
Court's concerns, one would do precisely what Minnesota
has done in Section 144.343(6): create a judicial mechanism to identify, and exempt from the strictures of the
law, those cases in which the minor is mature or in which
notification of the minor's parents is not in the minor's
best interests. The bypass procedure comports in all respects with our precedents [past decisions].

In providing for the bypass, Minnesota has done nothing
other than attempt to fit its legislation into the framework that we have supplied in our previous cases. The
simple fact is that our decision in *Belotti II* stands for the

proposition that a two-parent consent law is constitutional if it provides for a sufficient judicial bypass alternative, and it requires us to sustain the statute before us here. In *Belotti II*, the Court considered the constitutionality of a statute which required a physician to obtain, in most circumstances, the consent of both of a minor's parents before performing an abortion on the minor. Although eight Members of the Court concluded that the statute was unconstitutional, five indicated that they would uphold a two-parent consent statute with an adequate judicial bypass.

.... [F]ive Members of the Court in *Belotti II* found, either by express statement or by implication, that it was permissible under the Constitution for a State to require the consent of two parents, as long as it provides a consent substitute in the form of an adequate judicial bypass procedure.

.... As *Belotti II* dealt with the far more demanding requirement of two-parent consent, and approved of such a requirement when coupled with a judicial bypass alternative, I must conclude that these same principles validate a two-parent notice requirement when coupled with a judicial bypass alternative.

A second precedent that compels the conclusion that a two-parent notice law with a judicial bypass alternative is constitutional is our decision in *Matheson*. There we held that a two-parent notice statute without a bypass was constitutional as applied to immature minors whose best interests would be served by notice. Like the statute before the Court in *Matheson*, the Minnesota statute, as amended by subdivision 6, requires a physician to notify the par-

ents of those immature minors whose best interest will be
served by the communication.

If a two-parent notification law may be constitutional as
applied to immature minors whose best interests are
served by the law, but not as applied to minors who are
mature or whose best interests are not so served, a judicial
bypass is an expeditious and efficient means by which to
separate the applications of the law which are constitutional from those which are not. . . . If a judicial bypass is
mandated by the Constitution at all, it must be because a
general consent rule is unreasonable in at least some of its
applications, and the bypass is necessary to save the statute. No reason can be given for refusing to apply a similar analysis to the less demanding case of a notice statute.
It follows that a similar result should obtain: a law that
requires notice to one or both parents is constitutional
with a bypass. I thus concur in that portion of the judgment . . . which affirms the Court of Appeals' conclusion
that Section 144.343(6) is constitutional.

In this case, the Court rejects a legislature's judgment that
parents should at least be aware of their daughter's intention to seek an abortion, even if the State does not empower the parents to control the child's decision. That
judgment is rejected although it rests upon a tradition of a
parental role in the care and upbringing of children that
is as old as civilization itself. Our precedents do not permit this result.

It is true that for all too many young women the prospect
of two parents, perhaps even one parent, sustaining her
with support that is compassionate and committed is an illusion. Statistics on drug and alcohol abuse by parents
and documentations of child neglect and mistreatment are

but fragments of the evidence showing the tragic reality that becomes day-to-day life for thousands of minors. But the Court errs in serious degree when it commands its own solution to the cruel consequences of individual misconduct, parental failure, and social ills. The legislative authority is entitled to attempt to meet these wrongs by taking reasonable measures to recognize and promote the primacy of the family tie, a concept which this Court now seems intent on declaring a constitutional irrelevance.

OHIO v. AKRON CENTER
FOR REPRODUCTIVE HEALTH

EXCERPTS

"A free and enlightened society may decide that each of its members should attain a clearer, more tolerant understanding of the profound philosophic choices confronted by a woman who is considering whether to seek an abortion. Her decision will embrace her own destiny and personal dignity, and the origins of the other human life that life within the embryo. The State is entitled to assume that, for most of its people, the beginnings of that understanding will be within the family, society's most intimate association. It is both rational and fair for the State to conclude that, in most instances, the family will strive to give a lonely or even terrified minor advice that is both compassionate and mature."

Justice Anthony Kennedy

"A minor needs no statute to seek the support of loving parents. Where trust and confidence exist within the family structure, it is likely that communication already exists. If that compassionate support is lacking, an unwanted pregnancy is a poor way to generate it."

Justice Harry Blackmun

In Brief

Question: Is Ohio's abortion for minors law unconstitutional?

Lower Court: U.S. District Court, Northern Ohio
U.S. Court of Appeals, Sixth Circuit

Law: Ohio House Bill 319 (1985)

Parties: State of Ohio
Akron Center for Reproductive Health

Counsel: For Ohio: Rita Eppler
For Akron Center: Linda Sogg

Arguments: November 29, 1989

Decision: June 25, 1990

Majority: Chief Justice Rehnquist, Justices White, Stevens, O'Connor, Scalia, Kennedy

Minority: Justices Blackmun, Brennan, Marshall

Decision by: Justice Kennedy (p. 49)

Concurrences: Justice Scalia (p. 58)
Justice Stevens (p. 58)

Dissents: Justice Blackmun (p. 60)

Offical Text: U.S. Reports, Vol. 497
Lower Court: Federal Supplement, Vol. 633, p. 1123
Federal Reporter 2d, Vol. 854, p. 852

THE AKRON II COURT

Chief Justice William Rehnquist
Appointed Associate Justice 1971 by Richard M. Nixon
Appointed Chief Justice 1986 by Ronald W. Reagan

Associate Justice William Brennan
Appointed 1956 by Dwight D. Eisenhower

Associate Justice Byron White
Appointed 1962 by John F. Kennedy

Associate Justice Thurgood Marshall
Appointed 1967 by Lyndon B. Johnson

Associate Justice Harry Blackmun
Appointed 1970 by Richard M. Nixon

Associate Justice John Paul Stevens
Appointed 1975 by Gerald R. Ford

Associate Justice Sandra Day O'Connor
Appointed 1981 by Ronald W. Reagan

Associate Justice Antonin Scalia
Appointed 1986 by Ronald W. Reagan

Associate Justice Anthony Kennedy
Appointed 1988 by Ronald W. Reagan

OHIO v. AKRON CENTER FOR REPRODUCTIVE HEALTH

June 25, 1990

JUSTICE KENNEDY: The Court of Appeals held invalid an Ohio statute that, with certain exceptions, prohibits any person from performing an abortion on an unmarried, unemancipated, minor woman absent notice to one of the woman's parents or a court order of approval. We reverse, for we determine that the statute accords with our precedents on parental notice and consent in the abortion context and does not violate the Fourteenth Amendment.

The Ohio Legislature, in November 1985, enacted Amended Substitute House Bill 319 . . . . Section 2919.12(B), the cornerstone of this legislation, makes it a criminal offense, except in four specified circumstances, for a physician or other person to perform an abortion on an unmarried woman under eighteen years of age.

The first and second circumstances in which a physician may perform an abortion relate to parental notice and consent. First, a physician may perform an abortion if he provides "at least twenty-four hours actual notice, in person or by telephone," to one of the women's parents (or her guardian or custodian) of his intention to perform the abortion. The physician, as an alternative, may notify a minor's adult brother, sister, stepparent, or grandparent, if the minor and the other relative each file an affidavit in the juvenile court stating that the minor fears physical, sexual, or severe emotional abuse from one of her parents. If the physician cannot give the notice "after a reasonable effort," he may perform the abortion after "at least forty-eight hours constructive notice" by both ordinary and certified mail. Second, a physician may perform an abortion on the minor if one of her parents (or her guardian or custodian) has consented to the abortion in writing.

The third and fourth circumstances depend on a judicial procedure that allows a minor to bypass the notice and consent provisions just described. The statute allows a physician to perform an abortion without notifying one of the minor's parents or receiving the parent's consent if a juvenile court issues an order authorizing the minor to consent, or if a juvenile court or court of appeals, by its inaction, provides constructive authorization for the minor to consent.

The bypass procedure requires the minor to file a complaint in the juvenile court, stating (1) that she is pregnant; (2) that she is unmarried, under 18 years of age, and unemancipated; (3) that she desires to have an abortion without notifying one of her parents; (4) that she has sufficient maturity and information to make an intelligent decision whether to have an abortion without such notice, *or* that one of her parents has engaged in a pattern of physical, sexual, or emotional abuse against her, *or* that notice is not in her best interests; and (5) that she has or has not retained an attorney. . . .

The juvenile court must hold a hearing at the earliest possible time, but not later than the fifth business day after the minor files the complaint. The court must render its decision immediately after the conclusion of the hearing. Failure to hold the hearing within this time results in constructive authorization for the minor to consent to the abortion. At the hearing the court must appoint a guardian . . . and an attorney to represent the minor if she has not retained her own counsel. The minor must prove her allegation of maturity, pattern of abuse, or best interests by clear and convincing evidence, and the juvenile court must conduct the hearing to preserve the anonymity of the complainant, keeping all papers confidential.

The minor has the right to expedited review. The statute provides that, within four days after the minor files a notice of appeal, the clerk of the juvenile court shall deliver the notice of appeal and record to the state court of appeals. The clerk of the court of appeals dockets [places on the court's calendar] the appeal upon receipt of these items. The minor must file her brief within four days after the docketing. If she desires an oral argument, the court of appeals must hold one within five days after the docketing and must issue a decision immediately after oral argument. If she waives the right to an oral argument, the court of appeals must issue a decision within five days after the docketing. If the court of appeals does not comply with these time limits, a constructive order results authorizing the minor to consent to the abortion.

Appellees in this action include the Akron Center for Reproductive Health, a facility that provides abortions; Max Pierre Gaujean, M.D., a physician who performs abortions at the Akron Center; and Rachael Roe, an unmarried, unemancipated minor woman, who sought an abortion at the facility. In March 1986, days before the effective date of HB 319, [Akron Center] . . . challenge[d] the constitutionality of the statute in the United States District Court for the Northern District of Ohio. The District Court . . . issued a preliminary injunction [court order stopping an action] and later a permanent injunction preventing the State of Ohio from enforcing the statute.

The Court of Appeals for the Sixth Circuit affirmed [confirmed], concluding that HB 319 had six constitutional defects. . . . The State of Ohio, on appeal . . . challenges the Court of Appeals' decision in its entirety. . . .

We have decided five cases addressing the constitutionality of parental notice or parental consent statutes in the abortion context (*Planned Parenthood of Central Missouri v. Danforth, Belotti v. Baird, H.L. v. Matheson, Planned Parenthood Association of Kansas City, Missouri, Inc. v. Ashcroft,* and *Akron v. Akron Center for Reproductive Health, Inc.*). We do not need to determine whether a statute that does not accord with these cases would violate the Constitution, for we conclude that HB 319 is consistent with them.

. . . . In the case now before us, we have no difficulty concluding that HB 319 allows a minor to show maturity in conformity with the plurality opinion in *Belotti.* The statute permits the minor to show that she "is sufficiently mature and well enough informed to decide intelligently whether to have an abortion."

. . . . The statute requires the juvenile court to authorize the minor's consent where the court determines that the abortion is in the minor's best interest and in cases where the minor has shown a pattern of physical, sexual, or emotional abuse.

. . . . Section 2151.85(D) [of the Ohio statute] provides that "[t]he [juvenile] court shall not notify the parents, guardian, or custodian of the complainant that she is pregnant or that she wants to have an abortion." Section 2151.85(F) further states:

"Each hearing under this section shall be conducted in a manner that will preserve the anonymity of the complainant. The complaint and all other papers and records that pertain to an action commenced under this section shall be kept confidential and are not public records."

Section 2505.073(B), in a similar fashion, requires the court of appeals to preserve the minor's anonymity and confidentiality of all papers on appeal. The State, in addition, makes it a criminal offense for an employee to disclose documents not designated as public records.

. . . . Confidentiality differs from anonymity, but we do not believe that the distinction has constitutional significance in the present context. The distinction has not played a part in our previous decisions, and, even if the *Belotti* plurality is taken as setting the standard, we do not find complete anonymity critical. HB 319, like the statutes in *Belotti* and *Ashcroft*, takes reasonable steps to prevent the public from learning of the minor's identity. . . . HB 319, like many sophisticated judicial procedures, requires participants to provide identifying information for administrative purposes, not for public disclosure.

. . . . HB 319, as noted above, requires the trial court to make its decision within five "business day[s]" after the minor files her complaint; requires the court of appeals to docket an appeal within four "days" after the minor files a notice of appeal; and requires the court of appeals to render a decision within five "days" after docketing the appeal.

The District Court and the Court of Appeals assumed that all of the references to days . . . meant business days as opposed to calendar days. They calculated, as a result, that the procedure could take up to 22 calendar days because the minor could file at a time during the year in which the 14 business days needed for the bypass procedure would encompass three Saturdays, three Sundays, and two legal holidays. [Akron Center] maintain[s] . . . that a 3-week delay could increase by a substantial measure both the costs and the medical risks of an abortion. They conclude, as did those courts, that HB 319 does not satisfy the *Belotti* plurality's expedition requirement.

. . . . Interpreting the term "days" in Section 2505.073(A) to mean business days instead of calendar days seems inappropriate and unnecessary because of the express and contrasting use of "business day[s]" in Section 2151.85(B)(1). . . . The Court of Appeals should not have invalidated the Ohio statute . . . based upon a worst-case analysis that may never occur. . . . Moreover, under our precedents [past decisions], the mere possibility that the procedure may require up to twenty-two days in a rare case is plainly insufficient to invalidate the statute. . . .

We discern no constitutional defect in the statute. Absent a demonstrated pattern of abuse or defiance, a State may expect that its judges will follow mandated procedural requirements. There is no showing that the time limitations imposed by HB 319 will be ignored. . . .

The minor, under the statutory scheme and the requirements prescribed by the Ohio Supreme Court, must choose among three pleading forms. The first alleges only maturity and the second alleges only best interests. She may not attempt to prove both maturity and best interests unless she chooses the third form, which alleges both of these facts. . . .

Even on the assumption that the pleading scheme could produce some initial confusion because few minors would have counsel when pleading, the simple and straightforward procedure does not deprive the minor of an opportunity to prove her case. It seems unlikely that the Ohio courts will treat a minor's choice of complaint form without due care and understanding for her unrepresented status. In addition, we note that the minor does not make a binding election by the initial choice of pleading form. The minor, under HB 319, receives appointed counsel after filing the complaint and may move [ask] for leave to amend the pleadings. Regardless of whether Ohio could have written a simpler statute, HB 319 survives a facial challenge.

. . . . The confidentiality provisions, the expedited procedures, and the pleading form requirements, on their face, satisfy the dictates of minimal due process. We see little risk of erroneous deprivation under these provisions and no need to require additional procedural safeguards. . . . [G]iven that the statute provides definite and reasonable deadlines, the constructive authorization provision, Section 2151.85(B)(1), also comports with due process on its face.

. . . . In *Akron*, the Court found unconstitutional a requirement that the attending physician provide the information and counseling relevant to informed consent. Although the Court did not disapprove of informing a woman of the health risks of an abortion, it explained that "[t]he State's interest is in ensuring that the woman's consent is informed and unpressured; the critical factor is whether she obtains the necessary information and counseling from a qualified person, not the identity of the person from whom she obtains it." . . .

We upheld, in *Matheson*, a statute that required a physician to notify the minor's parents. The distinction between notifying a minor's parents and informing a woman of the routine risks of an abortion has ample justification. . . . We continue to believe that a State may require the physician himself or herself to take reasonable steps to notify a minor's parent because the parent often will provide important medical data to the physician. . . .

The conversation with the physician, in addition, may enable a parent to provide better advice to the minor. The parent who must respond to an event with complex philosophical and emotional dimensions is given some access to an experienced and, in an ideal case, detached physician who can assist the parent in approaching the problem in a mature and balanced way. This access may benefit both the parent and child in a manner not possible through notice by less qualified persons.

Any imposition on a physician's schedule, by requiring him to give notice when the minor does not have consent from one of her parents or court authorization, must be evaluated in light of the complete statutory scheme. The statute allows the physician to send notice by mail if he cannot reach the minor's parent "after a reasonable effort," and also allows him to forgo notice in the event of certain emergencies. These provisions are an adequate recognition of the physician's professional status. . . . [W]e find the physician notification requirement unobjectionable.

The Ohio statute, in sum, does not impose an undue, or otherwise unconstitutional, burden on a minor seeking an abortion. We believe, in addition, that the legislature acted in a rational manner in enacting HB 319. A free and enlightened society may decide that each of its members should attain a clearer, more tolerant understanding of the profound philosophic choices confronted by a woman who is considering whether to seek an abortion. Her decision will embrace her own destiny and personal dignity, and the origins of the other human life that lie within the embryo. The State is entitled to assume that, for most of its people, the beginnings of that understanding will be within the family, society's most intimate association. It is both rational and fair for the State to conclude that, in most instances, the family will strive to give a lonely or even terrified minor advice that is both compassionate and mature. The statute in issue here is a rational way to further those ends. It would deny all dignity to the family to say that the State cannot take this reasonable step in regulating its health professions to ensure that, in most cases, a young woman will receive guidance and understanding from a parent. We uphold HB 319 . . . and reverse the Court of Appeals.

It is so ordered.

JUSTICE SCALIA, concurring: I join the opinion of the
Court, because I agree that the Ohio statute neither deprives minors of procedural due process nor contradicts
our holdings regarding the constitutional right to abortion. I continue to believe, however, as I said in my separate concurrence last Term in *Webster v. Reproductive
Health Services*, that the Constitution contains no right to
abortion. It is not to be found in the longstanding traditions of our society, nor can it be logically deduced from
the text of the Constitution - not, that is, without volun-
teering a judicial answer to the nonjusticiable question of
when human life begins. Leaving this matter to the political process is not only legally correct, it is pragmatically
so. That alone - and not lawyerly dissection of federal judicial precedents - can produce compromises satisfying a
sufficient mass of the electorate that this deeply felt issue
will cease distorting the remainder of our democratic
process. The Court should end its disruptive intrusion
into this field as soon as possible.

JUSTICE STEVENS, concurring in part and concurring in
the judgment: .... The State may presume that, in most
of its applications, the statute will reasonably further its
legitimate interest in protecting the welfare of its minor
citizens. In some of its applications, however, the one-
parent notice requirement will not reasonably further that
interest. There will be exceptional situations in which notice will cause a realistic risk of physical harm to the
pregnant woman, will cause trauma to an ill parent, or
will enable the parent to prevent the abortion for reasons
that are unrelated to the best interests of the minor. The
Ohio statute recognizes that possibility by providing a judicial bypass. The question in this case is whether that
statutory protection for the exceptional case is so obvious-

ly inadequate that the entire statute should be invalidated.
I am not willing to reach that conclusion before the statute has been implemented and the significance of its restrictions evaluated in the light of its administration. I
therefore agree that the Court of Appeals' judgment must
be reversed. . . .

We have . . . squarely held that a requirement of preabor-
tion parental notice in all cases involving pregnant minors
is unconstitutional. Although it need not take the form of
a judicial bypass, the State must provide an adequate
mechanism for cases in which the minor is mature or notice would not be in her best interests.

. . . . [W]hile a judicial bypass may not be necessary to
take care of the cases in which the minor is mature or parental notice would not be in her best interests - and, indeed, may not be the preferable mechanism - the Court
has held that some provision must be made for such cases.

The Ohio statute, on its face, provides a sufficient procedure for those cases. . . . The requirement that the minor
prove maturity or best interests by clear and convincing
evidence is supported by the presumption that notification to a parent will in most circumstances be in the min-
or's best interests. . . . I have more concern about the possible delay in the bypass procedure, but the statute permits the Ohio courts to expedite the procedure upon a
showing of good cause, and sensitive administration of the
deadlines may demonstrate that my concern is unwarranted.

There is some tension between the statutory requirement
that the treating physician notify the minor's parent and

our decision in *Akron* that a State may not require the attending physician to personally counsel an abortion patient. One cannot overlook the possibility that this provision was motivated more by a legislative interest in placing obstacles in the woman's path to an abortion than by a
genuine interest in fostering informed decisionmaking. I
agree with the Court, however, that the Ohio statute requires only that the physician take "reasonable steps" to
notify a minor's parent and that such notification may
contribute to the decisionmaking process. Accordingly, I
am unable to conclude that this provision is unconstitutional on its face.

JUSTICE BLACKMUN (joined by Justices Brennan and
Marshall), dissenting: The constitutional right to "control
the quintessentially intimate, personal, and life-directing
decision whether to carry a fetus to term" does "not mature and come into being magically only when one attains
the state-defined age of majority. Minors, as well as
adults, are protected by the Constitution and possess constitutional rights." Although the Court "has recognized
that the State has somewhat broader authority to regulate
the activities of children than of adults," in doing so, the
State nevertheless must demonstrate that there is a
"*significant state interest* in conditioning an abortion . . .
that is not present in the case of an adult." . . .

"Particular sensitivity" is mandated because "there are few
situations in which denying a minor the right to make an
important decision will have consequences so grave and
indelible." It should be obvious that "considering her
probable education, employment skills, financial resources,
and emotional maturity, unwanted motherhood may be ex-
ceptionally burdensome for a minor."

The State of Ohio has acted with particular *in*sensitivity
in enacting the statute the Court today upholds. Rather
than create a judicial-bypass system that reflects the sensitivity necessary when dealing with a minor making this
deeply intimate decision, Ohio has created a tortuous
maze. Moreover, the State has failed utterly to show that
it has any significant state interest in deliberately placing
its pattern of obstacles in the path of the pregnant minor
seeking to exercise her constitutional right to terminate a
pregnancy. The challenged provisions of the Ohio statute
are merely "poorly disguised elements of discouragement
for the abortion decision."

. . . . I conclude . . . that, because of the minor's emotional
vulnerability and financial dependency on her parents,
and because of the "unique nature of the abortion decision," and its consequences, a parental-notice statute is tan-
tamount to a parental-consent statute. As a practical matter, a notification requirement will have the same deterrent effect on a pregnant minor seeking to exercise her
constitutional right as does a consent statute. Thus a notice statute, like a consent statute, must contain a bypass
procedure that comports with the standards set forth in
Belotti II. Because I disagree with the Court's conclusion
that the Ohio bypass procedure complies with the dictates
of *Belotti II* and its progeny, I would strike down Ohio . . .
Bill 319.

. . . . The language of the Ohio statute purports to follow
the standards for a bypass procedure that are set forth in
Belotti II, but at each stage along the way, the statute deliberately places "substantial state-created obstacles in the
pregnant [minor's] path to an abortion," in the legislative
hope that she will stumble, perhaps fall, and at least en-

suring that she "conquer a multi-faceted obstacle course" before she is able to exercise her constitutional right to an abortion.   The majority considers each provision in a piecemeal fashion, never acknowledging or assessing the "degree of burden that the entire regime of abortion regulations places" on the minor.

The obstacle course begins when the minor first enters the courthouse to fill out the complaint forms. The "pleading trap," as it appropriately was described by the Court of Appeals, requires the minor to choose among three forms. The first alleges *only* maturity; the second alleges *only* that the abortion is in her best interest. Only if the minor chooses the third form, which alleges both, may the minor attempt to prove both maturity *and* best interest as is her right under *Belotti II*. . . .   The constitutionality of a procedural provision cannot be analyzed on the basis that it may have no effect. If the pleading requirement prevents some minors from showing either that they are mature or that an abortion would be in their best interests, it plainly is unconstitutional.

The majority fails to elucidate *any* state interest in setting up this barricade for the young pregnant woman - a barricade that will "serve only to confuse . . . her and to heighten her anxiety." . . .

It is ludicrous to confound the pregnant minor, forced to go to court at this time of crisis in her life, with alternative complaint forms that must later be rescinded by appointed counsel and replaced by the only form that is constitutionally valid.   Moreover, this ridiculous pleading scheme leaves to the judge's discretion whether the minor may amend her pleading and attempt to prove both her maturity and best interest. To allow the resolution of this vital issue to turn on a judge's discretion does not comport with *Belotti II*'s declaration that the minor who "fails to satisfy the court that she is competent to make this decision independently . . . *must* be permitted to show that an abortion nevertheless would be in her best interests."

As the pregnant minor attempts to find her way through the labyrinth set up by the State of Ohio, she encounters yet another obstruction even before she has completed the complaint form. . . . The Ohio statute does not safeguard that right [of anonymity]. Far from keeping the identity of the minor anonymous, the statute requires the minor to sign her full name and the name of one of her parents on the complaint form. Acknowledging that "[c]onfidentiality differs from anonymity," the majority simply asserts that "complete anonymity" is not "critical." That easy conclusion is irreconcilable with *Bellotti*'s anonymity requirement. The definition of "anonymous" is "not named or identified." Complete anonymity, then, appears to be the only kind of anonymity that a person could possibly have. . . .

As the District Court pointed out, there are no indications of how a clerk's office, large or small, is to ensure that the records of abortion cases will be distinguished from the records of all other cases that are available to the public. Nor are there measures for sealing the record after the case is closed to prevent its public availability. This Court is well aware that, unless special care is taken, court documents of an intimate nature will find their way to the press and public. The State has offered no justification for its failure to provide specific guidelines to be followed by the Juvenile Court to ensure anonymity for the pregnant minor - even though it has in place a procedure to assure the anonymity of juveniles who have been adjudicated delinquent or unruly.

. . . . A minor, whose very purpose in going through a judicial-bypass proceeding is to avoid notifying a hostile or abusive parent, would be most alarmed at signing her name and the name of her parent on the complaint form. Generalized statements concerning the confidentiality of records would be of small comfort, even if she were aware of them.   True anonymity is essential to an effective, meaningful bypass. In the face of the forms that the minor must actually deal with, the State's assurances that the minor's privacy will be protected ring very hollow.   I would not permit the State of Ohio to force a minor to forgo her anonymity in order to obtain a waiver of the parental-notification requirement.

Because a "pregnant adolescent . . . cannot preserve for long the possibility of aborting, which effectively expires in a matter of weeks from the onset of pregnancy," this Court has required that the State "must assure" that the "resolution of the issue, and any appeals that may follow, will be completed with . . . sufficient expedition to provide an effective opportunity for an abortion to be obtained." Ohio's judicial-bypass procedure can consume up to three weeks of a young woman's pregnancy. I would join the Sixth Circuit, the District Court, and the other federal courts that have held that a time span of this length fails to guarantee a sufficiently expedited procedure.

. . . . The Court ignores the fact that the medical risks surrounding abortion increase as pregnancy advances and that such delay may push a woman into her second trimester, where the medical risks, economic costs, and state regulation increase dramatically. Minors, who are more likely to seek later abortions than adult women, and who usually are not financially independent, will suffer acutely from any delay. Because a delay of up to 22 days may limit significantly a woman's ability to obtain an abortion, I agree with the conclusions of the District Court and the Court of Appeals that the statute violates this Court's command that a judicial-bypass proceeding be conducted with sufficient speed to maintain "an effective opportunity for an abortion to be obtained."

The Ohio statute provides that if the juvenile or appellate courts fail to act within the statutory time frame, an abortion without parental notification is "constructively" authorized. Although Ohio's Legislature may have intended this provision to expedite the bypass procedure, the confusion that will result from the constructive-authorization provision will add further delay to the judicial-bypass proceeding, and is yet one more obstruction in the path of the pregnant minor. The physician risks civil damages, criminal penalties, including imprisonment, as well as revocation of his license for disobeying the statute's commands, but the statute provides for no formal court order or other relief to safeguard the physician from these penalties. . . . There is no doubt that the nebulous authorization envisioned by this statute "in conjunction with a statute imposing strict civil and criminal liability . . . could have a profound chilling effect on the willingness of physicians to perform abortions. . . ." I agree with the Court of Appeals that the "practical effect" of the "pocket approval" provision is to frustrate the minor's right to an expedient disposition of her petition.

If the minor is able to wend her way through the intricate
course of preliminaries Ohio has set up for her and at
least reaches the court proceeding, the State shackles her
even more tightly with still another "extra layer and burden of regulation on the abortion decision." The minor
must demonstrate by "clear and convincing evidence" either (1) her maturity; (2) or that one of her parents has
engaged in a pattern of physical, sexual, or emotional
abuse against her; or (3) that notice to a parent is not in
her best interest." The imposition of this heightened
standard of proof unduly burdens the minor's right to
seek an abortion and demonstrates a fundamental misun-
derstanding of the real nature of a court-bypass proceeding.

.... By imposing such a stringent standard of proof, this
Ohio statute improperly places the risk of an erroneous
decision on the minor, the very person whose fundamental
right is at stake. Even if the judge is satisfied that the
minor is mature or that an abortion is in her best interest,
the court may not authorize the procedure unless it addi-
tionally finds that the evidence meets a "clear and convincing" standard of proof.

.... [I]t is not the quantity of the evidence presented
that is crucial in the bypass proceeding; rather, the crucial
factors are the nature of the minor's statements to the
judge and her demeanor. Contrary to the majority's theory, if the minor presents evidence that she is mature, she
still must *satisfy* the judge that this is so, even without
this heightened standard of proof. The use of a heightened standard in the very special context of *Bellotti*'s
court-bypass procedure does little to facilitate a fair and
reliable result and imports an element from the adversari-

al process into this unique inquiry where it has no right-
ful place.

Although I think the provision is constitutionally infirm
for all minors, I am particularly concerned about the effect it will have on sexually or physically abused minors.
I agree that parental interest in the welfare of their children is "particularly strong where a *normal* family relationship exists." A minor needs no statute to seek the support of loving parents. Where trust and confidence exist
within the family structure, it is likely that communication already exists. If that compassionate support is lacking, an unwanted pregnancy is a poor way to generate it.

Sadly, not all children in our country are fortunate
enough to be members of loving families. For too many
young pregnant women, parental involvement in this most
intimate decision threatens harm, rather than promises
comfort. The Court's selective blindness to this stark social reality is bewildering and distressing. Lacking the
protection that young people typically find in their intimate family associations, these minors are desperately in
need of constitutional protection. The sexually or physically abused minor may indeed be "lonely or even terrified," not of the abortion procedure, but of an abusive
family member. The Court's placid reference to the
"compassionate and mature" advice the minor will receive
from within the family must seem an unbelievable and
cruel irony to those children trapped in violent families.

Under the system Ohio has set up, a sexually abused min-
or must go to court and demonstrate to a complete stranger by clear and convincing evidence that she has been the
victim of a pattern of sexual abuse. When asked at argu-

ment what kind of evidence a minor would be required to
adduce [offer] at her bypass hearing, the State answered
that the minor would tell her side to the judge and the
judge would consider how well "the minor is able to articulate what her particular concerns are." The court procedure alone, in many cases, is extremely traumatic. The
State and the Court are impervious to the additional burden imposed on the abused minor who, as any experienced
social worker or counselor knows, is often afraid and
ashamed to reveal what has happened to her to anyone
outside the home. The Ohio statute forces that minor, despite her very real fears, to experience yet one more hard-
ship. She must attempt, in public, and before strangers, to
"articulate what her particular concerns are" with sufficient clarity to meet the State's "clear and convincing evidence" standard. The upshot is that for the abused minor
the risk of error entails a risk of violence.

I would affirm [confirm] the judgments below. . . . The
pleading requirements, the so-called and fragile guarantee
of anonymity, the insufficiency of the expedited procedures, the constructive-authorization provision, and the
"clear and convincing evidence" requirement singly and
collectively cross the limit of constitutional acceptance.

Even if the Ohio statute complied with the *Belotti II* requirements for a constitutional court bypass, I would conclude that the Ohio procedure is unconstitutional because
it requires the physician's personal and nondelegable obligation to give the required statutory notice. Particularly
when viewed in context with the other impediments this
statute places in the minor's path, there is more than a
"possibility" that the physician-notification provision "was
motivated more by a legislative interest in placing obsta-

cles in the woman's path to an abortion, than by a genuine interest in fostering informed decisionmaking." . . . [T]he State has never claimed that personal notice by the physician was required to effectuate an interest in the minor's health until the matter reached this Court. . . . If these chimerical health concerns now asserted in fact were the true motivation behind this provision, I seriously doubt that the State would have taken so long to say so.

Even if the State's interest in the health of the minor were the motivation behind the provision, the State never explains why it is that a physician interested in obtaining information, or a parent interested in providing information to a physician cannot do so following the actual notification by some other competent professional, such as a nurse or counselor. And the State and the majority never explain why, if the physician's ability to garner information from the parents is of such paramount importance that only the physician may notify the parent, the statute allows the physician to send notice by mail if he or she cannot reach the minor's parent "after a reasonable effort."

The State's asserted interest in the minor's health care is especially ironic in light of the statute's interference with her physician's experienced professional judgment. . . . I have no doubt that the attending physician, better than the Ohio Legislature, will know when a consultation with the parent is necessary. . . . The strictures of this Ohio law not only unduly burden the minor's right to an abortion, but impinge on the physician's professional discretion in the practice of medicine.

The Ohio Legislature, in its wisdom, in 1985 enacted its anti-abortion statute. That statute . . . has been held unconstitutional by the United States District Court for the Northern District of Ohio and by the Court of Appeals for the Sixth Circuit. It is now, however, upheld on that challenge by a majority of this Court. The majority opinion takes up each challenged provision in turn; concludes, with brief comment, that it is within the bounds of the plurality opinion in *Bellotti II*, and moves on routinely and in the same fashion to the succeeding provisions, one by one. A plurality then concludes . . . with hyperbole that can have but one result: to further incite an American press, public, and pulpit already inflamed by the pronouncement made by a plurality of this Court last Term in *Webster v. Reproductive Health Services.* The plurality indulges in paternalistic comments about "profound philosophic choices"; the "woman's own destiny and personal dignity"; the "origins of the other human life that lie within the embryo"; the family as "society's most intimate association"; the striving of the family to give to the minor "advice that is both compassionate and mature"; and the desired assumption that "in most cases" the woman will receive "guidance and understanding from a parent."

Some of this may be so "in most cases" and, it is to be hoped, in judges' own and other warm and protected, nurturing family environments. But those "most cases" need not rely on constitutional protections that are so vital for others. I have cautioned before that there is "another world 'out there'" that the Court "either chooses to ignore or refuses to recognize." It is the unfortunate denizens of that world, often frightened and forlorn, lacking the comfort of loving parental guidance and mature advice, who most need the constitutional protection that the Ohio Legislature set out to make as difficult as possible to obtain.

That that Legislature set forth with just such a goal is evident from the statute it spawned. The underlying nature of the Ohio statute is proclaimed by its strident and offensively restrictive provisions. It is as though the Legislature said: "If the courts of the United States insist on upholding a limited right to an abortion, let us make that abortion as difficult as possible to obtain" because, basically, whether on professed moral or religious grounds or whatever, "we believe that is the way it must be." This often may be the way legislation is enacted, but few are the instances where the injustice is so evident and the impediments so gross as those inflicted by the Ohio Legislature on these vulnerable and powerless young women.

RUST v. SULLIVAN

EXCERPTS

"Congress' refusal to fund abortion counseling and advocacy leaves a pregnant woman with the same choices as if the government had chosen not to fund family-planning services at all."

Justice Harry Blackmun

"In a society that abhors censorship and in which policymakers have traditionally placed the highest value on the freedom to communicate, it is unrealistic to conclude that statutory authority to regulate conduct implicitly authorized the Executive to regulate speech."

Justice John Paul Stevens

In Brief

Question: May the federal government impose a "gag rule" on federally-funded family planning services?

Lower Court: U.S. District Court, Southern New York
U.S. Court of Appeals, Second Circuit

Law: Public Health Service Act, Title X

Parties: Irving Rust, representing Title X
grantees and doctors
Louis Sullivan, Secretary,
U.S. Department of
Health & Human Services

Counsel: For Rust: Laurence Tribe
For Sullivan: Kenneth Starr

Arguments: October 30, 1990

Decision: May 23, 1991

Majority: Chief Justice Rehnquist, Justices White, Scalia, Kennedy, Souter

Minority: Justices Marshall, Blackmun, Stevens, O'Connor

Decision by: Chief Justice Rehnquist (p. 77)

Dissents: Justice Blackmun (p. 93)
Justice Stevens (p. 103)
Justice O'Connor (p. 106)

Offical Text: U.S. Reports, Vol. 500
Lower Court: Federal Supplement, Vol. 690, p. 1261
Federal Reporter 2d, Vol. 889, p. 401

THE RUST COURT

Chief Justice William Rehnquist
Appointed Associate Justice 1971 by Richard M. Nixon
Appointed Chief Justice 1986 by Ronald W. Reagan

Associate Justice Byron White
Appointed 1962 by John F. Kennedy

Associate Justice Thurgood Marshall
Appointed 1967 by Lyndon B. Johnson

Associate Justice Harry Blackmun
Appointed 1970 by Richard M. Nixon

Associate Justice John Paul Stevens
Appointed 1975 by Gerald R. Ford

Associate Justice Sandra Day O'Connor
Appointed 1981 by Ronald W. Reagan

Associate Justice Antonin Scalia
Appointed 1986 by Ronald W. Reagan

Associate Justice Anthony Kennedy
Appointed 1988 by Ronald W. Reagan

Associate Justice David Souter
Appointed 1991 by George Bush

RUST v. SULLIVAN

May 23, 1991

CHIEF JUSTICE REHNQUIST: These cases [*Rust v. Sullivan* and its companion, *New York v. Sullivan*] concern a . . . challenge to Department of Health and Human Services (HHS) regulations which limit the ability of Title X fund recipients to engage in abortion-related activities. . . .

In 1970, Congress enacted Title X of the Public Health Service Act, which provides federal funding for family-planning services. The Act authorizes the Secretary to "make grants to and enter into contracts with public or nonprofit private entities to assist in the establishment and operation of voluntary family planning projects which shall offer a broad range of acceptable and effective family planning methods and services." Grants and contracts under Title X must "be made in accordance with such regulations as the Secretary may promulgate." Section 1008 of the Act, however, provides that "[n]one of the funds appropriated under this subchapter shall be used in programs where abortion is a method of family planning." That restriction was intended to ensure that Title X funds would "be used only to support preventive family planning services, population research, infertility services, and other related medical, informational, and educational activities."

In 1988, the Secretary promulgated new regulations designed to provide "'clear and operational guidance' to grantees about how to preserve the distinction between Title X programs and abortion as a method of family planning." The regulations clarify, through the definition of the term "family planning," that Congress intended Title X funds "to be used only to support *preventive* family planning services." Accordingly, Title X services are limited to "preconceptual counseling, education, and general reproductive health care," and expressly exclude "pregnancy care (including obstetric or prenatal care)." The regulations "focus the emphasis of the Title X program on its traditional mission: The provision of preventive family planning services specifically designed to enable individuals to determine the number and spacing of their children, while clarifying that pregnant women must be referred to appropriate prenatal care services."

The regulations attach three principal conditions on the grant of federal funds for Title X projects. First, the regulations specify that a "Title X project may not provide counseling concerning the use of abortion as a method of family planning or provide referral for abortion as a method of family planning." Because Title X is limited to preconceptional services, the program does not furnish services related to childbirth. Only in the context of a referral out of the Title X program is a pregnant woman given transitional information. Title X projects must refer every pregnant client "for appropriate prenatal and/or social services by furnishing a list of available providers that promote the welfare of the mother and the unborn child." The list may not be used indirectly to encourage or promote abortion. . . . The Title X project is expressly prohibited from referring a pregnant woman to an abortion provider, even upon specific request. One permissible response to such an inquiry is that "the project does not consider abortion an appropriate method of family planning and therefore does not counsel or refer for abortion."

Second, the regulations broadly prohibit a Title X project from engaging in activities that "encourage, promote or advocate abortion as a method of family planning." Forbidden activities include lobbying for legislation that would increase the availability of abortion as a method of family planning, developing or disseminating materials advocating abortion as a method of family planning, providing speakers to promote abortion as a method of family planning, using legal action to make abortion available in any way as a method of family planning, and paying dues to any group that advocates abortion as a method of family planning as a substantial part of its activities.

Third, the regulations require that Title X projects be organized so that they are "physically and financially separate" from prohibited abortion activities. To be deemed physically and financially separate, "a Title X project must have an objective integrity and independence from prohibited activities. . . . The regulations provide a list of nonexclusive factors for the Secretary to consider in conducting a case-by-case determination of objective integrity and independence, such as the existence of separate accounting records and separate personnel, and the degree of physical separation of the project from facilities for prohibited activities.

Petitioners are Title X grantees and doctors who supervise Title X funds suing on behalf of themselves and their patients [Rust et al.]. Respondent is the Secretary of the Department of Health and Human Services [Sullivan]. . . . [Rust] challenged the regulations on the grounds that they were not authorized by Title X and that they violate the First and Fifth Amendment rights of Title X clients and the First Amendment rights of Title X health providers.

After initially granting [Rust] a preliminary injunction [court order stopping an action], the District Court rejected [Rust's] statutory and constitutional challenges to the regulations and granted summary judgment in favor of the Secretary.

A panel of the Court of Appeals for the Second Circuit affirmed [confirmed]. . . . [T]he Court of Appeals determined that the regulations were a permissible construction of the statute that legitimately effectuated Congressional intent. . . .

[T]he Court of Appeals rejected [Rust's] Fifth Amendment challenge. It held that the regulations do not impermissibly burden a woman's right to an abortion because the "government may validly choose to favor childbirth over abortion and to implement that choice by funding medical services relating to childbirth but not those relating to abortion." . . .

The court likewise found that the "Secretary's implementation of Congress's decision not to fund abortion counseling, referral or advocacy also does not, under applicable Supreme Court precedent, constitute a . . . violation of the First Amendment rights of health care providers or of women." The court explained that . . . the government has no obligation to subsidize even the exercise of fundamental rights, including "speech rights." The court also held that the regulations do not violate the First Amendment by "condition[ing] receipt of a benefit on the relinquishment of constitutional rights" because Title X grantees and their employees remain free to say whatever they wish about abortion outside the Title X project." Finally, the court rejected [Rust's] contention that the regulations "facially discriminate on the basis of the viewpoint of the speech involved."

.... [W]e are concerned only with the question whether, on their face, the regulations are both authorized by the Act, and can be construed [interpreted] in such a manner that they can be applied to a set of individuals without infringing upon constitutionally protected rights. . . .

We begin with an examination of the regulations concerning abortion counseling, referral, and advocacy, which every Court of Appeals has found to be authorized by the statute, and then turn to the "program integrity requirement," with respect to which the courts below have adopted conflicting positions. We then address [Rust's] claim that the regulations must be struck down because they raise a substantial constitutional question.

We need not dwell on the plain language of the statute because we agree with every court to have addressed the issue that the language is ambiguous. The language of Section 1008 - that "[n]one of the funds appropriated under this subchapter shall be used in programs where abortion is a method of family planning" - does not speak directly to the issues of counseling, referral, advocacy, or program integrity. If a statute is "silent or ambiguous with respect to the specific issue, the question for the court is whether the agency's answer is based on a permissible construction of the statute."

The Secretary's construction of Title X may not be disturbed as an abuse of discretion if it reflects a plausible construction of the plain language of the statute and does not otherwise conflict with Congress' expressed intent. . . .

[S]ubstantial deference is accorded to the interpretation of the authorizing statute by the agency authorized with administering it.

The broad language of Title X plainly allows the Secretary's construction of the statute. By its own terms, Section 1008 prohibits the use of Title X funds "in programs where abortion is a method of family planning." Title X does not define the term "method of family planning," nor does it enumerate what types of medical and counseling services are entitled to Title X funding. Based on the broad directives provided by Congress in Title X in general and Section 1008 in particular, we are unable to say that the Secretary's construction of the prohibition in Section 1008 to require a ban on counseling, referral, and advocacy within the Title X project, is impermissible.

. . . . At no time did Congress directly address the issues of abortion counseling, referral, or advocacy. The parties' attempts to characterize highly generalized, conflicting statements in the legislative history into accurate revelations of congressional intent are unavailing.

When we find, as we do here, that the legislative history is ambiguous and unenlightening on the matters with respect to which the regulations deal, we customarily defer to the expertise of the agency. . . .

This Court has rejected the argument that an agency's interpretation "is not entitled to deference because it represents a sharp break with prior interpretations" of the statute in question. In *Chevron*, we held that a revised interpretation deserves deference because "[a]n initial agency interpretation is not instantly carved in stone" and "the agency, to engage in informed rulemaking, must consider varying interpretations and the wisdom of its policy on a continuing basis." An agency is not required to "'establish rules of conduct to last forever,'" but rather "must be given ample latitude to 'adapt [its] rules and policies to the demands of changing circumstances.'"

We find that the Secretary amply justified his change of interpretation with a "reasoned analysis." The Secretary explained that the regulations are a result of his determination, in the wake of the critical reports of the General Accounting Office (GAO) and the Office of the Inspector General (OIG), that prior policy failed to implement properly the statute and that it was necessary to provide "clear and operational guidance to grantees to preserve the distinction between Title X programs and abortion as a method of family planning." He also determined that the new regulations are more in keeping with the original intent of the statute, are justified by client experience under the prior policy, and are supported by a shift in attitude against the "elimination of unborn children by abortion." We believe that these justifications are sufficient to support the Secretary's revised approach. Having concluded that the plain language and legislative history are ambiguous as to Congress' intent in enacting Title X, we must defer to the Secretary's permissible construction of the statute.

We turn next to the "program integrity" requirements embodied at Section 59.9 of the regulations, mandating separate facilities, personnel, and records. These requirements are not inconsistent with the plain language of Title X. . . .

We agree that the program integrity requirements are based on a permissible construction of the statute and are not inconsistent with Congressional intent. As noted, the legislative history is clear about very little, and program integrity is no exception. . . .

[T]he cornerstone of the conclusion that in Title X Congress intended a comprehensive, integrated system of family planning services is the statement in the statute requiring state health authorities applying for Title X funds to submit "a state plan for a coordinated and comprehensive program of family planning services." This statement is, on its face, ambiguous as to Congress' intent in enacting Title X and the prohibition of Section 1008. Placed in context, the statement merely requires that a State health authority submit a plan for a "coordinated and comprehensive program of family planning services" in order to be eligible for Title X funds. By its own terms, the language evinces Congress' intent to place a duty on state entities seeking federal funds; it does not speak either to an overall view of family planning services or to the Secretary's responsibility for implementing the statute. Likewise, the statement in the original House Report on Title X that the Act was "not intended to interfere with or limit programs conducted in accordance with State or local laws" and supported through non-Title X funds is equally unclear. This language directly follows the statement that it is the "intent of both Houses that the funds authorized under this legislation be used only to support preventive family planning services. . . . The conferees have adopted the language contained in Section 1008, which prohibits the use of such funds for abortion, in order to make this intent clear." When placed in context and read in light of the express prohibition of Section 1008, the statements fall short of evidencing a congressional intent that would render the Secretary's interpretation of the statute impermissible.

. . . . It is well established that legislative history which does not demonstrate a clear and certain congressional intent cannot form the basis for enjoining [stopping] the regulations. The Secretary based the need for the separation requirements "squarely on the congressional intent that abortion not be a part of a Title X funded program." Indeed, if one thing is clear from the legislative history, it is that Congress intended that Title X funds be kept separate and distinct from abortion-related activities. It is undisputed that Title X was intended to provide primarily prepregnancy preventive services. Certainly the Secretary's interpretation of the statute that separate facilities are necessary, especially in light of the express prohibition of Section 1008, cannot be judged unreasonable. Accordingly, we defer to the Secretary's reasoned determination that the program integrity requirements are necessary to implement the prohibition.

. . . . Congress forbade the use of appropriated funds in programs where abortion is a method of family planning. It authorized the Secretary to promulgate regulations implementing this provision. The extensive litigation regarding governmental restrictions on abortion since our decision in *Roe v. Wade* suggests that it was likely that any set of regulations promulgated by the Secretary - other than the ones in force prior to 1988 and found by him to be relatively toothless and ineffectual - would be challenged on constitutional grounds. . . . [W]e hold that the regulations promulgated by the Secretary do not raise the sort of "grave and doubtful constitutional questions" that would lead us to assume Congress did not intend to authorize their issuance. Therefore, we need not invalidate the regulations in order to save the statute from unconstitutionality.

. . . . There is no question but that the statutory prohibition contained in Section 1008 is constitutional. In *Maher v. Roe*, we upheld a state welfare regulation under which Medicaid recipients received payments for services related to childbirth, but not for nontherapeutic abortions. The Court rejected the claim that this unequal subsidization worked a violation of the Constitution. We held that the government may "make a value judgment favoring childbirth over abortion, and . . . implement that judgment by the allocation of public funds." Here the Government is exercising the authority it possesses under *Maher* and *Harris v. McRae* to subsidize family planning services which will lead to conception and child birth, and declining to "promote or encourage abortion." The Government can, without violating the Constitution, selectively fund a program to encourage certain activities it believes to be in the public interest, without at the same time funding an alternate program which seeks to deal with the problem in another way. In so doing, the Government has not discriminated on the basis of viewpoint; it has merely chosen to fund one activity to the exclusion of the other. "[A] legislature's decision not to subsidize the exercise of a fundamental right does not infringe the right." . . .

The challenged regulations implement the statutory prohibition by prohibiting counseling, referral, and the provision of information regarding abortion as a method of family planning. They are designed to ensure that the limits of the federal program are observed. The Title X program is designed not for prenatal care, but to encourage family planning. A doctor who wished to offer prenatal care to a project patient who became pregnant could properly be prohibited from doing so because such service is outside the scope of the federally funded program. The regulations prohibiting abortion counseling and referral are of the same ilk; "no funds appropriated for the project may be used in programs where abortion is a method of family planning," and a doctor employed by the project may be prohibited in the course of his project duties from counseling abortion or referring for abortion. This is not a case of the Government "suppressing a dangerous idea," but of a prohibition on a project grantee or its employees from engaging in activities outside of its scope.

To hold that the Government unconstitutionally discriminates on the basis of viewpoint when it chooses to fund a program dedicated to advance certain permissible goals, because the program in advancing those goals necessarily discourages alternate goals, would render numerous government programs constitutionally suspect. When Congress established a National Endowment for Democracy to encourage other countries to adopt democratic principles, it was not constitutionally required to fund a program to encourage competing lines of political philosophy such as Communism and Fascism. . . . [W]hen the government appropriates public funds to establish a program it is entitled to define the limits of that program.

. . . . On their face, we do not read the regulations to bar abortion referral or counseling in such circumstances. Abortion counseling as a "method of family planning" is prohibited, and it does not seem that a medically necessi-

tated abortion in such circumstances would be the equivalent of its use as a "method of family planning." Neither
Section 1008 nor the specific restrictions of the regulations would apply. Moreover, the regulations themselves
contemplate that a Title X project would be permitted to
engage in otherwise prohibited abortion-related activity in
such circumstances. Section 59.8(a)(2) provides a specific
exemption for emergency care and requires Title X recipients "to refer the client immediately to an appropriate
provider of emergency medical services." Section
59.5(b)(1) also requires Title X projects to provide
"necessary referral to other medical facilities when medically indicated."

. . . . [Rust] argue[s] that . . . the government . . . may not
deny a benefit to a person on a basis that infringes his
constitutionally protected interests - especially, his interest
in freedom of speech."

[Rust's] reliance on these cases is unavailing, however, because here the government is not denying a benefit to
anyone, but is instead simply insisting that public funds
be spent for the purposes for which they were authorized. . . . The Title X *grantee* can continue to perform
abortions, provide abortion-related services, and engage in
abortion advocacy; it simply is required to conduct those
activities through programs that are separate and independent from the project that receives Title X funds.

In contrast, our "unconstitutional conditions" cases involve
situations in which the government has placed a condition
on the *recipient* of the subsidy rather than on a particular
program or service, thus effectively prohibiting the recipi-

ent from engaging in the protected conduct outside the scope of the federally funded program. . . .

The condition that federal funds will be used only to further the purposes of a grant does not violate constitutional rights. "Congress could, for example, grant funds to an organization dedicated to combating teenage drug abuse, but condition the grant by providing that none of the money received from Congress should be used to lobby state legislatures."

By requiring that the Title X grantee engage in abortion-related activity separately from activity receiving federal funding, Congress has . . . not denied it the right to engage in abortion-related activities. Congress has merely refused to fund such activities out of the public fisc, and the Secretary has simply required a certain degree of separation from the Title X project in order to ensure the integrity of the federally funded program.

. . . . Individuals who are voluntarily employed for a Title X project must perform their duties in accordance with the regulation's restrictions on abortion counseling and referral. The employees remain free, however, to pursue abortion-related activities when they are not acting under the auspices of the Title X project. The regulations, which govern solely the scope of the Title X project's activities, do not in any way restrict the activities of those persons acting as private individuals. The employees' freedom of expression is limited during the time that they actually work for the project; but this limitation is a consequence of their decision to accept employment in a project, the scope of which is permissibly restricted by the funding authority.

This is not to suggest that funding by the Government, even when coupled with the freedom of the fund recipients to speak outside the scope of the Government-funded project, is invariably sufficient to justify government control over the content of expression. ... It could be argued ... that traditional relationships such as that between doctor and patient should enjoy protection under the First Amendment from government regulation, even when subsidized by the Government. We need not resolve that question here, however, because the Title X program regulations do not significantly impinge upon the doctor-patient relationship. Nothing in them requires a doctor to represent as his own any opinion that he does not in fact hold. Nor is the doctor-patient relationship established by the Title X program sufficiently all-encompassing so as to justify an expectation on the part of the patient of comprehensive medical advice. The program does not provide post-conception medical care, and therefore a doctor's silence with regard to abortion cannot reasonably be thought to mislead a client into thinking that the doctor does not consider abortion an appropriate option for her. The doctor is always free to make clear that advice regarding abortion is simply beyond the scope of the program. In these circumstances, the general rule that the Government may choose not to subsidize speech applies with full force.

We turn now to [Rust's] argument that the regulations violate a woman's Fifth Amendment right to choose whether to terminate her pregnancy. ... The Government has no constitutional duty to subsidize an activity merely because the activity is constitutionally protected and may validly choose to fund childbirth over abortion and "'implement that judgment by the allocation of public funds'" for medical services relating to childbirth but not to those relating to abortion. The Government has no affirmative duty to "commit any resources to facilitating abortions," and its decision to fund childbirth but not abortion "places no governmental obstacle in the path of a woman who chooses to terminate her pregnancy, but rather, by means of unequal subsidization of abortion and other medical services, encourages alternative activity deemed in the public interest."

That the regulations do not impermissibly burden a woman's Fifth Amendment rights is evident from the line of cases beginning with *Maher* and *McRae* and culminating in our most recent decision in *Webster*. . . . Congress' refusal to fund abortion counseling and advocacy leaves a pregnant woman with the same choices as if the government had chosen not to fund family-planning services at all. The difficulty that a woman encounters when a Title X project does not provide abortion counseling or referral leaves her in no different position than she would have been if the government had not enacted Title X.

In *Webster* we stated that "[h]aving held that the State's refusal [in *Maher*] to fund abortions does not violate *Roe v. Wade*, it strains logic to reach a contrary result for the use of public facilities and employees." It similarly would strain logic, in light of the more extreme restrictions in those cases, to find that the mere decision to exclude abortion-related services from a federally funded *preconceptual* family planning program, is unconstitutional.

[Rust] also argue[s] that by impermissibly infringing on the doctor/patient relationship and depriving a Title X client of information concerning abortion as a method of family planning, the regulations violate a woman's Fifth Amendment right to medical self-determination and to make informed medical decisions free of government-imposed harm. . . .

Critical to our decisions in *Akron* and *Thornburgh* to invalidate a governmental intrusion into the patient/doctor dialogue was the fact that the laws in both cases required *all* doctors within their respective jurisdictions to provide *all* pregnant patients contemplating an abortion a litany of information, regardless of whether the patient sought the information or whether the doctor thought the information necessary to the patient's decision. Under the Secretary's regulations, however, a doctor's ability to provide, and a woman's right to receive, information concerning abortion and abortion-related services outside the context of the Title X project remains unfettered. It would undoubtedly be easier for a woman seeking an abortion if she could receive information about abortion from a Title X project, but the Constitution does not require that the Government distort the scope of its mandated program in order to provide that information.

[Rust] contend[s], however, that most Title X clients are effectively precluded by indigency and poverty from seeing a health care provider who will provide abortion-related services. But once again, even these Title X clients are in no worse position than if Congress had never enacted Title X. "The financial constraints that restrict an indigent woman's ability to enjoy the full range of constitutionally protected freedom of choice are the product not of governmental restrictions on access to abortion, but rather of her indigency."

The Secretary's regulations are a permissible construction of Title X and do not violate either the First or Fifth Amendments to the Constitution. Accordingly, the judgment of the Court of Appeals is affirmed [confirmed].

JUSTICE BLACKMUN (joined by Justices Marshall and Stevens in part, and Justice O'Connor in part), dissenting:
. . . . [T]he majority in these cases [*Rust v. Sullivan* and *New York v. Sullivan*] today unnecessarily passes upon important questions of constitutional law. In so doing, the Court, for the first time, upholds viewpoint-based suppression of speech solely because it is imposed on those dependent upon the Government for economic support. Under essentially the same rationale, the majority upholds direct regulation of dialogue between a pregnant woman and her physician when that regulation has both the purpose and the effect of manipulating her decision as to the continuance of her pregnancy. I conclude that the Secretary's regulation of referral, advocacy, and counseling activities exceeds his statutory authority, and, also, that the Regulations violate the First and Fifth Amendments of our Constitution. Accordingly, I dissent and would reverse the divided-vote judgment of the Court of Appeals.

. . . . Whether or not one believes that these Regulations are valid, it avoids reality to contend that they do not give rise to serious constitutional questions. The canon is applicable to this case not because "it was likely that [the Regulations] . . . would be challenged on constitutional grounds," but because the question squarely presented by the Regulations - the extent to which the Government may attach an otherwise unconstitutional condition to the receipt of a public benefit - implicates a troubled area of

our jurisprudence in which a court ought not entangle itself unnecessarily. . . .

[T]he Regulations impose viewpoint-based restrictions
upon protected speech and are aimed at a woman's decision whether to continue or terminate her pregnancy. In
both respects, they implicate core constitutional values. . . .

Nor is this a case in which the statutory language itself requires us to address a constitutional question. Section
1008 of the Public Health Service Act provides simply:
"None of the funds appropriated under this title shall be
used in programs where abortion is a method of family
planning." The majority concedes that this language "does
not speak directly to the issues of counseling, referral, advocacy, or program integrity," and that "the legislative history is ambiguous" in this respect. Consequently, the language of Section 1008 easily sustains [grants] a constitutionally trouble-free interpretation.

. . . . [I]t would appear that our duty to avoid passing unnecessarily upon important constitutional questions is
strongest where, as here, the language of the statute is de-
cidedly ambiguous. It is both logical and eminently pru-
dent to assume that when Congress intends to press the
limits of constitutionality in its enactments, it will express
that intent in explicit and unambiguous terms.

Because I conclude that a plainly constitutional construction of Section 1008 "is not only 'fairly possible' but entirely reasonable," I would reverse the judgment of the
Court of Appeals on this ground without deciding the
constitutionality of the Secretary's Regulations.

I also strongly disagree with the majority's disposition of [Rust's] constitutional claims. . . .

Until today, the Court never has upheld viewpoint-based suppression of speech simply because that suppression was a condition upon the acceptance of public funds. Whatever may be the Government's power to condition the receipt of its largess upon the relinquishment of constitutional rights, it surely does not extend to a condition that suppresses the recipient's cherished freedom of speech based solely upon the content or viewpoint of that speech. This rule is a sound one, for, as the Court often has noted: "'A regulation of speech that is motivated by nothing more than a desire to curtail expression of a particular point of view on controversial issues of general interest is the purest example of a "law . . . abridging the freedom of speech, or of the press."'" "[A]bove all else, the First Amendment means that government has no power to restrict expression because of its message, its ideas, its subject matter, or its content."

. . . . It cannot seriously be disputed that the counseling and referral provisions at issue in the present cases constitute content-based regulation of speech. Title X grantees may provide counseling and referral regarding any of a wide range of family planning and other topics, save abortion.

The Regulations are also clearly viewpoint-based. While suppressing speech favorable to abortion with one hand, the Secretary compels anti-abortion speech with the other. For example, the Department of Health and Human Services' own description of the Regulations makes plain that "Title X projects are *required* to facilitate access to prena-

tal care and social services, that might be needed by the
pregnant client to promote her well-being and that of her
child, while making it abundantly clear that the project is
not permitted to promote abortion by facilitating access to
abortion through the referral process."

Moreover, the Regulations command that a project refer
for prenatal care each woman diagnosed as pregnant, irrespective of the woman's expressed desire to continue or
terminate her pregnancy. If a client asks directly about
abortion, a Title X physician or counselor is required to
say, in essence, that the project does not consider abortion
to be an appropriate method of family planning. Both requirements are antithetical to the First Amendment.

The Regulations pertaining to "advocacy" are even more
explicitly viewpoint-based. These provide: "A Title X
project may not *encourage, promote or advocate* abortion
as a method of family planning." They explain: "This requirement prohibits actions to *assist* women to obtain
abortions or *increase* the availability or accessibility of
abortion for family planning purposes." The Regulations
do not, however, proscribe or even regulate anti-abortion
advocacy. These are clearly restrictions aimed at the suppression of "dangerous ideas."

Remarkably, the majority concludes that "the Government
has not discriminated on the basis of viewpoint; it has
merely chosen to fund one activity to the exclusion of the
other." But the majority's claim that the Regulations
merely limit a Title X project's speech to preventive or
preconceptional services, rings hollow in light of the
broad range of non-preventive services that the Regulations authorize Title X projects to provide. By refusing to

fund those family-planning projects that advocate abortion *because* they advocate abortion, the Government
plainly has targeted a particular viewpoint. The
majority's reliance on the fact that the Regulations pertain solely to funding decisions simply begs the question.
Clearly, there are some bases upon which government may
not rest its decision to fund or not to fund. For example,
the Members of the majority surely would agree that government may not base its decision to support an activity
upon considerations of race. As demonstrated above, our
cases make clear that ideological viewpoint is a similarly
repugnant ground upon which to base funding decisions.

. . . . [I]n addition to their impermissible focus upon the
viewpoint of regulated speech, the provisions intrude
upon a wide range of communicative conduct, including
the very words spoken to a woman by her physician. By
manipulating the content of the doctor/patient dialogue,
the Regulations upheld today force each of the petitioners
"to be an instrument for fostering public adherence to an
ideological point of view [he or she] finds unacceptable."
This type of intrusive, ideologically based regulation of
speech . . . cannot be justified simply because it is a condition upon the receipt of a governmental benefit.

The Court concludes that the challenged Regulations do
not violate the First Amendment rights of Title X staff
members because any limitation of the employees' freedom of expression is simply a consequence of their decision to accept employment at a federally funded project.
But it has never been sufficient to justify an otherwise
unconstitutional condition upon public employment that
the employee may escape the condition by relinquishing
his or her job. It is beyond question "that a government

may not require an individual to relinquish rights guaranteed him by the First Amendment as a condition of public employment." ...

The majority attempts to circumvent this principle by emphasizing that Title X physicians and counselors "remain free . . . to pursue abortion-related activities when they are not acting under the auspices of the Title X project." . . . Under the majority's reasoning, the First Amendment could be read to tolerate *any* governmental restriction upon an employee's speech so long as that restriction is limited to the funded workplace. This is a dangerous proposition, and one the Court has rightly rejected in the past.

. . . . In addressing the family-planning needs of their clients, the physicians and counselors who staff Title X projects seek to provide them with the full range of information and options regarding their health and reproductive freedom. Indeed, the legitimate expectations of the patient and the ethical responsibilities of the medical profession demand no less. . . . When a client becomes pregnant, the full range of therapeutic alternatives includes the abortion option, and Title X counselors' interest in providing this information is compelling.

The Government's articulated interest in distorting the doctor/patient dialogue - ensuring that federal funds are not spent for a purpose outside the scope of the program - falls far short of that necessary to justify the suppression of truthful information and professional medical opinion regarding constitutionally protected conduct. Moreover, the offending Regulation is not narrowly tailored to serve this interest. . . . By failing to balance or even to consider

the free speech interests claimed by Title X physicians
against the Government's asserted interest in suppressing
the speech, the Court falters in its duty to implement the
protection that the First Amendment clearly provides for
this important message.

Finally, it is of no small significance that the speech the
Secretary would suppress is truthful information regarding constitutionally protected conduct of vital importance
to the listener. One can imagine no legitimate governmental interest that might be served by suppressing such
information. Concededly, the abortion debate is among
the most divisive and contentious issues that our Nation
has faced in recent years. "But freedom to differ is not
limited to things that do not matter much. That would be
a mere shadow of freedom. The test of its substance is
the right to differ as to things that touch the heart of the
existing order."

By far the most disturbing aspect of today's ruling is the
effect it will have on the Fifth Amendment rights of the
women who, supposedly, are beneficiaries of Title X programs. The majority rejects [Rust's] Fifth Amendment
claims summarily. . . .

Until today, the Court has allowed to stand only those restrictions upon reproductive freedom that, while limiting
the availability of abortion, have left intact a woman's
ability to decide without coercion whether she will continue her pregnancy to term. . . . Today's decision abandons
that principle, and with disastrous results.

. . . [T]his is not a case in which individuals seek government aid in exercising their fundamental rights. The

Fifth Amendment right asserted by [Rust] is the right of
a pregnant woman to be free from affirmative governmental *interference* in her decision. *Roe v. Wade* and its
progeny are not so much about a medical procedure as
they are about a woman's fundamental right to self-
determination. Those cases serve to vindicate the idea
that "liberty," if it means anything, must entail freedom
from governmental domination in making the most intimate and personal of decisions. By suppressing medically
pertinent information and injecting a restrictive ideological message unrelated to considerations of maternal
health, the Government places formidable obstacles in the
path of Title X clients' freedom of choice and thereby violates their Fifth Amendment rights.

It is crystal-clear that the aim of the challenged provisions
- an aim the majority cannot escape noticing - is not simply to ensure that federal funds are not used to perform
abortions," but to "reduce the incidence of abortion." As
recounted above, the Regulations require Title X physicians and counselors to provide information pertaining
only to childbirth, to refer a pregnant woman for prenatal
care irrespective of her medical situation, and, upon direct
inquiry, to respond that abortion is not an "appropriate
method" of family planning.

The undeniable message conveyed by this forced speech,
and the one that the Title X client will draw from it, is
that abortion nearly always is an improper medical option.
Although her physician's words, in fact, are strictly con-
trolled by the Government and wholly unrelated to her
particular medical situation, the Title X client will reasonably construe them as professional advice to forgo her
right to obtain an abortion. As would most rational pa-

tients, many of these women will follow that perceived advice and carry their pregnancy to term, despite their needs to the contrary and despite the safety of the abortion procedure for the vast majority of them. Others, delayed by the Regulations' mandatory prenatal referral, will be prevented from acquiring abortions during the period in which the process is medically sound and constitutionally protected.

In view of the inevitable effect of the Regulations, the majority's conclusion that "[t]he difficulty that a woman encounters when a Title X project does not provide abortion counseling or referral leaves her in no different position than she would have been if the government had not enacted Title X," is insensitive and contrary to common human experience. Both the purpose and result of the challenged Regulations is to deny women the ability voluntarily to decide their procreative destiny. For these women, the Government will have obliterated the freedom to choose as surely as if it had banned abortions outright. The denial of this freedom is not a consequence of poverty but of the Government's ill-intentioned distortion of information it has chosen to provide.

The substantial obstacles to bodily self-determination that the Regulations impose are doubly offensive because they are effected by manipulating the very words spoken by physicians and counselors to their patients. In our society, the doctor/patient dialogue embodies a unique relationship of trust. The specialized nature of medical science and the emotional distress often attendant to health-related decisions requires that patients place their complete confidence, and often their very lives, in the hands of medical professionals. One seeks a physician's aid not only for medication or diagnosis, but also for guidance, professional judgment, and vital emotional support. Accordingly, each of us attaches profound importance and authority to the words of advice spoken by the physician.

It is for this reason that we have guarded so jealously the doctor/patient dialogue from governmental intrusion. . . . The majority's approval of the Secretary's Regulations flies in the face of our repeated warnings that regulations tending to "confine the attending physician in an undesired and uncomfortable straitjacket in the practice of his profession," cannot endure.

The majority attempts to distinguish our holdings in *Akron* and *Thornburgh* on the post-hoc basis that the governmental intrusions into the doctor/patient dialogue invalidated in those cases applied to *all* physicians within a jurisdiction while the Regulations now before the Court pertain to the narrow class of healthcare professionals employed at Title X projects. But the rights protected by the Constitution are *personal* rights. And for the individual woman, the deprivation of liberty by the Government is no less substantial because it affects few rather than many. It cannot be that an otherwise unconstitutional infringement of choice is made lawful because it touches only some of the Nation's pregnant women and not all of them.

The manipulation of the doctor/patient dialogue achieved through the Secretary's Regulations is clearly an effort "to deter a woman from making a decision that, with her physician, is hers to make." As such, it violates the Fifth Amendment.

.... The majority professes to leave undisturbed the free speech protections upon which our society has come to rely, but one must wonder what force the First Amendment retains if it is read to countenance the deliberate manipulation by the Government of the dialogue between a woman and her physician. ... [I]f a right is found to be unenforceable, even against flagrant attempts by government to circumvent it, then it ceases to be a right at all. This, I fear, may be the effect of today's decision.

JUSTICE STEVENS, dissenting: In my opinion, the Court has not paid sufficient attention to the language of the controlling statute or to the consistent interpretation accorded the statute by the responsible cabinet officers during four different Presidencies and 18 years.

The relevant text of the "Family Planning Services and Population Research Act of 1970" has remained unchanged since its enactment. The preamble to the Act states that it was passed:

"To promote public health and welfare by expanding, improving, and better coordinating the family planning services and population research activities of the Federal Government, and for other purposes."

The declaration of congressional purposes emphasizes the importance of educating the public about family planning services. Thus, Section 2 of the Act states, in part, that the purpose of the Act is:

"(1) to assist in making comprehensive voluntary family planning services readily available to all persons desiring such services;

".... (5) to develop and make readily available information (including educational materials) on family planning and population growth to all persons desiring such information."

In contrast to the statutory emphasis on making relevant information readily available to the public, the statute contains no suggestion that Congress intended to authorize the suppression or censorship of any information by any Government employee or by any grant recipient.

Section 6 of the Act authorizes the provision of federal funds to support the establishment and operation of voluntary family planning projects. The section also empowers the Secretary to promulgate regulations imposing conditions on grant recipients to ensure that "such grants will be effectively utilized for the purposes for which made." Not a word in the statute, however, authorizes the Secretary to impose any restrictions on the dissemination of truthful information or professional advice by grant recipients.

The word "prohibition" is used only once in the Act. Section 6, which adds to the Public Health Service Act the new Title X, covering the subject of population research and voluntary planning programs, includes the following provision:

"PROHIBITION OF ABORTION

"SEC. 1008. None of the funds appropriated under this title shall be used in programs where abortion is a method of family planning."

Read in the context of the entire statute, this prohibition is plainly directed at conduct, rather than the dissemination of information or advice, by potential grant recipients.

The original regulations promulgated in 1971 by the Secretary of Health, Education and Welfare so interpreted the statute. This "'contemporaneous construction of [the] statute by the men charged with the responsibility of setting its machinery in motion'" is entitled to particular respect. The regulations described the kind of services that grant recipients had to provide in order to be eligible for federal funding, but they did not purport to regulate or restrict the kinds of advice or information that recipients might make available to their clients. Conforming to the language of the governing statute, the regulations provided that "[t]he project will not *provide* abortions as a method of family planning." Like the statute itself, the regulations prohibited conduct, not speech.

The same is true of the regulations promulgated in 1986 by the Secretary of Health and Human Services. They also prohibited grant recipients from performing abortions but did not purport to censor or mandate any kind of speech.

The entirely new approach adopted by the Secretary in 1988 was not, in my view, authorized by the statute. The new regulations did not merely reflect a change in a policy determination that the Secretary had been authorized by Congress to make. Rather, they represented an assumption of policymaking responsibility that Congress had not delegated to the Secretary. In a society that abhors censorship and in which policymakers have tradition

ally placed the highest value on the freedom to communicate, it is unrealistic to conclude that statutory authority
to regulate conduct implicitly authorized the Executive to
regulate speech.

Because I am convinced that the 1970 Act did not authorize the Secretary to censor the speech of grant recipients
or their employees, I would hold the challenged regulations invalid and reverse the judgment of the Court of
Appeals. . . .

JUSTICE O'CONNOR, dissenting: "[W]here an otherwise
acceptable construction of a statute would raise serious
constitutional problems, the Court will construe the statute to avoid such problems unless such construction is
plainly contrary to the intent of Congress." . . .

"It is a fundamental rule of judicial restraint . . . that this
Court will not reach constitutional questions in advance
of the necessity of deciding them." . . .

This Court acts at the limits of its power when it invali-
dates a law on constitutional grounds. In recognition of
our place in the constitutional scheme, we must act with
"great gravity and delicacy" when telling a coordinate
branch that its actions are absolutely prohibited absent
constitutional amendment. In this case, we need only tell
the Secretary that his regulations are not a reasonable interpretation of the statute; we need not tell Congress that
it cannot pass such legislation. If we rule solely on statutory grounds, Congress retains the power to force the constitutional question by legislating more explicitly. It may
instead choose to do nothing. That decision should be left
to Congress; we should not tell Congress what it cannot do

before it has chosen to do it. It is enough in this case to conclude that neither the language nor the history of Section 1008 compels the Secretary's interpretation, and that the interpretation raises serious First Amendment concerns. On this basis alone, I would reverse the judgment of the Court of Appeals and invalidate the challenged regulations.

PLANNED PARENTHOOD v. CASEY

EXCERPTS

"Liberty finds no refuge in a jurisprudence of doubt."

> Justices Sandra O'Connor,
> Anthony Kennedy, and
> David Souter

"Reason finds no refuge in this jurisprudence of confusion."

> Chief Justice William Rehnquist

"I am 83 years old. I cannot remain on this Court forever, and when I do step down, the confirmation process for my successor well may focus on the issue before us today. That, I regret, may be exactly where the choice between the two worlds will be made."

> Justice Harry Blackmun

In Brief

Question: Are the Pennsylvania abortion laws constitutional?

Lower Court: U.S. District Court, Eastern Pennsylvania
U.S. Court of Appeals, Third Circuit

Law: Pennsylvania Abortion Control Act (1982)

Parties: Planned Parenthood of Southeastern Pennsylvania
Robert Casey, Governor, Pennsylvania

Counsel: For Planned Parenthood: Kathryn Kolbert
For Casey: Ernest Preate, Jr.

Arguments: April 22, 1992

Decision: June 29, 1992

Majority: Justices Blackmun, Stevens, O'Connor, Kennedy, Souter

Minority: Chief Justice Rehnquist, Justices White, Scalia, Thomas

Decision by: Justices O'Connor, Kennedy, Souter (p. 113)

Concurring in part/Dissenting in part:

Justice Stevens (p. 152)
Justice Blackmun (p. 159)
Chief Justice Rehnquist (p. 173)
Justice Scalia (p. 192)

Offical Text: U.S. Reports, Vol. 505
Lower Court: Federal Supplement, Vol. 744, p. 1323
Federal Reporter 2d, Vol. 947, p. 682

THE CASEY COURT

Chief Justice William Rehnquist
Appointed Associate Justice 1971 by Richard M. Nixon
Appointed Chief Justice 1986 by Ronald W. Reagan

Associate Justice Byron White
Appointed 1962 by John F. Kennedy

Associate Justice Harry Blackmun
Appointed 1970 by Richard M. Nixon

Associate Justice John Paul Stevens
Appointed 1975 by Gerald R. Ford

Associate Justice Sandra Day O'Connor
Appointed 1981 by Ronald W. Reagan

Associate Justice Antonin Scalia
Appointed 1986 by Ronald W. Reagan

Associate Justice Anthony Kennedy
Appointed 1988 by Ronald W. Reagan

Associate Justice David Souter
Appointed 1991 by George Bush

Associate Justice Clarence Thomas
Appointed 1992 by George Bush

PLANNED PARENTHOOD v. CASEY

June 29, 1992

JUSTICES O'CONNOR, KENNEDY and SOUTER (joined in part by Justice Stevens): Liberty finds no refuge in a jurisprudence of doubt. Yet 19 years after our holding that the Constitution protects a woman's right to terminate her pregnancy in its early states, that definition of liberty is still questioned. Joining the respondents [Casey] as *amicus curiae* [friends of the Court], the United States, as it has done in five other cases in the last decade, again asks us to overrule *Roe*.

At issue in these cases are five provisions of the Pennsylvania Abortion Control Act of 1982 as amended in 1988 and 1989. . . . The Act requires that a woman seeking an abortion give her informed consent prior to the abortion procedure, and specifies that she be provided with certain information at least 24 hours before the abortion is performed. For a minor to obtain an abortion, the Act requires the informed consent of one of her parents, but provides for a judicial bypass option if the minor does not wish to or cannot obtain a parent's consent. Another provision of the Act requires that, unless certain exceptions apply, a married woman seeking an abortion must sign a statement indicating that she has notified her husband of her intended abortion. The Act exempts compliance with these three requirements in the event of a "medical emergency," which is defined in Section 3203 of the Act. In addition to the above provisions regulating the perform-

ance of abortions, the Act imposes certain reporting requirements on facilities that provide abortion services.

Before any of these provisions took effect, the petitioners,
who are five abortion clinics and one physician representing himself as well as a class of physicians who provide
abortion services, brought this suit seeking declaratory
and injunctive relief. Each provision was challenged as
unconstitutional on its face. The District Court entered a
preliminary injunction [court order stopping an action]
against the enforcement of the regulations, and, after a
3-day bench trial, held all the provisions at issue here unconstitutional, entering a permanent injunction against
Pennsylvania's enforcement of them. The Court of Appeals for the Third Circuit affirmed in part and reversed
in part, upholding all of the regulations except for the
husband notification requirement.

. . . . We disagree with that analysis [that none of the enactments can be upheld without overruling *Roe v. Wade*];
but we acknowledge that our decisions after *Roe* cast
doubt upon the meaning and reach of its holding. Further, the Chief Justice [Williams Rehnquist] admits that
he would overrule the central holding of *Roe* and adopt
the rational relationship test as the sole criterion of constitutionality. State and federal courts as well as legislatures
throughout the Union must have guidance as they seek to
address this subject in conformance with the Constitution.
Given these premises, we find it imperative to review
once more the principles that define the rights of the
woman and the legitimate authority of the State respecting the termination of pregnancies by abortion procedures.

After considering the fundamental constitutional questions resolved by *Roe*, principles of institutional integrity,
and the rule of *stare decisis* [let past decisions stand], we
are led to conclude this: the essential holding of *Roe v.
Wade* should be retained and once again reaffirmed.

It must be stated at the outset and with clarity that *Roe*'s
essential holding, the holding we reaffirm, has three parts.
First is a recognition of the right of the woman to choose
to have an abortion before viability and to obtain it without undue interference from the State. Before viability,
the State's interests are not strong enough to support a
prohibition of abortion or the imposition of a substantial
obstacle to the woman's effective right to elect the procedure. Second is a confirmation of the State's power to restrict abortions after fetal viability, if the law contains exceptions for pregnancies which endanger a woman's life
or health. And third is the principle that the State has legitimate interests from the outset of the pregnancy in protecting the health of the woman and the life of the fetus
that may become a child. These principles do not contra-
dict one another; and we adhere to each.

Constitutional protection of the woman's decision to terminate her pregnancy derives from the Due Process
Clause of the Fourteenth Amendment. It declares that no
State shall "deprive any person of life, liberty, or property, without due process of law." The controlling word in
the case before us is "liberty." Although a literal reading
of the Clause might suggest that it governs only the
procedures by which a State may deprive persons of liberty, for at least 105 years, at least since *Mulger v. Kansas*,
the Clause has been understood to contain a substantive
component as well, one "barring certain government ac-

tions regardless of the fairness of the procedures used to implement them." As Justice Brandeis (joined by Justice Holmes) observed, " . . . all fundamental rights comprised within the term liberty are protected by the Federal Constitution from invasion by the States." . . .

The most familiar of the substantive liberties protected by the Fourteenth Amendment are those recognized by the Bill of Rights. We have held that the Due Process Clause of the Fourteenth Amendment incorporates most of the Bill of Rights against the States. It is tempting, as a means of curbing the discretion of federal judges, to suppose that liberty encompasses no more than those rights already guaranteed to the individual against federal interference by the express provisions of the first eight amendments to the Constitution. But of course this Court has never accepted that view.

It is also tempting, for the same reason, to suppose that the Due Process Clause protects only those practices, defined at the most specific level, that were protected against government interference by other rules of law when the Fourteenth Amendment was ratified. But such a view would be inconsistent with our law. It is a promise of the Constitution that there is a realm of personal liberty which the government may not enter. We have vindicated this principle before. Marriage is mentioned nowhere in the Bill of Rights and interracial marriage was illegal in most States in the 19th century, but the Court was no doubt correct in finding it to be an aspect of liberty protected against state interference by the substantive component of the Due Process Clause in *Loving v. Virginia*. . . .

It is settled now, as it was when the Court heard arguments in *Roe v. Wade*, that the Constitution places limits on a State's right to interfere with a person's most basic decisions about family and parenthood, as well as bodily integrity.

The inescapable fact is that adjudication of substantive due process claims may call upon the Court in interpreting the Constitution to exercise that same capacity which by tradition courts always have exercised: reasoned judgment. Its boundaries are not susceptible of expression as a simple rule. That does not mean we are free to invalidate state policy choices with which we disagree; yet neither does it permit us to shrink from the duties of our office. . . .

Men and women of good conscience can disagree, and we suppose some always shall disagree, about the profound moral and spiritual implications of terminating a pregnancy, even in its spiritual implications of terminating a pregnancy, even in its earliest stage. Some of us as individuals find abortion offensive to our most basic principles of morality, but that cannot control our decision. Our obligation is to define the liberty of all, not to mandate our own moral code. The underlying constitutional issue is whether the State can resolve these philosophic questions in such a definitive way that a woman lacks all choice in the matter, except perhaps in those rare circumstances in which the pregnancy is itself a danger to her own life or health, or is the result of rape or incest.

It is conventional constitutional doctrine that where reasonable people disagree the government can adopt one position or the other. That theorem, however, assumes a

state of affairs in which the choice does not intrude upon
a protected liberty. Thus, while some people might disagree about whether or not the flag should be saluted, or
disagree about the proposition that it may not be defiled,
we have ruled that a State may not compel or enforce one
view or the other.

Our law affords constitutional protection to personal decisions relating to marriage, procreation, contraception, family relationships, child rearing, and education. Our cases
recognize "the right of the *individual*, married or single, to
be free from unwarranted governmental intrusion into
matters so fundamentally affecting a person as the decision whether to bear or beget a child. Our precedents
"have respected the private realm of family life which the
state cannot enter." These matters, involving the most intimate and personal choices a person may make in a lifetime, choices central to personal dignity and autonomy,
are central to the liberty protected by the Fourteenth
Amendment. At the heart of liberty is the right to define
one's own concept of existence, of meaning, of the universe, and of the mystery of human life. Beliefs about
these matters could not define the attributes of personhood were they formed under compulsion of the State.

These considerations begin our analysis of the woman's
interest in terminating her pregnancy but cannot end it,
for this reason: though the abortion decision may originate within the zone of conscience and belief, it is more
than a philosophic exercise. Abortion is a unique act. It
is an act fraught with consequences for others; for the
woman who must live with the implications of her decision; for the persons who perform and assist in the procedure; for the spouse, family, and society which must con-

front the knowledge that these procedures exist, procedures some deem nothing short of an act of violence against innocent human life; and, depending on one's beliefs, for the life or potential life that is aborted. Though abortion is conduct, it does not follow that the State is entitled to proscribe it in all instances. That is because the liberty of the woman is at stake in a sense unique to the human condition and so unique to the law. The mother who carries a child to full term is subject to anxieties, to physical constraints, to pain that only she must bear. That these sacrifices have from the beginning of the human race been endured by woman with a pride that ennobles her in the eyes of others and gives to the infant a bond of love cannot alone be grounds for the State to insist she make the sacrifice. Her suffering is too intimate and personal for the State to insist, without more, upon its own vision of the woman's role, however dominant that vision has been in the course of our history and our culture. The destiny of the woman must be shaped to a large extent on her own conception of her spiritual imperatives and her place in society.

It should be recognized, moreover, that in some critical respects the abortion decision is of the same character as the decision to use contraception, to which *Griswold v. Connecticut, Eisenstadt v. Baird,* and *Carey v. Population Services International,* afford constitutional protection. We have no doubt as to the correctness of those decisions. They support the reasoning in *Roe* relating to the woman's liberty because they involve personal decisions concerning not only the meaning of procreation but also human responsibility and respect for it. As with abortion, reasonable people will have differences of opinion about these matters. One view is based on such reverence for the wonder of creation that any pregnancy ought to be welcomed and carried to full term no matter how difficult it will be to provide for the child and ensure its well-being. Another is that the inability to provide for the nurture and care of the infant is a cruelty to the child and an anguish to the parent. These are intimate views with infinite variations, and their deep, personal character underlay our decisions in *Griswold*, *Eisenstadt*, and *Carey*. The same concerns are present when the woman confronts the reality that, perhaps despite her attempts to avoid it, she has become pregnant.

It was this dimension of personal liberty that *Roe* sought to protect, and its holding invoked the reasoning and the tradition of the precedents we have discussed, granting protection to substantive liberties of the person. *Roe* was, of course, an extension of those cases and, as the decision itself indicated, the separate States could act in some degree to further their own legitimate interests in protecting pre-natal life. The extent to which the legislatures of the States might act to outweigh the interests of the woman in choosing to terminate her pregnancy was a subject of debate both in *Roe* itself and in decisions following it.

While we appreciate the weight of the arguments made on behalf of the State in the case before us, arguments which in their ultimate formulation conclude that *Roe* should be overruled, the reservations any of us may have in reaffirming the central holding of *Roe* are outweighed by the explication of individual liberty we have given combined with the force of *stare decisis*. We turn now to that doctrine.

The obligation to follow precedent begins with necessity, and a contrary necessity marks its outer limit. With [Supreme Court Justice Benjamin] Cardozo, we recognize that no judicial system could do society's work if it eyed each issue afresh in every case that raised it. Indeed, the very concept of the rule of law underlying our own Constitution requires such continuity over time that a respect for precedent is, by definition, indispensable. At the other extreme, a different necessity would make itself felt if a prior judicial ruling should come to be seen so clearly as error that its enforcement was for that very reason doomed.

.... [I]n this case we may inquire whether *Roe*'s central rule has been found unworkable; whether the rule's limitation on state power could be removed without serious inequity to those who have relied upon it or significant damage to the stability of the society governed by the rule in question; whether the law's growth in the intervening years has left *Roe*'s central rule a doctrinal anachronism discounted by society; and whether *Roe*'s premises of fact have so far changed in the ensuing two decades as to render its central holding somehow irrelevant or unjustifiable in dealing with the issue it addressed.

Although *Roe* has engendered opposition, it has in no sense proven "unworkable," representing as it does a simple limitation beyond which a state law is unenforceable. While *Roe* has, of course, required judicial assessment of state laws affecting the exercise of the choice guaranteed against government infringement, and although the need for such review will remain as a consequence of today's decision, the required determinations fall within judicial competence.

.... The Constitution serves human values, and while the
effect of reliance on *Roe* cannot be exactly measured, neither can the certain cost of overruling *Roe* for people
who have ordered their thinking and living around that
case be dismissed.

No evolution of legal principle has left *Roe*'s doctrinal
footings weaker than they were in 1973. No development
of constitutional law since the case was decided has implicitly or explicitly left *Roe* behind as a mere survivor of
obsolete constitutional thinking.

It will be recognized, of course, that *Roe* stands at an in-
tersection of two lines of decisions, but in whichever doctrinal category one reads the case, the result for present
purposes will be the same. The *Roe* Court itself placed its
holding in the succession of cases most prominently exem-
plified by *Casey v. Connecticut.* When it is so seen, *Roe* is
clearly in no jeopardy, since subsequent constitutional developments have neither disturbed, nor do they threaten
to diminish, the scope of recognized protection accorded
to the liberty relating to intimate relationships, the family,
and decisions about whether or not to beget or bear a
child.

Roe, however, may be seen not only as an exemplar of
Griswold liberty but as a rule (whether or not mistaken)
of personal autonomy and bodily integrity, with doctrinal
affinity to cases recognizing limits on governmental power to mandate medical treatment or to bar its rejection. If
so, our cases since *Roe* accord with *Roe*'s view that a
State's interest in the protection of life falls short of justifying any plenary override of individual liberty claims.

Finally, one could classify *Roe* as *sui generis* [unique]. If the case is so viewed, then there clearly has been no erosion of its central determination. The original holding resting on the concurrence of seven Members of the Court in 1973 was expressly affirmed by a majority of six in 1983, and by a majority of five in 1986, expressing adherence to the constitutional ruling despite legislative efforts in some States to test its limits. More recently, in *Webster v. Reproductive Health Services*, although two of the present authors questioned the trimester framework in a way consistent with our judgment today, a majority of the Court either decided to reaffirm or declined to address the constitutional validity of the central holding of *Roe*.

Nor will courts building upon *Roe* be likely to hand down erroneous decisions as a consequence. Even on the assumption that the central holding of *Roe* was in error, that error would go only to the strength of the state interest in fetal protection, not to the recognition afforded by the Constitution to the woman's liberty. . . .

If indeed the woman's interest in deciding whether to bear and beget a child had not been recognized as in *Roe*, the State might as readily restrict a woman's right to choose to carry a pregnancy to term as to terminate it, to further asserted state interests in population control, or eugenics, for example. Yet *Roe* has been sensibly relied upon to counter any such suggestions. . . .

We have seen how time has overtaken some of *Roe*'s factual assumptions; advances in maternal health care allow for abortions safe to the mother later in pregnancy than was true in 1973, and advances in neonatal care have ad-

vanced viability to a point somewhat earlier. But these
facts go only to the scheme of time limits on the realization of competing interests, and the divergences from the
factual premises of 1973 have no bearing on the validity
of *Roe*'s central holding, that viability marks the earliest
point at which the State's interest in fetal life is constitutionally adequate to justify a legislative ban on nontherapeutic abortions. The soundness or unsoundness of that
constitutional judgment in no sense turns on whether viability occurs at approximately 28 weeks, as was usual at
the time of *Roe*, at 23 to 24 weeks, as it sometimes does
today, or at some moment even slightly earlier in pregnancy, as it may if fetal respiratory capacity can somehow be
enhanced in the future. Whenever it may occur, the attainment of viability may continue to serve as the critical
fact, just as it has done since *Roe* was decided; which is to
say that no change in *Roe*'s factual underpinning has left
its central holding obsolete, and none supports an argument for overruling it.

The sum of the precedential inquiry to this point shows
Roe's underpinnings unweakened in any way affecting its
central holding. While it has engendered disapproval, it
has not been unworkable. An entire generation has come
of age free to assume *Roe*'s concept of liberty in defining
the capacity of women to act in society, and to make reproductive decisions; no erosion of principle going to liberty or personal autonomy has left *Roe*'s central holding a
doctrinal remnant; *Roe* portends no developments at odds
with other precedent [past decisions] for the analysis of
personal liberty; and no changes of fact have rendered viability more or less appropriate as the point at which the
balance of interests tips. Within the bounds of normal
stare decisis analysis, then, and subject to the considera-

tions on which it customarily turns, the stronger argument is for affirming *Roe*'s central holding, with whatever degree of personal reluctance any of us may have, not for overruling it.

In a less significant case, *stare decisis* analysis could, and would, stop at the point we have reached. But the sustained and widespread debate *Roe* has provoked calls for some comparison between that case and others of comparable dimension that have responded to national controversies and taken on the impress of the controversies addressed. Only two such decisional lines from the past century present themselves for examination, and in each instances the result reached by the Court accorded with the principles we apply today.

. . . . *West Coast Hotel* and *Brown* each rested on facts, or an understanding of facts, changed from those which furnished the claimed justifications for the earlier constitutional resolutions [in *Adkins* and *Plessy*]. Each case was comprehensible as the Court's response to facts that the country could understand, or had come to understand already, but which the Court of an earlier day, as its own declarations disclosed, had not been able to perceive. As the decisions were thus comprehensible they were also defensible, not merely as the victories of one doctrinal school over another by dint of numbers (victories though they were), but as applications of constitutional principle to facts as they had not been seen by the Court before. In constitutional adjudication as elsewhere in life, changed circumstances may impose new obligations, and the thoughtful part of the Nation could accept each decision to overrule a prior case as a response to the Court's constitutional duty.

Because the case before us presents no such occasion it
could be seen as no such response. Because neither the
factual underpinnings of *Roe*'s central holding nor our
understanding of it has changed (and because no other indication of weakened precedent has been shown) the
Court could not pretend to be reexamining the prior law
with any justification beyond a present doctrinal disposition to come out differently from the Court of 1973. To
overrule prior law for no other reason than that would
run counter to the view repeated in our cases, that a decision to overrule should rest on some special reason over
and above the belief that a prior case was wrongly decided.

The examination of the conditions justifying the repudiation of *Adkins* by *West Coast Hotel* and *Plessy* by *Brown*
is enough to suggest the terrible price that would have
been paid if the Court had not overruled as it did. In the
present case, however, as our analysis to this point makes
clear, the terrible price would be paid for overruling. Our
analysis would not be complete, however, without explaining why overruling *Roe*'s central holding would not only
reach an unjustifiable result under principles of *stare
decisis*, but would seriously weaken the Court's capacity
to exercise the judicial power and to function as the Supreme Court of a Nation dedicated to the rule of law. To
understand why this would be so it is necessary to understand the source of this Court's authority, the conditions
necessary for its preservation, and its relationship to the
country's understanding of itself as a constitutional Re-
public.

The root of American governmental power is revealed
most clearly in the instance of the power conferred by the

Constitution upon the Judiciary of the United States and specifically upon this Court. As Americans of each succeeding generation are rightly told, the Court cannot buy support for its decisions by spending money and, except to a minor degree, it cannot independently coerce obedience to its decrees. The Court's power lies, rather, in its legitimacy, a product of substance and perception that shows itself in the people's acceptance of the Judiciary as fit to determine what the Nation's law means and to declare what it demands.

The underlying substance of this legitimacy is of course the warrant for the Court's decisions in the Constitution and the lesser sources of legal principle on which the Court draws. That substance is expressed in the Court's opinions, and our contemporary understanding is such that a decision without principled justification would be no judicial act at all. . . . The Court must take care to speak and act in ways that allow people to accept its decisions on the terms the Court claims for them, as grounded truly in principle, not as compromises with social and political pressures having, as such, no bearing on the principled choices that the Court is obliged to make. Thus, the Court's legitimacy depends on making legally principled decisions under circumstances in which their principled character is sufficiently plausible to be accepted by the Nation.

. . . . People understand that some of the Constitution's language is hard to fathom and that the Court's Justices are sometimes able to perceive significant facts or to understand principles of law that eluded their predecessors and that justify departures from existing decisions. However upsetting it may be to those most directly affected when one judicially derived rule replaced another, the country can accept some correction of error without necessarily questioning the legitimacy of the Court.

In two circumstances, however, the Court would almost certainly fail to receive the benefit of the doubt in overruling prior cases. There is, first, a point beyond which frequent overruling would overtax the country's belief in the Court's good faith. . . . There is a limit to the amount of error that can plausibly be imputed to prior courts. . . . The legitimacy of the Court would fade with the frequency of its vacillation.

That first circumstance can be described as hypothetical; the second is to the point here and now. Where, in the performance of its judicial duties, the Court decides a case in such a way as to resolve the sort of intensely divisive controversy reflected in *Roe* and those rare, comparable cases, its decision has a dimension that the resolution of the normal case does not carry. It is the dimension present whenever the Court's interpretation of the Constitution calls the contending sides of a national controversy to end their national division by accepting a common mandate rooted in the Constitution.

The Court is not asked to do this very often, having thus addressed the Nation only twice in our lifetime, in the decisions of *Brown* and *Roe*. But when the Court does act in this way, its decision requires an equally rare precedential force to counter the inevitable efforts to overturn it and to thwart its implementation. . . . [O]nly the most convincing justification under accepted standards of precedent could suffice to demonstrate that a later decision overruling the first was anything but a surrender to political pressure, and an unjustified repudiation of the principle on which the Court staked its authority in the first instance. So to overrule under fire in the absence of the most compelling reason to reexamine a watershed decision would subvert the Court's legitimacy beyond any serious question.

. . . . The promise of constancy, once given, binds its maker for as long as the power to stand by the decision survives and the understanding of the issue has not changed so fundamentally as to render the commitment obsolete. From the obligation of this promise this Court cannot and should not assume any exemption when duty requires it to decide a case in conformance with the Constitution. A willing breach of it would be nothing less than a breach of faith, and no Court that broke its faith with the people could sensibly expect credit for principle in the decision by which it did that.

. . . . Like the character of an individual, the legitimacy of the Court must be earned over time. So, indeed, must be the character of a Nation of people who aspire to live according to the rule of law. Their belief in themselves as such a people is not readily separable from their understanding of the Court invested with the authority to decide their constitutional cases and speak before all others for their constitutional ideals. If the Court's legitimacy should be undermined, then, so would the country be in its very ability to see itself through its constitutional ideals. The Court's concern with legitimacy is not for the sake of the Court but for the sake of the Nation to which it is responsible.

The Court's duty in the present case is clear. In 1973, it confronted the already-divisive issue of governmental power to limit personal choice to undergo abortion, for which it provided a new resolution based on the due process guaranteed by the Fourteenth Amendment. Whether or not a new social consensus is developing on that issue, its divisiveness is no less today than in 1973, and pressure to overrule the decision, like pressure to retain it, has grown only more intense. A decision to overrule *Roe*'s essential holding under the existing circumstances would address error, if error there was, at the cost of both profound and unnecessary damage to the Court's legitimacy, and to the Nation's commitment to the rule of law. It is therefore imperative to adhere to the essence of *Roe*'s original decision, and we do so today.

From what we have said so far it follows that it is a constitutional liberty of the woman to have some freedom to terminate her pregnancy. We conclude that the basic decision in *Roe* was based on a constitutional analysis which we cannot now repudiate. The woman's liberty is not so unlimited, however, that from the outset the State cannot show its concern for the life of the unborn, and at a later point in fetal development the State's interest in life has sufficient force so that the right of the woman to terminate the pregnancy can be restricted.

That brings us, of course, to the point where much criticism has been directed at *Roe*, a criticism that always inheres when the Court draws a specific rule from what in the Constitution is but a general standard. We conclude, however, that the urgent claims of the woman to retain the ultimate control over her destiny and her body, claims implicit in the meaning of liberty, require us to perform

that function. Liberty must not be extinguished for want
of a line that is clear. And it falls to us to give some real
substance to the woman's liberty to determine whether to
carry her pregnancy to full term.

We conclude the line should be drawn at viability, so that
before that time the woman has a right to choose to terminate her pregnancy. We adhere to this principle for two
reasons. First, as we have said, is the doctrine of stare
decisis. Any judicial act of line-drawing may seem somewhat arbitrary, but *Roe* was a reasoned statement, elabo-
rated with great care. We have twice reaffirmed it in the
face of great opposition. Although we must overrule
those parts of *Thornburgh* and *Akron I* which, in our
view, are inconsistent with *Roe*'s statement that the State
has a legitimate interest in promoting the life or potential
life of the unborn, the central premise of those cases represents an unbroken committee by this Court to the essential holding of *Roe*. It is that premise which we reaffirm
today.

The second reason is that the concept of viability, as we
noted in *Roe*, is the time at which there is a realistic possibility of maintaining and nourishing a life outside the
womb, so that the independent existence of the second life
can in reason and all fairness by the object of state protection that now overrides the rights of the woman. . . . To
be sure, as we have said, there may be some medical developments that affect the precise point of viability, but this
is an imprecision within tolerable limits given that the
medical community and all those who must apply its discoveries will continue to explore the matter. The viability
line also has, as a practical matter, an element of fairness.
In some broad sense it might be said that a woman who

fails to act before viability has consented to the State's intervention on behalf of the developing child.

The woman's right to terminate her pregnancy before viability is the most central principle of *Roe v. Wade.* It is a rule of law and a component of liberty we cannot renounce.

On the other side of the equation is the interest of the State in the protection of potential life. The *Roe* Court recognized the State's "important and legitimate interest in protecting the potentiality of human life." The weight to be given this state interest, not the strength of the woman's interest, was the difficult question faced in *Roe.* We do not need to say whether each of us, had we been Members of the Court when the valuation of the State interest came before it as an original matter, would have concluded, as the *Roe* Court did, that its weight is insufficient to justify a ban on abortions prior to viability even when it is subject to certain exceptions. The matter is not before us in the first instance, and coming as it does after nearly 20 years of litigation in *Roe's* wake we are satisfied that the immediate question is not the soundness of *Roe's* resolution of the issue, but the precedential force that must be accorded to its holding. And we have concluded that the essential holding of *Roe* should be reaffirmed.

Yet it must be remembered that *Roe v. Wade* speaks with clarity in establishing not only the woman's liberty but also the State's "important and legitimate interest in potential life." That portion of the decision in *Roe* has been given too little acknowledgement and implementation by the Court in its subsequent cases. . . .

Roe established a trimester framework to govern abortion regulations. Under this elaborate but rigid construct, almost no regulation at all is permitted during the first trimester of pregnancy; regulations designed to protect the woman's health, but not to further the State's interest in potential life, are permitted during the second trimester; and during the third trimester, when the fetus is viable, prohibitions are permitted provided the life or health of the mother is not at stake. Most of our cases since *Roe* have involved the application of rules derived from the trimester framework.

The trimester framework no doubt was erected to ensure that the woman's right to choose not become so subordinate to the State's interest in promoting fetal life that her choice exists in theory but not in fact. We do not agree, however, that the trimester approach is necessary to accomplish this objective. A framework of this rigidity was unnecessary and in its later interpretation sometimes contradicted the State's permissible exercise of its powers.

Though the woman has a right to choose to terminate or continue her pregnancy before viability, it does not at all follow that the State is prohibited from taking steps to ensure that this choice is thoughtful and informed. Even in the earliest stages of pregnancy, the State may enact rules and regulations designed to encourage her to know that there are philosophic and social arguments of great weight that can be brought to bear in favor of continuing the pregnancy to full term and that there are procedures and institutions to allow adoption of unwanted children as well as a certain degree of state assistance if the mother chooses to raise the child herself. "'[T]he Constitution does not forbid a State or city, pursuant to democratic

processes, from expressing a preference for normal childbirth.'" It follows that States are free to enact laws to
provide a reasonable framework for a woman to make a
decision that has such profound and lasting meaning.
This, too, we find consistent with *Roe*'s central premises,
and indeed the inevitable consequence of our holding that
the State has an interest in protecting the life of the unborn.

We reject the trimester framework, which we do not consider to be part of the essential holding of *Roe*.... A logical reading of *Roe* itself, and a necessary reconciliation of
the liberty of the woman and the interest of the State in
promoting prenatal life, require, in our view, that we
abandon the trimester framework as a rigid prohibition on
all previability regulation aimed at the protection of fetal
life. The trimester framework suffers from these basic
flaws: in its formulation it misconceives the nature of the
pregnant woman's interest; and in practice it undervalues
the State's interest in potential life, as recognized in *Roe*.

As our jurisprudence relating to all liberties save perhaps
abortion has recognized, not every law which makes a
right more difficult to exercise is, ipso facto [in fact], an
infringement of that right. ...

The fact that a law which serves a valid purpose, one not
designed to strike at the right itself, has the incidental effect of making it more difficult or more expensive to pro-
cure an abortion cannot be enough to invalidate it. Only
where state regulation imposes an undue burden on a
woman's ability to make this decision does the power of
the State reach into the heart of the liberty protected by
the Due Process Clause.

For the most part, the Court's early abortion cases adhered to this view. . . .

These considerations of the nature of the abortion right illustrate that it is an overstatement to describe it as a right to decide whether to have an abortion "without interference from the State." All abortion regulations interfere to some degree with a woman's ability to decide whether to terminate her pregnancy. It is, as a consequence, not surprising that despite the protestations contained in the original *Roe* opinion to the effect that the Court was not recognizing an absolute right, the Court's experience applying the trimester framework has led to the striking down of some abortion regulations which in no real sense deprived women of the ultimate decision. Those decisions went too far because the right recognized by *Roe* is a right "to be free from unwarranted governmental intrusion into matters to fundamentally affecting a person as the decision whether to bear or beget a child." Not all governmental intrusion is of necessity unwarranted; and that brings us to the other basic flaw in the trimester framework: even in *Roe*'s terms, in practice it undervalues the State's interest in the potential life within the woman.

. . . . The trimester framework . . . does not fulfill *Roe*'s own promise that the State has an interest in protecting fetal life or potential life. *Roe* began the contradiction by using the trimester framework to forbid any regulation of abortion designed to advance that interest before viability. Before viability, *Roe* and subsequent cases treat all governmental attempts to influence a woman's decision on behalf of the potential life within her as unwarranted. This treatment is, in our judgment, incompatible with the recognition that there is a substantial state interest in potential life throughout pregnancy.

The very notion that the State has a substantial interest in potential life leads to the conclusion that not all regulations must be deemed unwarranted. Not all burdens on the right to decide whether to terminate a pregnancy will be undue. In our view, the undue burden standard is the appropriate means of reconciling the State's interest with the woman's constitutionally protected liberty.

. . . . Because we set forth a standard of general application to which we intend to adhere, it is important to clarify what is meant by an undue burden.

A finding of an undue burden is a shorthand for the conclusion that a state regulation has the purpose or effect of placing a substantial obstacle in the path of a woman seeking an abortion of a nonviable fetus. A statute with this purpose is invalid because the means chosen by the State to further the interest in potential life must be calculated to inform the woman's free choice, not hinder it. And a statute which, while furthering the interest in potential life or some other valid state interest, has the effect of placing a substantial obstacle in the path of a woman's choice cannot be considered a permissible means of serving its legitimate ends. . . . In our considered judgment, an undue burden is an unconstitutional burden. Understood another way, we answer the question, left open in previous opinions discussing the undue burden formulation, whether a law designed to further the State's interest in fetal life which imposes an undue burden on the woman's decision before fetal viability could be constitutional. . . .

Some guiding principles should emerge. What is at stake is the woman's right to make the ultimate decision, not a right to be insulated from all others in doing so. Regulations which do no more than create a structural mechanism by which the State, or the parent or guardian of a minor, may express profound respect for the life of the unborn are permitted, if they are not a substantial obstacle to the woman's exercise of the right to choose. Unless it has that effect on her right of choice, a state measure designed to persuade her to choose childbirth over abortion will be upheld if reasonably related to that goal. Regulations designed to foster the health of a woman seeking an abortion are valid if they do not constitute an undue burden.

. . . . To protect the central right recognized by *Roe v. Wade* while at the same time accommodating the State's profound interest in potential life, we will employ the undue burden analysis as explained in this opinion. An undue burden exists, and therefore a provision of law is invalid, if its purpose or effect is to place a substantial obstacle in the path of a woman seeking an abortion before the fetus attains viability.

We reject the rigid trimester framework of *Roe v. Wade.* To promote the State's profound interest in potential life, throughout pregnancy the State may take measures to ensure that the woman's choice is informed, and measures designed to advance this interest will not be invalidated as long as their purpose is to persuade the woman to choose childbirth over abortion. These measures must not be an undue burden on the right.

As with any medical procedure, the State may enact regulations to further the health or safety of a woman seeking
an abortion. Unnecessary health regulations that have the
purpose or effect of presenting a substantial obstacle to a
woman seeking an abortion impose an undue burden on
the right.

Our adoption of the undue burden analysis does not dis-
turb the central holding of *Roe v. Wade*, and we reaffirm
that holding. Regardless of whether exceptions are made
for particular circumstances, a State may not prohibit any
woman from making the ultimate decision to terminate
her pregnancy before viability.

We also reaffirm *Roe*'s holding that "subsequent to viability, the State in promoting its interest in the potentiality
of human life may, if it chooses, regulate, and even proscribe, abortion except where it is necessary, in appropriate medical judgment, for the preservation of the life or
health of the mother."

. . . . The Court of Appeals applied what it believed to be
the undue burden standard and upheld each of the provisions except for the husband notification requirement.
We agree generally with this conclusion, but refine the
undue burden analysis in accordance with the principles
articulated above. . . .

Because it is central to the operation of various other requirements, we begin with the statute's definition of medical emergency. Under the statute, a medical emergency is

"[t]hat condition which, on the basis of the physician's
good faith clinical judgment, so complicates the medi-

cal condition of a pregnant woman as to necessitate the immediate abortion of her pregnancy to avert her death or for which a delay will create serious risk of substantial and irreversible impairment of a major bodily function."

. . . . We . . . conclude that, as construed by the Court of Appeals, the medical emergency definition imposes no undue burden on a woman's abortion right.

We next consider the informed consent requirement. Except in a medical emergency, the statute requires that at least 24 hours before performing an abortion a physician inform the woman of the nature of the procedure, the health risks of the abortion and of childbirth, and the "probable gestational age of the unborn child." The physician or a qualified nonphysician must inform the woman of the availability of printed materials published by the State describing the fetus and providing information about medical assistance for childbirth, information about child support from the father, and a list of agencies which provide adoption and other services as alternatives to abortion. An abortion may not be performed unless the woman certifies in writing that she has been informed of the availability of these printed materials and has been provided them if she chooses to view them.

Our prior decisions establish that as with any medical procedure, the State may require a woman to give her written informed consent to an abortion. In this respect, the statute is unexceptional. . . .

To the extent *Akron I* and *Thornburgh* find a constitutional violation when the government requires, as it does

here, the giving of truthful, nonmisleading information
about the nature of the procedure, the attendant health
risks and those of childbirth, and the "probable gestational
age" of the fetus, those cases go too far, are inconsistent
with *Roe*'s acknowledgment of an important interest in
potential life, and are overruled. . . . In attempting to ensure that a woman apprehend the full consequences of her
decision, the State furthers the legitimate purpose of re-
ducing the risk that a woman may elect an abortion, only
to discover later, with devastating psychological consequences, that her decision was not fully informed. If the
information the State requires to be made available to the
woman is truthful and not misleading, the requirement
may be permissible.

We also see no reason why the State may not require doctors to inform a woman seeking an abortion of the availability of materials relating to the consequences to the fetus, even when those consequences have no direct relation
to her health. . . . A requirement that the physician make
available information similar to that mandated by the statute here was described in *Thornburgh* as "an outright attempt to wedge the Commonwealth's message discourag-
ing abortion into the privacy of the informed-consent dialogue between the woman and her physician." We conclude, however, that informed choice need not be defined
in such narrow terms that all considerations of the effect
on the fetus are made irrelevant. As we have made clear,
we depart from the holdings of *Akron I* and *Thornburgh*
to the extent that we permit a State to further its legitimate goal of protecting the life of the unborn by enacting
legislation aimed at ensuring a decision that is mature and
informed, even when in so doing the State expresses a
preference for childbirth over abortion. In short, requir-

ing that the woman be informed of the availability of information relating to fetal development and the assistance available should she decide to carry the pregnancy to full term is a reasonable measure to insure an informed choice, one which might cause the woman to choose childbirth over abortion. This requirement cannot be considered a substantial obstacle to obtaining an abortion, and, it follows, there is no undue burden.

. . . . [I]t is worth noting that the statute now before us does not require a physician to comply with the informed consent provisions "if he or she can demonstrate by a preponderance of the evidence, that he or she reasonably believed that furnishing the information would have resulted in a severely adverse effect on the physical or mental health of the patient." In this respect, the statute does not prevent the physician from exercising his or her medical judgment.

. . . . [A] requirement that a doctor give a woman certain information as part of obtaining her consent to an abortion is, for constitutional purposes, no different from a requirement that a doctor give certain specific information about any medical procedure.

All that is left of [Casey's] argument is an asserted First Amendment right of a physician not to provide information about the risks of abortion, and childbirth, in a manner mandated by the State. To be sure, the physician's First Amendment rights not to speak are implicated, but only as part of the practice of medicine, subject to reasonable licensing and regulation by the State. We see no constitutional infirmity in the requirement that the physician provide the information mandated by the State here.

The Pennsylvania statute also requires us to reconsider the holding in *Akron I* that the State may not require that a physician, as opposed to a qualified assistant, provide information relevant to a woman's informed consent. Since there is no evidence on this record that requiring a doctor to give the information as provided by the statute would amount in practical terms to a substantial obstacle to a woman seeking an abortion, we conclude that it is not an undue burden. Our cases reflect the fact that the Constitution gives the States broad latitude to decide that particular functions may be performed only by licensed professionals, even if an objective assessment might suggest that those same tasks could be performed by others. Thus, we uphold the provision as a reasonable means to insure that the woman's consent is informed.

Our analysis of Pennsylvania's 24-hour waiting period between the provision of the information deemed necessary to informed consent and the performance of an abortion under the undue burden standard requires us to reconsider the premise behind the decision in *Akron I* invalidating a parallel requirement. In *Akron I* we said: "Nor are we convinced that the State's legitimate concern that the woman's decision be informed is reasonably served by requiring a 24-hour delay as a matter of course." We consider that conclusion to be wrong. The idea that important decisions will be more informed and deliberate if they follow some period of reflection does not strike us as unreasonable, particularly where the statute directs that important information become part of the background of the decision. The statute, as construed by the Court of

Appeals, permits avoidance of the waiting period in the event of a medical emergency and the record evidence shows that in the vast majority of cases, a 24-hour delay does not create any appreciable health risk. In theory, at least, the waiting period is a reasonable measure to implement the State's interest in protecting the life of the unborn, a measure that does not amount to an undue burden.

Whether the mandatory 24-hour waiting period is nonetheless invalid because in practice it is a substantial obstacle to a woman's choice to terminate her pregnancy is a closer question. . . . [T]he District Court found that for those women who have the fewest financial resources, those who must travel long distances, and those who have difficulty explaining their whereabouts to husbands, employers, or others, the 24-hour waiting period will be "particularly burdensome."

These findings are troubling in some respects, but they do not demonstrate that the waiting period constitutes an undue burden. . . . [U]nder the undue burden standard a State is permitted to enact persuasive measures which favor childbirth over abortion, even if those measures do not further a health interest. And while the waiting period does limit a physician's discretion, that is not, standing alone, a reason to invalidate it. In light of the construction given the statute's definition of medical emergency by the Court of Appeals, and the District Court's findings, we cannot say that the waiting period imposes a real health risk.

. . . . A particular burden is not of necessity a substantial obstacle. Whether a burden falls on a particular group is a distinct inquiry from whether it is a substantial obstacle even as to the women in that group.... [W]e are not convinced that the 24-hour waiting period constitutes an undue burden.

We are left with the argument that the various aspects of the informed consent requirement are unconstitutional because they place barriers in the way of abortion on demand. Even the broadest reading of *Roe*, however, has not suggested that there is a constitutional right to abortion on demand. Rather, the right protected by *Roe* is a right to decide to terminate a pregnancy free of undue interference by the State. Because the informed consent requirement facilitates the wise exercise of that right it cannot be classified as an interference with the right *Roe* protects. The informed consent requirement is not an undue burden on that right.

Section 3209 of Pennsylvania's abortion law provides, except in cases of medical emergency, that no physician shall perform an abortion on a married woman without receiving a signed statement from the woman that she has notified her spouse that she is about to undergo an abortion. The woman has the option of providing an alternative signed statement certifying that her husband is not the man who impregnated her; that her husband could not be located; that the pregnancy is the result of spousal sexual assault which she has reported; or that the woman believes that notifying her husband will cause him or someone else to inflict bodily injury upon her. A physician who performs an abortion on a married woman without receiving the appropriate signed statement will have his or her license revoked, and is liable to the husband for damages.

. . . . The vast majority of women notify their male part-
ners of their decision to obtain an abortion. In many
cases in which married women do not notify their husbands, the pregnancy is the result of an extramarital af-
fair. Where the husband is the father, the primary reason
women do not notify their husbands is that the husband
and wife are experiencing marital difficulties, often ac-
companied by incidents of violence.

. . . . In well-functioning marriages, spouses discuss important intimate decisions such as whether ot bear a child.
But there are millions of women in this country who are
the victims of regular physical and psychological abuse at
the hands of their husbands. Should these women become
pregnant, they may have very good reasons for not wish-
ing to inform their husbands of their decision to obtain an
abortion. Many may have justifiable fears of physical
abuse, but may be no less fearful of the consequences of
reporting prior abuse to the Commonwealth of Pennsylvania. Many may have a reasonable fear that notifying their
husbands will provoke further instances of child abuse;
these women are not exempt from Section 3209's notification requirement. Many may fear devastating forms of
psychological abuse from their husbands, including abuse
from their husbands, including verbal harrassment, threats
of future violence, the destruction of possessions, physical
confinement to the home, the withdrawal of financial support, or the disclosure of the abortion to family and
friends. These methods of psychological abuse may act as
even more of a deterrent to notification than the possibility of physical violence, but women who are the victims of
the abuse are not exempt from Section 3209's notification
requirement. And many women who are pregnant as a result of sexual assaults by their husbands will be unable to

avail themselves of the exception for spousal sexual assault, because the exception requires that the woman have notified law enforcement authorities within 90 days of the assault, and her husband will be notified of her report once an investigation begins. If anything in this field is certain, it is that victims of spousal sexual assault are extremely reluctant to report the abuse to the government; hence, a great many spousal rape victims will not be exempt from the notification requirement imposed by Section 3209.

The spousal notification requirement is thus likely to prevent a significant number of women from obtaining an abortion. It does not merely make abortions a little more difficult or expensive to obtain; for many women, it will impose a substantial obstacle. We must not blind ourselves to the fact that the significant number of women who fear for their safety and the safety of their children are likely to be deterred from procuring an abortion as surely as if the Commonwealth had outlawed abortion in all cases.

. . . . Legislation is measured for consistency with the Constitution by its impact on those whose conduct it affects. . . . The proper focus of constitutional inquiry is the group for whom the law is a restriction, not the group for whom the law is irrelevant.

. . . . The unfortunate yet persisting conditions we document above will mean that in a large fraction of cases in which Section 3209 is relevant, it will operate as a substantial obstacle to a woman's choice to undergo an abortion. It is an undue burden, and therefore invalid.

This conclusion is in no way inconsistent with our decisions upholding parental notification or consent requirements. Those enactments, and our judgment that they are constitutional, are based on the quite reasonable assumption that minors will benefit from consultation with their parents and that children will often not realize that their parents have their best interests at heart. We cannot adopt a parallel assumption about adult women.

We recognize that a husband has a "deep and proper concern and interest . . . in his wife's pregnancy and in the growth and development of the fetus she is carrying." With regard to the children he has fathered and raised, the Court has recognized his "cognizable and substantial" interest in their custody. If this case concerned a State's ability to require the mother to notify the father before taking some action with respect to a living child raised by both, therefore, it would be reasonable to conclude as a general matter that the father's interest in the welfare of the child and the mother's interest are equal.

Before birth, however, the issue takes on a very different cast. It is an inescapable biological fact that state regulation with respect to the child a woman is carrying will have a far greater impact on the mother's liberty than on the father's. . . . The Constitution protects individuals, men and women alike, from unjustified state interference, even when that interference is enacted into law for the benefit of their spouses.

There was a time, not so long ago, when a different understanding of the family and of the Constitution prevailed. In *Bradwell v. Illinois*, three Members of this Court reaffirmed the common-law principle that "a woman had no

legal existence separate from her husband, who was regarded as her head and representative in the social state;
and, notwithstanding some recent modifications of this
civil status, many of the special rules of law flowing from
and dependent upon this cardinal principle still exist in
full force in most States." Only one generation has passed
since this Court observed that "woman is still regarded as
the center of home and family life," with attendant
"special responsibilities" that precluded full and independent legal status under the Constitution. These views, of
course, are no longer consistent with our understanding of
the family, the individual, or the Constitution.

.... For the great many women who are victims of abuse
inflicted by their husbands, or whose children are the victims of such abuse, a spousal notice requirement enables
the husband to wield an effective veto over his wife's decision. ... The women most affected by this law - those
who most reasonably fear the consequences of notifying
their husbands that they are pregnant - are in the gravest
danger.

The husband's interest in the life of the child his wife is
carrying does not permit the State to empower him with
this troubling degree of authority over his wife. ... A
husband has no enforceable right to require a wife to ad-
vise him before she exercises her personal choices. If a
husband's interest in the potential life of the child outweighs a wife's liberty, the State could require a married
woman to notify her husband before she uses a postfertili-
zation contraceptive. Perhaps next in line would be a statute requiring pregnant married women to notify their
husbands before engaging in conduct causing risks to the
fetus. After all, if the husband's interest in the fetus'

safety is a sufficient predicate for state regulation, the State could reasonably conclude that pregnant wives should notify their husbands before drinking alcohol or smoking. Perhaps married women should notify their husbands before using contraceptives or before undergoing any type of surgery that may have complications affecting the husband's interest in his wife's reproductive organs. And if a husband's interest justifies notice in any of these cases, one might reasonably argue that it justifies exactly what the *Danforth* Court held it did not justify - a requirement of the husband's consent as well. A State may not give to a man the kind of dominion over his wife that parents exercise over their children.

Section 3209 embodies a view of marriage consonant with the common-law status of married women but repugnant to our present understanding of marriage and of the nature of the rights secured by the Constitution. Women do not lose their constitutionally protected liberty when they marry. The Constitution protects all individuals, male or female, married or unmarried, from the abuse of governmental power, even where that power is employed for the supposed benefit of a member of the individual's family. These considerations confirm our conclusion that Section 3209 is invalid.

We next consider the parental consent provision. Except in a medical emergency, an unemancipated young woman under 18 may not obtain an abortion unless she and one of her parents (or guardian) provides informed consent as defined above. If neither a parent nor a guardian provides consent, a court may authorize the performance of an abortion upon a determination that the young woman is mature and capable of giving informed consent and has in fact given her informed consent, or that an abortion would be in her best interests.

We have been over most of this ground before. Our cases establish, and we reaffirm today, that a State may require a minor seeking an abortion to obtain the consent of a parent or guardian, provided that there is an adequate judicial bypass procedure. Under these precedents, in our view, the one-parent consent requirement and judicial bypass procedure are constitutional.

Under the recordkeeping and reporting requirements of the statute, every facility which performs abortions is required to file a report stating its name and address as well as the name and address of any related entity, such as a controlling or subsidiary organization. In the case of state-funded institutions, the information becomes public.

For each abortion performed, a report must be filed identifying: the physician (and the second physician where required); the facility; the referring physician or agency; the woman's age; the number of prior pregnancies and prior abortions she has had; gestational age; the type of abortion procedure; the date of the abortion; whether there were any pre-existing medical conditions which would complicate pregnancy; medical complications with the abortion; where applicable, the basis for the determination that the abortion was medically necessary; the weight of the aborted fetus; and whether the woman was married, and if so, whether notice was provided or the basis for the failure to give notice. Every abortion facility must also file quarterly reports showing the number of abortions performed broken down by trimester. In all events, the identity of each woman who has had an abortion remains confidential.

. . . . We think that . . . all the provision at issue here except that relating to spousal notice are constitutional. Although they do not relate to the State's interest in informing the woman's choice, they do relate to health. The collection of information with respect to actual patients is a vital element of medical research, and so it cannot be said that the requirements serve no purpose other than to make abortions more difficult. Nor do we find that the requirements impose a substantial obstacle to a woman's choice. At most they might increase the cost of some abortions by a slight amount. While at some point increased cost could become a substantial obstacle, there is no such showing on the record before us.

Subsection (12) of the reporting provision requires the reporting of, among other things, a married woman's "reason for failure to provide notice" to her husband. This provision in effect requires women, as a condition of obtaining an abortion, to provide the Commonwealth with the precise information we have already recognized that many women have pressing reasons not to reveal. Like the spousal notice requirement itself, this provision places an undue burden on a woman's choice, and must be invalidated for that reason.

Our Constitution is a covenant running from the first generation of Americans to us and then to future generations. It is a coherent succession. Each generation must learn anew that the Constitution's written terms embody ideas and aspirations that must survive more ages than one. We accept our responsibility no to retreat from interpreting the full meaning of the covenant in light of all of our precedents. We invoke it once again to define the freedom guaranteed by the Constitution's own promise, the promise of liberty.

The judgment . . . is affirmed [confirmed]. . . .

It is so ordered.

JUSTICE STEVENS, concurring in part and dissenting in part: . . . . The Court is unquestionably correct in concluding that the doctrine of stare decisis has controlling significance in a case of this kind. . . . The central holding of *Roe v. Wade* has been a "part of our law" for almost two decades. The societal costs of overruling *Roe* at this late date would be enormous. *Roe* is an integral part of a correct understanding of both the concept of liberty and the basic equality of men and women.

Stare decisis also provides a sufficient basis for my agreement with the joint opinion's reaffirmation of *Roe*'s post-viability analysis. Specifically, I accept the proposition that "[i]f the State is interested in protecting fetal life after viability, it may go so far as to proscribe abortion during that period, except when it is necessary to preserve the life or health of the mother."

I also accept what is implicit in the Court's analysis, namely, a reaffirmation of *Roe*'s explanation of *why* the State's obligation to protect the life or health of the mother must take precedence over any duty to the unborn. The Court in *Roe* carefully considered, and rejected, the State's argument "that the fetus is a 'person' within the language and meaning of the Fourteenth Amendment." After analyzing

the usage of "person" in the Constitution, the Court concluded that that word "has application only postnatally."
Commenting on the contingent property interests of the
unborn that are generally represented by guardians ad li-
tem [court-appointed guardians for minors], the Court
noted: "Perfection of the interests involved, again, has
generally been contingent upon live birth. In short, the
unborn have never been recognized in the law as persons
in the whole sense." Accordingly, an abortion is not "the
termination of life entitled to Fourteenth Amendment
protection." From this holding, there was no dissent; indeed, no member of the Court has ever questioned this
fundamental proposition. Thus, as a matter of federal
constitutional law, a developing organism that is not yet a
"person" does not have what is sometimes described as a
"right to life." This has been and, by the Court's holding
today, remains a fundamental premise of our constitutional law governing reproductive autonomy.

My disagreement with the joint opinion begins with its
understanding of the trimester framework established in
Roe. Contrary to the suggestion of the joint opinion, it is
not a "contradiction" to recognize that the State may have
a legitimate interest in potential human life and, at the
same time, to conclude that that interest does not justify
the regulation of abortion before viability (although other
interests, such as maternal health, may). The fact that the
State's interest is legitimate does not tell us when, if ever,
that interest outweighs the pregnant woman's interest in
personal liberty. It is appropriate, therefore, to consider
more carefully the nature of the interests at stake.

First, it is clear that, in order to be legitimate, the State's
interest must be secular; consistent with the First Amend-

ment the State may not promote a theological or sectarian interest. Moreover, as discussed above, the state interest in potential human life is not an interest in loco parentis [in place of a parent], for the fetus is not a person.

Identifying the State's interests - which the States rarely articulate with any precision - makes clear that the interest in protecting potential life is not grounded in the Constitution. It is, instead, an indirect interest supported by both humanitarian and pragmatic concerns. Many of our citizens believe that any abortion reflects an unacceptable disrespect for potential human life and the the performance of more than a million abortions each year is intolerable; many find third-trimester abortions performed when the fetus is approaching personhood particularly offensive. The State has a legitimate interest in minimizing such offense. The State may also have a broader interest in expanding the population, believing society would benefit from the services of additional productive citizens - or that the potential human lives might include the occasional Mozart or Curie. These are the kinds of concerns that comprise the State's interest in potential human life.

In counterpoise is the woman's constitutional interest in liberty. One aspect of this liberty is a right to bodily integrity, a right to control one's person. This right is neutral on the question of abortion: The Constitution would be equally offended by an absolute requirement that all women undergo abortions as by an absolute prohibition on abortions. "Our whole constitutional heritage rebels at the thought of giving government the power to control men's minds." The same holds true for the power to control women's bodies.

The woman's constitutional liberty interest also involves her freedom to decide matters of the highest privacy and the most personal nature. . . . The authority to make such traumatic and yet empowering decisions is an element of basic human dignity. As the joint opinion so eloquently demonstrates, a woman's decision to terminate her pregnancy is nothing less than a matter of conscience.

Weighing the State's interest in potential life and the woman's liberty interest, I agree with the joint opinion that the State may "'expres[s] a preference for normal childbirth,'" that the State may take steps to ensure that a woman's choice "is thoughtful and informed," and that "States are free to enact laws to provide a reasonable framework for a woman to make a decision that has such profound and lasting meaning." Serious questions arise, however, when a State attempts to "persuade the woman to choose childbirth over abortion." Decisional autonomy must limit the State's power to inject into a woman's most personal deliberations its own views of what is best. The State may promote its preferences by funding childbirth, by creating and maintaining alternatives to abortion, and by espousing the virtues of family; but it must respect the individual's freedom to make such judgments.

This theme runs throughout our decisions concerning reproductive freedom. . . .

In my opinion, the principles established in this long line of cases and the wisdom reflected in Justice Powell's opinion for the Court in *Akron* (and followed by the Court just six years ago in *Thornburgh*) should govern our decision today. Under these principles, [certain sections] of the Pennsylvania statute are unconstitutional. Those sections require a physician or counselor to provide the woman with a range of materials clearly designed to persuade her to choose not to undergo the abortion. While the State is free, pursuant to Section 3208 of the Pennsylvania law, to produce and disseminate such material, the State may not inject such information into the woman's deliberations just as she is weighing such an important choice.

Under this same analysis, [certain sections] of the Pennsylvania statute are constitutional. Those sections, which require the physician to inform a woman of the nature and risks of the abortion procedure and the medical risks of carrying to term, are neutral requirements comparable to those imposed in other medical procedures. Those sections indicate no effort by the State to influence the woman's choice in any way. If anything, such requirements *enhance*, rather than skew, the woman's decisionmaking.

The 24-hour waiting period required by [certain sections] of the Pennsylvania statute raises even more serious concerns. Such a requirement arguably furthers the State's interests in two ways, neither of which is constitutionally permissible.

First, it may be argued that the 24-hour delay is justified by the mere fact that it is likely to reduce the number of abortions, thus furthering the State's interest in potential life. But such an argument would justify any form of coercion that placed an obstacle in the woman's path. The State cannot further its interests by simply wearing down the ability of the pregnant woman to exercise her constitutional right.

Second, it can more reasonably be argued that the 24-hour delay furthers the State's interest in ensuring that the woman's decision is informed and thoughtful. But there is no evidence that the mandated delay benefits women or that it is necessary to enable the physician to convey any relevant information to the patient. The mandatory delay thus appears to rest on outmoded and unacceptable assumptions about the decisionmaking capacity of women. While there are well-established and consistently maintained reasons for the State to view with skepticism the ability of minors to make decisions, none of those reasons applies to an adult woman's decisionmaking ability. Just as we have left behind the belief that a woman must consult her husband before undertaking serious matters, so we must reject the notion that a woman is less capable of deciding matters of gravity.

In the alternative, the delay requirement may be premised on the belief that the decision to terminate a pregnancy is presumptively wrong. This premise is illegitimate. Those who disagree vehemently about the legality and morality of abortion agree about one thing: The decision to terminate a pregnancy is profound and difficult. No person undertakes such a decision lightly - and States may not presume that a woman has failed to reflect adequately merely because her conclusion differs from the State's preference. A woman who has, in the privacy of her thoughts and conscience, weighed the options and made her decision cannot be forced to reconsider all, simply because the State believes she has come to the wrong conclusion.

Part of the constitutional liberty to choose is the equal dignity to which each of us is entitled. A woman who decides to terminate her pregnancy is entitled to the same respect as a woman who decides to carry the fetus to term. The mandatory waiting period denies women that equal respect.

In my opinion, a correct application of the "undue burden" standard leads to the same conclusion concerning the constitutionality of these requirements. A state-imposed burden on the exercise of a constitutional right is measured both by its effects and by its character: A burden may be "undue" either because the burden is too severe or because it lacks a legitimate, rational justification.

The 24-hour delay requirement fails both parts of this test. . . .

The counseling provisions are similarly infirm. Whenever government commands private citizens to speak or to listen, careful review of the justification for that command is particularly appropriate. In this case, the Pennsylvania statute directs that counselors provide women seeking abortions with information concerning alternatives to abortion, the availability of medical assistance benefits, and the possibility of child-support payments. The statute requires that this information be given to *all* women seeking abortions, including those for whom such information is clearly useless, such as those who are married, those who have undergone the procedure in the past and are fully aware of the options, and those who are fully convinced that abortion is their only reasonable option. Moreover, the statute requires physicians to inform all of their patients of "the probable gestational age of the unborn child." This information is of little decisional value in most cases, because 90% of all abortions are performed

during the first trimester when fetal age has less rele-
vance than when the fetus nears viability. Nor can the information required by the statute be justified as relevant
to any "philosophic" or "social" argument, either favoring
or disfavoring the abortion decision in a particular case.
In light of all of these facts, I conclude that the information requirements in [these sections] do not serve a useful
purpose and thus constitute an undue burden on the woman's constitutional liberty to decide to terminate her pregnancy....

JUSTICE BLACKMUN, concurring in part, concurring in
the judgment in part, and dissenting in part: .... Three
years ago, in *Webster v. Reproductive Health Services*,
four Members of this Court appeared poised to "cas[t]
into darkness the hopes and visions of every woman in
this country" who had come to believe that the Constitution guaranteed her the right to reproductive choice. All
that remained between the promise of *Roe* and the darkness of the plurality was a single, flickering flame. Decisions since *Webster* gave little reason to hope that this
flame would cast much light. But now, just when so many
expected the darkness to fall, the flame has grown bright.

I do not underestimate the significance of today's joint
opinion. Yet I remain steadfast in my belief that the right
to reproductive choice is entitled to the full protection afforded by this Court before *Webster*. And I fear for the
darkness as four Justices anxiously await the single vote
necessary to extinguish the light.

Make no mistake, the joint opinion of Justices O'Connor,
Kennedy, and Souter is an act of personal courage and
constitutional principle. In contrast to previous decisions

in which Justices O'Connor and Kennedy postponed reconsideration of *Roe v. Wade*, the authors of the joint
opinion today join Justice Stevens and me in concluding
that "the essential holding of *Roe* should be retained and
once again reaffirmed." In brief, five Members of this
Court today recognize that "the Constitution protects a
woman's right to terminate her pregnancy in its early
stages."

A fervent view of individual liberty and the force of stare
decisis have led the Court to this conclusion. Today a majority reaffirms that the Due Process Clause of the Fourteenth Amendment establishes "a realm of personal liberty which the government may not enter" - a realm whose
outer limits cannot be determined by interpretations of
the Constitution that focus only on the specific practices
of States at the time the Fourteenth Amendment was
adopted. Included within this realm of liberty is "'the
right of the *individual*, married or single, to be free from
unwarranted governmental intrusion into matters so fundamentally affecting a person as the decision whether to
bear or beget a child.'" . . . Finally, the Court today recognizes that in the case of abortion, "the liberty of the woman is at stake in a sense unique to the human condition
and so unique to the law. The mother who carries a child
to full term is subject to anxieties, to physical constraints,
to pain that only she must bear."

The Court's reaffirmation of *Roe*'s central holding is also
based on the force of stare decisis. "[N]o erosion of principle going to liberty or personal autonomy has left *Roe*'s
central holding a doctrinal remnant; *Roe* portends no developments at odds with other precedent for the analysis
of personal liberty; and no changes of fact have rendered

viability more or less appropriate as the point at which the balance of interests tips." Indeed, the Court acknowledges that *Roe*'s limitation on state power could not be removed "without serious inequity to those who have relied upon it or significant damage to the stability of the society governed by the rule in question." In the 19 years since *Roe* was decided, that case has shaped more than reproductive planning - "an entire generation has come of age free to assume *Roe*'s concept of liberty in defining the capacity of women to act in society, and to make reproductive decisions." The Court understands that, having "call[ed] the contending sides . . . to end their national division by accepting a common mandate rooted in the Constitution," a decision to overrule *Roe* "would seriously weaken the Court's capacity to exercise the judicial power and to function as the Supreme Court of a Nation dedicated to the rule of law." What has happened today should serve as a model for future Justices and a warning to all who have tried to turn this Court into yet another political branch.

In striking down the Pennsylvania statute's spousal notification requirement, the Court has established a framework for evaluating abortion regulations that responds to the social context of women facing issues of reproductive choice. . . . Whatever may have been the practice when the Fourteenth Amendment was adopted, the Court observes, "[w]omen do not lose their constitutionally protected liberty when they marry. The Constitution protects all individuals, male or female, married or unmarried, from the abuse of governmental power, even where that power is employed for the supposed benefit of a member of the individual's family."

Lastly, while I believe that the joint opinion errs in failing to invalidate the other regulations, I am pleased that the joint opinion has not ruled out the possibility that these regulations may be shown to impose an unconstitutional burden. The joint opinion makes clear that its specific holdings are based on the insufficiency of the record before it. I am confident that in the future evidence will be produced to show that "in a large fraction of the cases in which [these regulations are] relevant, [they] will operate as a substantial obstacle to a woman's choice to undergo an abortion."

Today, no less than yesterday, the Constitution and decisions of this Court require that a State's abortion restrictions be subjected to the strictest judicial scrutiny. Our precedents and the joint opinion's principles require us to subject all non-de minimis [significant] abortion regulations to strict scrutiny. Under this standard, the Pennsylvania statute's provisions requiring content-based counseling, a 24-hour delay, informed parental consent, and reporting of abortion-related information must be invalidated.

The Court today reaffirms the long recognized rights of privacy and bodily integrity. . . . [The] Court . . . has held that the fundamental right of privacy protects citizens against governmental intrusion in such intimate family matters as procreation, childrearing, marriage, and contraceptive choice. . . . In *Roe v. Wade*, this Court correctly applied these principles to a woman's right to choose abortion.

State restrictions on abortion violate a woman's right of privacy in two ways. First, compelled continuation of a pregnancy infringes upon a woman's right to bodily integrity by imposing substantial physical intrusions and significant risks of physical harm. . . . [R]estrictive abortion laws force women to endure physical invasions far more substantial than those this Court has held to violate the constitutional principle of bodily integrity in other contexts.

Further, when the State restricts a woman's right to terminate her pregnancy, it deprives a woman of the right to make her own decision about reproduction and family planning - critical life choices that this Court long has deemed central to the right to privacy. . . . Because motherhood has a dramatic impact on a woman's educational prospects, employment opportunities, and self-determination, restrictive abortion laws deprive her of basic control over her life. . . .

A State's restrictions on a woman's right to terminate her pregnancy also implicate constitutional guarantees of gender equality. State restrictions on abortion compel women to continue pregnancies they otherwise might terminate. By restricting the right to terminate pregnancies, the State conscripts women's bodies into its service, forcing women to continue their pregnancies, suffer the pains of childbirth, and in most instances, provide years of maternal care. The State does not compensate women for their services; instead, it assumes that they own this duty as a matter of course. This assumption - that women can simply be forced to accept the "natural" status and incidents of motherhood - appears to rest upon a conception of women's role that has triggered the protection of the Equal Protection Clause. The joint opinion recognizes that these assumptions about women's place in society "are no longer consistent with our understanding of the family, the individual, or the Constitution."

The Court has held that limitations on the right of privacy are permissible only if they survive "strict" constitutional scrutiny - that is, only if the governmental entity imposing the restriction can demonstrate that the limitation is both necessary and narrowly tailored to serve a compelling governmental interest.

. . . . *Roe* identified two relevant State interests: "an interest in preserving and protecting the health of the pregnant woman" and an interest in "protecting the potentiality of human life." With respect to the State's interest in the health of the mother, "the 'compelling' point . . . is at approximately the end of the first trimester," because it is at that point that the mortality rate in abortion approaches that in childbirth. With respect to the State's interest in potential life, "the 'compelling' point is at viability," because it is at that point that the fetus "presumably has the capability of meaningful life outside the mother's womb." . . .

In my view, application of this analytical framework is no less warranted than when it was approved by seven Members of this Court in *Roe.* Strict scrutiny of state limitations on reproductive choice still offers the most secure protection of the woman's right to make her own reproductive decisions, free from state coercion. . . . [T]he *Roe* framework is far more administrable, and far less manipulable, than the "undue burden" standard adopted by the joint opinion.

Nonetheless, three criticisms of the trimester framework continue to be uttered. First, the trimester framework is attacked because is key elements do not appear in the text of the Constitution. My response to this attack remains the same as it was in *Webster*:

"Were this a true concern, we would have to abandon most of our constitutional jurisprudence. [T]he 'critical elements' of countless constitutional doctrines nowhere appear in the Constitution's text. . . . [T]he Constitution makes no mention of the rational-basis test, or the specific verbal formulations of intermediate and strict scrutiny by which this Court evaluates claims under the Equal Protection Clause. The reason is simple. Like the *Roe* framework, these tests or standards are not, and do not purport to be, rights protected by the Constitution. Rather, they are judge-made methods for evaluating and measuring the strength and scope of constitutional rights or for balancing the constitutional rights of individuals against the competing interests of government."

The second criticism is that the framework more closely resembles a regulatory code than a body of constitutional doctrine. Again, my answer remains the same as in *Webster*.

"[I]f this were a true and genuine concern, we wold have to abandon vast areas of our constitutional jurisprudence. . . . That numerous constitutional doctrines result in narrow differentiations between similar circumstances does not mean that this Court has abandoned adjudication in favor of regulation."

The final, and more genuine, criticism of the trimester framework is that it fails to find the State's interest in potential human life compelling throughout pregnancy. . . . [A] State's interest in protecting fetal life is not grounded in the Constitution. Nor, consistent with our Establishment Clause, can it be a theological or sectarian interest. It is, instead, a legitimate interest grounded in humanitarian or pragmatic concerns.

But while a State has "legitimate interests from the outset of the pregnancy in protecting the health of the woman and the life of the fetus that may become a child," legitimate interests are not enough. To overcome the burden of strict scrutiny, the interests must be compelling. . . .

Roe's trimester framework does not ignore the State's interest in prenatal life. . . . But

"[s]erious questions arise when a State attempts to 'persuade the woman to choose childbirth over abortion.' Decisional autonomy must limit the State's power to inject into a woman's most personal deliberations its own views of what is best. . . ."

Roe's requirement of strict scrutiny as implemented through a trimester framework should not be disturbed. No other approach has gained a majority, and no other is more protective of the woman's fundamental right. Lastly, no other approach properly accommodates the woman's constitutional right with the State's legitimate interests.

. . . . A State may not, under the guise of securing informed consent, "require the delivery of information

'designed to influence the woman's informed choice between abortion or childbirth.'" Rigid requirements that a
specific body of information be imparted to a woman in
all cases, regardless of the needs of the patient, improperly intrude upon the discretion of the pregnant woman's
physician and thereby impose an '"undesired and uncomfortable straitjacket.'"

Measured against these principles, some aspects of the
Pennsylvania informed-consent scheme are unconstitutional. While it is unobjectionable for the Commonwealth
to require that the patient be informed of the nature of
the procedure, the health risks of the abortion and of
childbirth, and the probable gestational age of the unborn
child, I remain unconvinced that there is a vital state need
for insisting that the information be provided by a physician rather than a counselor. . . .

[Certain sections] of the Act further requires that the
physician or a qualified non-physician inform the woman
that printed materials are available from the Commonwealth that describe the fetus and provide information
about medical assistance for childbirth, information about
child support from the father, and a list of agencies offer-
ing that provide adoption and other services as alternatives to abortion. *Thornburgh* invalidated biased patient-
counseling requirements virtually identical to the one at
issue here. . . .

"This type of compelled information is the antithesis of
informed consent," and goes far beyond merely describing
the general subject matter relevant to the woman's decision. "That the Commonwealth does not, and surely
would not, compel similar disclosure of every possible

peril of necessary surgery or of simple vaccination, reveals the anti-abortion character of the statute and its real
purpose."

The 24-hour waiting period following the provision of the
foregoing information is also clearly unconstitutional. . . .
In *Akron* this Court invalidated a similarly arbitrary or
inflexible waiting period because, as here, it furthered no
legitimate state interest.

. . . . [T]he mandatory delay rests either on outmoded or
unacceptable assumptions about the decisionmaking capacity of women or the belief that the decision to terminate the pregnancy is presumptively wrong. The requirement that women consider this obvious and slanted information for an additional 24 hours contained in these provisions will only influence the woman's decision in improper ways. The vast majority of women will know this
information - of the few that do not, it is less likely that
their minds will be changed by this information than it
will be either by the realization that the State opposes
their choice or the need once again to endure abuse and
harassment on return to the clinic.

Except in the case of a medical emergency, Section 3206
requires a physician to obtain the informed consent of a
parent or guardian before performing an abortion on an
unemancipated minor or an incompetent woman. . . . Although the Court "has recognized that the State has somewhat broader authority to regulate the activities of children than of adults," the State nevertheless must demonstrate that there is a "*significant state interest* in conditioning an abortion . . . that is not present in the case of
an adult." The requirement of an in-person visit would

carry with it the risk of a delay of several days or possibly weeks, even where the parent is willing to consent. While the State has an interest in encouraging parental involvement in the minor's abortion decision, Section 3206 is not narrowly drawn to serve that interest.

Finally, the Pennsylvania statute requires every facility performing abortions to report its activities to the Commonwealth. . . . The Commonwealth attempts to justify its required reports on the ground that the public has a right to know how its tax dollars are spent. A regulation designed to inform the public about public expenditures does not further the Commonwealth's interest in protecting maternal health. Accordingly, such a regulation cannot justify a legally significant burden on a woman's right to obtain an abortion.

. . . . The Commonwealth has failed to show that the name of the referring physician either adds to the pool of scientific knowledge concerning abortion or is reasonably related to the Commonwealth's interest in maternal health. I therefore agree with the District Court's conclusion that the confidential reporting requirements are unconstitutional insofar as they require the name of the referring physician and the basis for his or her medical judgment.

In sum, I would affirm the judgment. . . .

At long last, the Chief Justice and those who have joined him admit it. Gone are the contentions that the issue need not be (or has not been) considered. There, on the first page, for all to see, is what was expected: "We believe that *Roe* was wrongly decided, and that it can and should be overruled consistently with our traditional approach to stare decisis in constitutional cases." If there is much reason to applaud the advances made by the joint opinion today, there is far more to fear from The Chief Justice's opinion.

The Chief Justice's criticism of *Roe* follows from his stunted conception of individual liberty. While recognizing that the Due Process Clause protects more than simple physical liberty, he then goes on to construe this Court's personal-liberty cases as establishing only a laundry list of particular rights, rather than a principled account of how these particular rights are grounded in a more general right of privacy. This constricted view is reinforced by The Chief Justice's exclusive reliance on tradition as a source of fundamental rights. . . . In The Chief Justice's world, a woman considering whether to terminate a pregnancy is entitled to no more protection than adulterers, murderers, and so-called "sexual deviates." Given The Chief Justice's exclusive reliance on tradition, people using contraceptives seem the next likely candidate for his list of outcasts.

Even more shocking that The Chief Justice's cramped notion of individual liberty is his complete omission of any discussion of the effects that compelled childbirth and motherhood have on women's lives. The only expression of concern with women's health is purely instrumental - for The Chief Justice, only women's *psychological* health is a concern, and only to the extent that he assumes that every woman who decides to have an abortion does so without serious consideration of the moral implications of her decision. In short, the Chief Justice's view of the State's compelling interest in maternal health has less to do with health than it does with compelling women to be maternal.

Nor does The Chief Justice give any serious consideration to the doctrine of stare decisis. For The Chief Justice, the facts that gave rise to *Roe* are surprisingly simple: "women become pregnant, there is a point somewhere, depending on medical technology, where a fetus becomes viable, and women give birth to children." This characterization of the issue thus allows The Chief Justice quickly to discard the joint opinion's reliance argument by asserting that "reproductive planning could take virtually immediate account of" a decision overruling *Roe.*

The Chief Justice's narrow conception of individual liberty and stare decisis leads him to propose the same standard of review proposed by the plurality in *Webster.* "States may regulate abortion procedures in ways rationally related to a legitimate state interest." The Chief Justice then further weakens the test by providing an insurmountable requirement for facial challenges: petitioners must "'show that no set of circumstances exists under which the [provision] would be valid.'" In short, in his view, petitioners must prove that the statute cannot constitutionally be applied to *anyone.* Finally, in applying his standard to the spousal-notification provision, The Chief Justice contends that the record lacks any "hard evidence" to support the joint opinion's contention that a "large fraction" of women who prefer not to notify their husbands involve situations of battered women and unreported spousal assault. Yet throughout the explication of his standard, The Chief Justice never explains what hard evidence is, how large a fraction is required, or how a battered woman is supposed to pursue an as-applied challenge.

Under his standard, States can ban abortion if that ban is rationally related to a legitimate state interest - a standard which the United States calls "deferential, but not toothless." Yet when pressed at oral argument to describe the teeth, the best protection that the Solicitor General could offer to women was that a prohibition, enforced by criminal penalties, *with no exception for the life of the mother*, "could raise very serious questions." Perhaps, the Solicitor General offered, the failure to include an exemption for the life of the mother would be "arbitrary and capricious." If, as The Chief Justice contends,, the undue burden test is made out of whole cloth, the so-called "arbitrary and capricious" limit is the Solicitor General's "new clothes."

Even if it is somehow "irrational" for a State to require a woman to risk her life for her child, what protection is offered for women who become pregnant through rape or incest? Is there anything arbitrary or capricious about a State's prohibiting the sins of the father from being visited upon his offspring?

But, as we are reassured, there is always the protection of the democratic process. While there is much to be praised about our democracy, our country since its founding has recognized that there are certain fundamental liberties that are not to be left to the whims of an election. A woman's right to reproductive choice is one of those fundamental liberties. Accordingly, that liberty need not seek refuge at the ballot box.

In one sense, the Court's approach is worlds apart from that of The Chief Justice and Justice Scalia. And yet, in another sense, the distance between the two approaches is short - the distance is but a single vote.

I am 83 years old. I cannot remain on this Court forever, and when I do step down, the confirmation process for my successor well may focus on the issue before us today. That, I regret, may be exactly where the choice between the two worlds will be made.

CHIEF JUSTICE REHNQUIST (joined by Justices White, Scalia, and Thomas), concurring in the judgment in part and dissenting in part: The joint opinion, following its newly-minted variation on stare decisis, retains the outer shell of *Roe v. Wade*, but beats a wholesale retreat from the substance of that case. We believe that *Roe* was wrongly decided, and that it can and should be overruled consistently with our traditional approach to stare decisis in constitutional cases. We would adopt the approach of the plurality in *Webster v. Reproductive Health Services*, and uphold the challenged provisions of the Pennsylvania statute in their entirety.

. . . . Unfortunately for those who must apply this Court's decisions, the reexamination undertaken today leaves the Court no less divided than beforehand. Although they reject the trimester framework that formed the underpinning of *Roe*, Justices O'Connor, Kennedy, and Souter adopt a revised undue burden standard to analyze the challenged regulations. We conclude, however, that such an outcome is an unjustified constitutional compromise, one which leaves the Court in a position to closely scrutinize all types of abortion regulations despite the fact that it lacks the power to do so under the Constitution.

In *Roe*, the Court opined that the State "does have an important and legitimate interest in preserving and protecting the health of the pregnant woman, . . . and that it has still another important and legitimate interest in protecting the potentiality of human life." In the companion case of *Doe v. Bolton*, the Court referred to its conclusion in *Roe* "that a pregnant woman does not have an absolute constitutional right to an abortion on her demand." But while the language and holdings of these cases appeared to leave States free to regulate abortion procedures in a variety of ways, later decisions based on them have found considerably less latitude for such regulations than might have been expected.

. . . . We have held that a liberty interest protected under the Due Process Clause of the Fourteenth Amendment will be deemed fundamental if it is "implicit in the concept of ordered liberty." . . .

In construing the phrase "liberty" incorporated in the Due Process Clause of the Fourteenth Amendment, we have recognized that its meaning extends beyond freedom from physical restraint. In *Pierce v. Society of Sisters*, we held that it included a parent's right to send a child to private school; in *Meyer v. Nebraska*, we held that it included a right to teach a foreign language in a parochial school. Building on these cases, we have held that that the term "liberty" includes a right to marry; a right to procreate; and a right to use contraceptives. But a reading of these opinions makes clear that they do not endorse any all-encompassing "right of privacy."

In *Roe v. Wade*, the Court recognized a "guarantee of personal privacy" which "is broad enough to encompass a woman's decision whether or not to terminate her pregnancy." We are now of the view that, in terming this right fundamental, the Court in *Roe* read the earlier opinions upon which it based its decision much too broadly. Unlike marriage, procreation and contraception, abortion "involves the purposeful termination of potential life." The abortion decision must therefore "be recognized as sui generis [unique], different in kind from the others that the Court has protected under the rubric of personal or family privacy and autonomy." One cannot ignore the fact that a woman is not isolated in her pregnancy, and that the decision to abort necessarily involves the destruction of a fetus.

Nor do the historical traditions of the American people support the view that the right to terminate one's pregnancy is "fundamental." The common law which we inherited from England made abortion after "quickening" an offense. At the time of the adoption of the Fourteenth Amendment, statutory prohibitions or restrictions on abortion were commonplace; in 1868, at least 28 of the then-37 States and 8 Territories had statutes banning or limiting abortion. By the turn of the century virtually every State had a law prohibiting or restricting abortion on its books. By the middle of the present century, a liberalization trend had set in. But 21 of the restrictive abortion laws in effect in 1868 were still in effect in 1973 when *Roe* was decided, and an overwhelming majority of the States prohibited abortion unless necessary to preserve the life or health of the mother. On this record, it can scarcely be said that any deeply rooted tradition of relatively unrestricted abortion in our history supported the classification of the right to abortion as "fundamental" under the Due Process Clause of the Fourteenth Amendment.

We think, therefore, both in view of this history and of our decided cases dealing with substantive liberty under the Due Process Clause, that the Court was mistaken in *Roe* when it classified a woman's decision to terminate her pregnancy as a "fundamental right" that could be abridged only in a manner which withstood "strict scrutiny." . . .

We believe that the sort of constitutionally imposed abortion code of the type illustrated by our decisions following *Roe* is inconsistent "with the notion of a Constitution cast in general terms, as ours is, and usually speaking in general principles, as ours does." The Court in *Roe* reached too far when it analogized the right to abort a fetus to the rights involved in *Pierce, Meyer, Loving*, and *Griswold*, and thereby deemed the right to abortion fundamental.

The joint opinion of Justices O'Connor, Kennedy, and Souter cannot bring itself to say that *Roe* was correct as an original matter, but the authors are of the view that "the immediate question is not the soundness of *Roe*'s resolution of the issue, but the precedential force that must be accorded to its holding." Instead of claiming that *Roe* was correct as a matter of original constitutional interpretation, the opinion therefore contains an elaborate discussion of stare decisis. This discussion of the principle of stare decisis appears to be almost entirely dicta [non-binding discussion within an opinion], because the joint opinion does not apply that principle in dealing with *Roe*. . . .

Stare decisis is defined in Black's Law Dictionary as meaning "to abide by, or adhere to, decided cases." Whatever the "central holding" of *Roe* that is left after the joint opinion finishes dissecting it is surely not the result of that principle. While purporting to adhere to precedent, the joint opinion instead revises it. *Roe* continues to exist, but only in the way a storefront on a western movie set exists: a mere facade to give the illusion of reality. . . .

In our view, authentic principles of stare decisis do not require that any portion of the reasoning in *Roe* be kept intact. . . . Our constitutional watch does not cease merely because we have spoken before on an issue; when it becomes clear that a prior constitutional interpretation is unsound we are obliged to reexamine the question.

The joint opinion discusses several stare decisis factors which, it asserts, point toward retaining a portion of *Roe*. Two of these factors are that the main "factual underpinning" of *Roe* has remained the same, and that its doctrinal foundation is no weaker now than it was in 1973. Of course, what might be called the basic facts which gave rise to *Roe* have remained the same - women become pregnant, there is a point somewhere, depending on medical technology, where a fetus becomes viable, and women give birth to children. But this is only to say that the same facts which gave rise to *Roe* will continue to give rise to similar cases. It is not a reason, in and of itself, why those cases must be decided in the same incorrect manner as was the first case to deal with the question. And surely there is no requirement, in considering whether to depart from stare decisis in a constitutional case, that a decision be more wrong now than it was at the time it was rendered. If that were true, the most outlandish con-

stitutional decision could survive forever, based simply on
the fact that it was no more outlandish later than it was
when originally rendered.

.... The joint opinion thus turns to what can only be described as an unconventional - and unconvincing - notion
of reliance, a view based on the surmise that the availability of abortion since *Roe* has led to "two decades of economic and social developments" that would be undercut if
the error of *Roe* were recognized. The joint opinion's assertion of this fact is undeveloped and totally conclusory.
In fact, one can not be sure to what economic and social
developments the opinion is referring. Surely it is dubi-
ous to suggest that women have reached their "places in
society" in reliance upon *Roe*, rather than as a result of
their determination to obtain higher education and com-
pete with men in the job market, and of society's increasing recognition of their ability to fill positions that were
previously thought to be reserved only for men.

In the end, having failed to put forth any evidence to
prove any true reliance, the joint opinion's argument is
based solely on generalized assertions about the national
psyche, on a belief that the people of this country have
grown accustomed to the *Roe* decision over the last 19
years and have "ordered their thinking and living around"
it. As an initial matter, one might inquire how the joint
opinion can view the "central holding" of *Roe* as so deeply
rooted in our constitutional culture, when it so casually
uproots and disposes of that same decision's trimester
framework. Furthermore, at various points in the past,
the same could have been said about this Court's erroneous decisions that the Constitution allowed "separate but
equal" treatment of minorities, or that "liberty" under the

Due Process Clause protected "freedom of contract." The "separate but equal" doctrine lasted 58 years after *Plessy*, and *Lochner*'s protection of contractual freedom lasted 32 years. However, the simple fact that a generation or more had grown used to these major decisions did not prevent the Court from correcting its errors in those cases, nor should it prevent us from correctly interpreting the Constitution here.

Apparently realizing that conventional stare decisis principles do not support its position, the joint opinion advances a belief that retaining a portion of *Roe* is necessary to protect the "legitimacy" of this Court. . . . [T]he joint opinion properly declares it to be this Court's duty to ignore the public criticism and protest that may arise as a result of a decision. Few would quarrel with this statement, although it may be doubted that Members of this Court, holding their tenure as they do during constitutional "good behavior," are at all likely to be intimidated by such public protests.

But the joint opinion goes on to state that when the Court "resolve[s] the sort of intensely divisive controversy reflected in *Roe* and those rare, comparable cases," its decision is exempt from reconsideration under established principles of stare decisis in constitutional case. This is so, the joint opinion contends, because in those "intensely divisive" cases the Court has "call[ed] the contending sides of a national division by accepting a common mandate rooted in the Constitution," and must therefore take special care not to be perceived as "surrender[ing] to political pressure" and continued opposition. This is a truly novel principle, one which is contrary to both the Court's historical practice and to the Court's traditional willingness to tolerate criticism of its opinions. Under this principle, when the Court has ruled on a divisive issue, it is apparently prevented from overruling that decision for the sole reason that it was incorrect, *unless opposition to the original decision has died away.*

The first difficulty with this principle lies in its assumption that cases which are "intensely divisive" can be readily distinguished from those that are not. The question of whether a particular issue is "intensely divisive" enough to qualify for special protection is entirely subjective and dependent on the individual assumptions of the members of this Court. In addition, because the Court's duty is to ignore public opinion and criticism on issues that come before it, its members are in perhaps the worst position to judge whether a decision divides the Nation deeply enough to justify such uncommon protection. Although many of the Court's decisions divide the populace to a large degree, we have not previously on that account shied away from applying normal rules of stare decisis when urged to reconsider earlier decisions. Over the past 21 years, for example, the Court has overruled in whole or in part 34 of its previous constitutional decisions.

. . . . In terms of public interest, however, *Roe,* so far as we know, was unique. But just as the Court should not respond to that sort of protest by retreating from the decision simply to allay the concerns of the protesters, it should likewise not respond by determining to adhere to the decision at all costs lest it *seem* to be retreating under fire. Public protests should not alter the normal application of stare decisis, lest perfectly lawful protest activity be penalized by the Court itself.

. . . . The joint opinion also agrees that the Court acted properly in rejecting the doctrine of "separate but equal" in *Brown*. In fact, the opinion lauds *Brown* in comparing it to *Roe.* This is strange, in that under the opinion's "legitimacy" principle the Court would seemingly have been forced to adhere to its erroneous decision in *Plessy* because of its "intensely divisive" character. To us, adherence to *Roe* today under the guise of "legitimacy" would seem to resemble more closely adherence to *Plessy* on the same ground. Fortunately, the Court did not choose that option in *Brown*, and instead frankly repudiated *Plessy.* The joint opinion concludes that such repudiation was justified only because of newly discovered evidence that segregation had the effect of treating one race as inferior to another. But it can hardly be argued that this was not urged upon those who decided *Plessy*, as Justice Harlan observed in his dissent that the law at issue "puts the brand of servitude and degradation upon a large class of our fellow-citizens," our equals before the law." It is clear that the same arguments made before the Court in *Brown* were made in *Plessy* as well. The Court in *Brown* simply recognized, as Justice Harlan had recognized beforehand, that the Fourteenth Amendment does not permit racial segregation. The rule of *Brown* is not tied to popular opinion about the evils of segregation; it is a judgment that the Equal Protection Clause does not permit racial segregation, no matter whether the public might come to believe that it is beneficial. On that ground it stands, and on that ground alone the Court was justified in properly concluding that the *Plessy* Court had erred.

There is also a suggestion in the joint opinion that the propriety of overruling a "divisive" decision depends in part on whether "most people" would now agree that it

should be overruled. Either the demise of opposition or
its progression to substantial popular agreement apparently is required to allow the Court to reconsider a divisive
decision. How such agreement would be ascertained, short
of a public opinion poll, the joint opinion does not say.
But surely even the suggestion is totally at war with the
idea of "legitimacy" in whose name it is invoked. The Judicial Branch derives its legitimacy, not from following
public opinion, but from deciding by its best lights whether legislative enactments of the popular branches of Government comport with the Constitution. The doctrine of
stare decisis is an adjunct of this duty, and should be no
more subject to the vagaries of public opinion than is the
basic judicial task.

. . . . The joint opinion asserts that, in order to protect its
legitimacy, the Court must refrain from overruling a controversial decision lest it be viewed as favoring those who
oppose the decision. But a decision to *adhere* to prior
precedent is subject to the same criticism, for in such a
case one can easily argue that the Court is responding to
those who have demonstrated in favor of the original decision. The decision in *Roe* has engendered large demonstrations, including repeated marches on this Court and on
Congress, both in opposition to and in support of that
opinion. A decision either way on *Roe* can therefore be
perceived as favoring one group or the other. But this
perceived dilemma arises only if one assumes, as the joint
opinion does, that the Court should make its decisions
with a view toward speculative public perceptions. . . .

Nearly a century ago, Justice David J. Brewer of this
Court, in an article discussing criticism of its decisions,
observed that "many criticisms may be, like their authors,

devoid of good taste, but better all sorts of criticism than no criticism at all." This was good advice to the Court then, as it is today. Strong and often misguided criticism of a decision should not render the decision immune from reconsideration, lest a fetish for legitimacy penalize freedom of expression.

The end result of the joint opinion's paeans of praise for legitimacy is the enunciation of a brand new standard for evaluating state regulation of a woman's right to abortion - the "undue burden" standard. As indicated above, *Roe v. Wade* adopted a "fundamental right" standard under which state regulations could survive only if they met the requirement of "strict scrutiny." While we disagree with that standard, it at least had a recognized basis in constitutional law at the time *Roe* was decided. The same cannot be said for the "undue burden" standard, which is created largely out of whole cloth by the authors of the joint opinion. It is a standard which even today does not command the support of a majority of this Court. And it will not, we believe, result in the sort of "simple limitation," easily applied, which the joint opinion anticipates. In sum, it is a standard which is not built to last.

In evaluating abortion regulations under that standard, judges will have to decide whether they place a "substantial obstacle" in the path of a woman seeking an abortion. In that this standard is based even more on a judge's subjective determinations than was the trimester framework, the standard will do nothing to prevent "judges from roaming at large in the constitutional field" guided only by their personal views. Because the undue burden standard is plucked from nowhere, the question of what is a "substantial obstacle" to abortion will undoubtedly engender a variety of conflicting views. For example, in the very matter before us now, the authors of the joint opinion would uphold Pennsylvania's 24-hour waiting period, concluding that a "particular burden" on some women is not a substantial obstacle. But the authors would at the same time strike down Pennsylvania's spousal notice provision, after finding that in a "large fraction" of cases the provision will be a substantial obstacle. And, while the authors conclude that the informed consent provisions do not constitute an "undue burden," Justice Stevens would hold that they do.

Furthermore, while striking down the spousal *notice* regulation, the joint opinion would uphold a parental *consent* restriction that certainly places very substantial obstacles in the path of a minor's abortion choice. The joint opinion is forthright in admitting that it draws this distinction based on a policy judgment that parents will have the best interests of their children at heart, while the same is not necessarily true of husbands as to their wives. This may or may not be a correct judgment, but it is quintessentially a legislative one. The "undue burden" inquiry does not in any way supply the distinction between parental consent and spousal consent which the joint opinion adopts. Despite the efforts of the joint opinion, the undue burden standard presents nothing more workable than the trimester framework which it discards today. Under the guise of the Constitution, this Court will still impart its own preference on the States in the form of a complex abortion code.

The sum of the joint opinion's labors in the name of stare decisis and "legitimacy" is this: *Roe v. Wade* stands as a sort of judicial Potemkin Village, which may be pointed out to passers by as a monument to the importance of adhering to precedent. But behind the facade, an entirely new method of analysis, without any roots in constitutional law, is imported to decide the constitutionality of state laws regulating abortion. Neither stare decisis nor "legitimacy" are truly served by such an effort.

We have stated above our belief that the Constitution does not subject state abortion regulations to heightened scrutiny. Accordingly, we think that the correct analysis is that set forth by the plurality opinion in *Webster.* A woman's interest in having an abortion is a form of liberty protected by the Due Process Clause, but States may regulate abortion procedures in ways rationally related to a legitimate state interest. . . .

This Court has held that it is certainly within the province of the States to require a woman's voluntary and informed consent to an abortion. Here, Pennsylvania seeks to further its legitimate interest in obtaining informed consent by ensuring that each woman "is aware not only of the reasons for having an abortion, but also of the risks associated with an abortion and the availability of assistance that might make the alternative of normal childbirth more attractive than it might otherwise appear."

We conclude that this provision of the statute is rationally related to the State's interest in assuring that a woman's consent to an abortion be a fully informed decision.

[A s]ection requires a physician to disclose certain information about the abortion procedure and its risks and alternatives. This requirement is certainly no large burden, as the Court of Appeals found that "the record shows that

the clinics, without exception, insist on providing this information to women before an abortion is performed."
We are of the view that this information "clearly is related to maternal health and to the State's legitimate purpose
in requiring informed consent." An accurate description
of the gestational age of the fetus and of the risks involved in carrying a child to term helps to further both
those interests and the State's legitimate interest in unborn life. . . . [W]e agree with the Court of Appeals that
a State "may rationally decide that physicians are better
qualified than counselors to impart this information and
answer questions about the medical aspects of the available alternatives."

[A s]ection compels the disclosure, by a physician or a
counselor, of information concerning the availability of
paternal child support and state-funded alternatives if the
woman decides to proceed with her pregnancy. . . . [T]his
required presentation of "balanced information" is rationally related to the State's legitimate interest in ensuring
that the woman's consent is truly informed, and in addition furthers the State's interest in preserving unborn life.
That the information might create some uncertainty and
persuade some women to forgo abortions does not lead to
the conclusion that the Constitution forbids the provision
of such information. Indeed, it only demonstrates that
this information might very well make a difference, and
that it is therefore relevant to a woman's informed
choice. . . .

[W]e do not feel bound to follow this Court's previous
holding that a State's 24-hour mandatory waiting period is
unconstitutional. . . . [S]uch a provision will result in de-
lays for some women that might not otherwise exist,

therefore placing a burden on their liberty. But the provision in no way prohibits abortions, and the informed consent and waiting period requirements do not apply in the case of a medical emergency. We are of the view that, in providing time for reflection and reconsideration, the waiting period helps ensure that a woman's decision to abort is a well-considered one, and reasonably furthers the State's legitimate interest in maternal health and in the unborn life of the fetus. It "is surely a small cost to impose to ensure that the woman's decision is well considered in light of its certain and irreparable consequences on fetal life, and the possible effects on her own."

In addition to providing her own informed consent, before an unemancipated woman under the age of 18 may obtain an abortion she must either furnish the consent of one of her parents, or must opt for the judicial procedure that allows her to bypass the consent requirement. Under the judicial bypass option, a minor can obtain an abortion if a state court finds that she is capable of giving her informed consent and has indeed given such consent, *or* determines that an abortion is in her best interests. Records of these court proceedings are kept confidential. The Act directs the state trial court to render a decision within three days of the woman's application, and the entire procedure, including appeal to Pennsylvania Superior Court, is to last no longer than eight business days. The parental consent requirement does not apply in the case of a medical emergency.

This provision is entirely consistent with this Court's previous decisions involving parental consent requirements. . . .

We think it beyond dispute that a State "has a strong and legitimate interest in the welfare of its young citizens, whose immaturity, inexperience, and lack of judgment may sometimes impair their ability to exercise their rights wisely." A requirement of parental consent to abortion, like myriad other restrictions placed upon minors in other contexts, is reasonably designed to further this important and legitimate state interest. In our view, it is entirely "rational and fair for the State to conclude that, in most instances, the family will strive to give a lonely or even terrified minor advice that is both compassionate and mature." We thus conclude that Pennsylvania's parental consent requirement should be upheld.

Section 3209 of the Act contains the spousal notification provision. It requires that, before a physician may perform an abortion on a married woman, the woman must sign a statement indicating that she has notified her husband of her planned abortion. A woman is not required to notify her husband if (1) her husband is not the father, (2) her husband, after diligent effort, cannot be located, (3) the pregnancy is the result of a spousal sexual assault that has been reported to the authorities, or (4) the woman has reason to believe that notifying her husband is likely to result in the infliction of bodily injury upon her by him or by another individual. In addition, a woman is exempted from the notification requirement in the case of a medical emergency.

. . . . [T]his case involves a much less intrusive requirement of spousal *notification*, not consent. Such a law requiring only notice to the husband "does not give any third party the legal right to make the [woman's] decision for her, or to prevent her from obtaining an abortion should she choose to have one performed." . . . Pennsylvania has incorporated exceptions in the notice provision. . . . [A] woman need not notify her husband if the pregnancy is result of a reported sexual assault, or if she has reason to believe that she would suffer bodily injury as a result of the notification. . . . [I]t is not enough . . . to show that, in some "worst-case" circumstances, the notice provision will operate as a grant of veto power to husbands. . . . [Planned Parenthood] must "show that no set of circumstances exists under which the [provision] would be valid." This they have failed to do.

The question before us is therefore whether the spousal notification requirement rationally furthers any legitimate state interests. We conclude that it does. First, a husband's interests in procreation within marriage and in the potential life of his unborn child are certainly substantial ones. The State itself has legitimate interests in both protecting these interests of the father and in protecting the potential life of the fetus, and the spousal notification requirement is reasonably related to advancing those state interests. By providing that a husband will usually know of his spouse's intent to have an abortion, the provision makes it more likely that the husband will participate in deciding the fate of his unborn child, a possibility that might otherwise have been denied him. This participation might in some cases result in a decision to proceed with the pregnancy. As Judge Alito observed in his dissent below, "[t]he Pennsylvania legislature could have rationally believed that some married women are initially inclined to obtain an abortion without their husbands' knowledge because of perceived problems - such as economic constraints, future plans, or the husbands' previously expressed opposition - that may be obviated by discussion prior to the abortion."

The State also has a legitimate interest in promoting "the integrity of the marital relationship." This Court has previously recognized "the importance of the marital relationship in our society." In our view, the spousal notice requirement is a rational attempt by the State to improve truthful communication between spouses and encourage collaborative decisionmaking, and thereby fosters marital integrity. . . . [I]n our view, it is unrealistic to assume that every husband-wife relationship is either (1) so perfect that this type of truthful and important communication will take place as a matter of course, or (2) so imperfect that, upon notice, the husband will react selfishly, violently, or contrary to the best interests of his wife. The spousal notice provision will admittedly be unnecessary in some circumstances, and possibly harmful in others, but "the existence of particular cases in which a feature of a statute performs no function (or is even counterproductive) ordinarily does not render the statute unconstitutional or even constitutionally suspect." The Pennsylvania Legislature was in a position to weigh the likely benefits of the provision against its likely adverse effects, and presumably concluded, on balance, that the provision would be beneficial. Whether this was a wise decision or not, we cannot say that it was irrational. We therefore conclude that the spousal notice provision comports with the Constitution.

The Act also imposes various reporting requirements. Section 3214(a) requires that abortion facilities file a report on each abortion performed. The reports do not include the identity of the women on whom abortions are performed, but they do contain a variety of information about the abortions. . . . We . . . conclude that these reporting requirements rationally further the State's legitimate interests in advancing the state of medical knowledge concerning maternal health and prenatal life, in gathering statistical information with respect to patients, an din ensuring compliance with other provisions of the Act.

Section 3207 of the Act requires each abortion facility to file a report with its name and address, as well as the names and addresses of any parent, subsidiary or affiliated organizations. Section 3214(f) further requires each facility to file quarterly reports stating the total number of abortions performed, broken down by trimester. Both of these reports are available to the public only if the facility received state funds within the preceding 12 months. . . . Records relating to the expenditure of public funds are generally available to the public under Pennsylvania law. As the Court of Appeals observed, "[w]hen a state provides money to a private commercial enterprise, there is a legitimate public interest in informing taxpayers who the funds are benefiting and what services the funds are supporting." These reporting requirements rationally further this legitimate state interest.

Finally, petitioners challenge the medical emergency exception provided for by the Act. The existence of a medical emergency exempts compliance with the Act's informed consent, parental consent, and spousal notice requirements. The Act defines a "medical emergency" as

"[t]hat condition which, on the basis of the physician's good faith clinical judgment, so complicates the medical condition of a pregnant woman as to necessitate the

immediate abortion of her pregnancy to avert her
death or for which a delay will create serious risk of
substantial and irreversible impairment of major bodily
function."

. . . . We observe that Pennsylvania's present definition of
medical emergency is almost an exact copy of that State's
definition at the time of this Court's ruling in *Thornburgh*, one which the Court made reference to with apparent approval.   We find that the interpretation of the
Court of Appeals in this case is eminently reasonable, and
that the provision thus should be upheld.   When a woman
is faced with any condition that poses a "significant threat
to [her] life or health," she is exempted from the Act's
consent and notice requirements and may proceed immediately with her abortion.

For the reasons stated, we therefore would hold that each
of the challenged provisions of the Pennsylvania statute is
consistent with the Constitution.   It bears emphasis that
our conclusion in this regard does not carry with it any
necessary approval of these regulations.   Our task is, as always, to decide only whether the challenged provisions of
a law comport with the United States Constitution.   If, as
we believe, these do, their wisdom as a matter of public
policy is for the people of Pennsylvania to decide.

JUSTICE SCALIA (joined by Chief Justice Rehnquist,
and Justices White and Thomas), concurring in the judgment in part and dissenting in part:

My views on this matter are unchanged from those I set
forth in my separate opinions in *Webster v. Reproductive
Health Services* and *Ohio v. Akron Center for Reproduc-*

Health. The States may, if they wish, permit abortion-on-demand, but the Constitution does not *require* them to do so. The permissibility of abortion, and the limitations upon it, are to be resolved like most important questions in our democracy: by citizens trying to persuade one another and then voting. As the Court acknowledges, "where reasonable people disagree the government can adopt one position or the other." The Court is correct in adding the qualification that this "assumes a state of affairs in which the choice does not intrude upon a protected liberty" - but the crucial part of that qualification is the penultimate word. A State's choice between two positions on which reasonable people can disagree is constitutional even when (as is often the case) it intrudes upon a "liberty" in the absolute sense. Laws against bigamy, for example - which entire societies of reasonable people disagree with - intrude upon men and women's liberty to marry and live with one another. But bigamy happens not to be a liberty specially "protected" by the Constitution.

That is, quite simply, the issue in this case: not whether the power of a woman to abort her unborn child is a "liberty" in the absolute sense; or even whether it is a liberty of great importance to many women. Of course it is both. The issue is whether it is a liberty protected by the Constitution of the United States. I am sure it is not. I reach that conclusion not because of anything so exalted as my views concerning the "concept of existence, of meaning, of the universe, and of the mystery of human life." Rather, I reach it for the same reason I reach the conclusion that bigamy is not constitutionally protected - because of two simple facts: (1) the Constitution says absolutely nothing about it, and (2) the longstanding traditions of American society have permitted it to be legally proscribed.

The Court destroys the proposition, evidently meant to represent my position, that "liberty" includes "only those practices, defined at the most specific level, that were protected against government interference by other rules of law when the Fourteenth Amendment was ratified." . . . The Court's statement that it is "tempting" to acknowledge the authoritativeness of tradition in order to "cur[b] the discretion of federal judges," is of course rhetoric rather than reality; no government official is "tempted" to place restraints upon his own freedom of action. . . . The Court's temptation is in the quite opposite and more natural direction - towards systematically eliminating checks upon its own power; and it succumbs.

. . . . [A]pplying the rational basis test, I would uphold the Pennsylvania statute in its entirety. I must, however, respond to a few of the more outrageous arguments in today's opinion, which it is beyond human nature to leave unanswered. I shall discuss each of them under a quotation from the Court's opinion to which they pertain.

"The inescapable fact is that adjudication of substantive due process claims may call upon the Court in interpreting the Constitution to exercise that same capacity which by tradition courts always have exercised: reasoned judgment."

Assuming that the question before us is to be resolved at such a level of philosophical abstraction, in such isolation from the traditions of American society, as by simply applying "reasoned judgment," I do not see how that could possibly have produced the answer the Court arrived at in *Roe v. Wade*. Today's opinion describes the methodology of *Roe*, quite accurately, as weighing against the woman's interest the State's "'important and legitimate interest in protecting the potentiality of human life.'" But "reasoned judgment" does not begin by begging the question, as *Roe* and subsequent cases unquestionably did by assuming that what the State is protecting is the mere "potentiality of human life." The whole argument of abortion opponents is that what the Court calls the fetus and what others call the unborn child *is a human life*. Thus, whatever answer *Roe* came up with after conducting its "balancing" is bound to be wrong, unless it is correct that the human fetus is in some critical sense merely potentially human. There is of course no way to determine that as a legal matter; it is in fact a value judgment. Some societies have considered newborn children not yet human, or the incompetent elderly no longer so.

The authors of the joint opinion, of course, do not squarely contend that *Roe v. Wade* was a *correct* application of "reasoned judgment"; merely that it must be followed, because of stare decisis. But in their exhaustive discussion of all the factors that go into the determination of when stare decisis should be observed and when disregarded, they never mention "how wrong was the decision on its face?" Surely, if "[t]he Court's power lies . . . in its legitimacy, a product of substance and perception," the "substance" part of the equation demands that plain error be acknowledged and eliminated. *Roe* was plainly wrong - even on the Court's methodology of "reasoned judgment," and even more so (of course) if the proper criteria of text and tradition are applied.

The emptiness of the "reasoned judgment" that produced *Roe* is displayed in plain view by the fact that, after more than 19 years of effort by some of the brightest (and most determined) legal minds in the country, after more than 10 cases upholding abortion rights in this Court, . . . the best the Court can do to explain how it is that the word "liberty" *must* be thought to include the right to destroy human fetuses is to rattle off a collection of adjectives that simply decorate a value judgment and conceal a political choice. The right to abort, we are told, inheres in "liberty" because it is among "a person's most basic decisions"; it involves a "most intimate and personal choic[e]"; it is "central to personal dignity and autonomy"; it "originate[s] within the zone of conscience and belief"; it is "too intimate and personal" for state interference; it reflects "intimate views" of a "deep, personal character"; it involves "intimate relationships," and notions of "personal autonomy and bodily integrity"; and it concerns a particularly "'important decisio[n].'" But it is obvious to anyone applying "reasoned judgment" that the same adjectives can be applied to many forms of conduct that this Court (including one of the Justices in today's majority) has held are *not* entitled to constitutional protection - because, like abortion, they are forms of conduct that have long been criminalized in American society. Those adjectives might be applied, for example, to homosexual sodomy, polygamy, adult incest, and suicide, all of which are equally "intimate" and "deep[ly] personal" decisions involving "personal autonomy and bodily integrity," and all of which can constitutionally be proscribed because it is our unquestionable constitutional tradition that they are proscribable. It is not reasoned judgment that supports the Court's decision; only personal predilection. Justice Curtis's warning is as timely today as it was 135 years ago:

"[W]hen a strict interpretation of the Constitution, according to the fixed rules which govern the interpretation of laws, is abandoned, and the theoretical opinions of individuals are allowed to control its meaning, we have no longer a Constitution; we are under the government of individual men, who for the time being have power to declare what the Constitution is, according to their own views of what it ought to mean."

"Liberty finds no refuge in a jurisprudence of doubt."

One might have feared to encounter this august and sonorous phrase in an opinion defending the real *Roe v. Wade,* rather than the revised version fabricated today by the authors of the joint opinion. The shortcomings of *Roe* did not include lack of clarity: Virtually all regulation of abortion before the third trimester was invalid. But to come across this phrase in the joint opinion - which calls upon federal district judges to apply an "undue burden" standard as doubtful in application as it is unprincipled in origin - is really more than one should have to bear.

. . . . Because the three Justices now wish to "set forth a standard of general application," the joint opinion announces that "it is important to clarify what is meant by an undue burden." I certainly agree with that, but I do not agree that the joint opinion succeeds in the announced endeavor. To the contrary, its efforts at clarification make clear only that the standard is inherently manipulable and will prove hopelessly unworkable in practice.

The joint opinion explains that a state regulation imposes an "undue burden" if it "has the purpose or effect of placing a substantial obstacle in the path of a woman seeking

an abortion of a nonviable fetus." An obstacle is
"substantial," we are told, if it is "calculated[,] [not] to inform the woman's free choice [but to] hinder it." This
latter statement cannot possibly mean what it says. *Any*
regulation of abortion that is intended to advance what
the joint opinion concedes is the State's "substantial" interest in protecting unborn life will be "calculated [to]
hinder" a decision to have an abortion. It thus seems more
accurate to say that the joint opinion would uphold abortion regulations only if they do not *unduly* hinder the
woman's decision. That, of course, brings us right back to
square one: Defining an "undue burden" as an "undue hindrance" (or a "substantial obstacle") hardly "clarifies" the
test. Consciously or not, the joint opinion's verbal shell
game will conceal raw judicial policy choices concerning
what is "appropriate" abortion legislation.

The ultimately standardless nature of the "undue burden"
inquiry is a reflection of the underlying fact that the concept has no principled or coherent legal basis. As The
Chief Justice points out, *Roe's* strict-scrutiny standard "at
least had a recognized basis in constitutional law at the
time *Roe* was decided," while "[t]he same cannot be said
for the 'undue burden' standard, which is created largely
out of whole cloth by the authors of the joint opinion."
The joint opinion . . . argues that the abortion right is
similar to other rights in that a law "not designed to strike
at the right itself, [but which] has the incidental effect of
making it more difficult or more expensive to [exercise
the right,]" is not invalid. I agree, indeed I have forceful-
ly urged, that a law of general applicability which places
only an incidental burden on a fundamental right does not
infringe that right, but that principle does not establish
the quite different (and quite dangerous) proposition that

a law which *directly* regulates a fundamental right will not be found to violate the Constitution unless it imposes an "undue burden." . . . The "undue burden" standard is not at all the generally applicable principle the joint opinion pretends it to be; rather, it is a unique concept created specially for this case, to preserve some judicial foothold in this ill-gotten territory. In claiming otherwise, the three Justices show their willingness to place all constitutional rights at risk in an effort to preserve what they deem the "central holding in *Roe.*"

The rootless nature of the "undue burden" standard, a phrase plucked out of context from our earlier abortion decisions, is further reflected in the fact that the joint opinion finds it necessary expressly to repudiate the more narrow formulations used in Justice O'Connor's earlier opinions. Those opinions stated that a statute imposes an "undue burden" if it imposes "*absolute* obstacles or *severe* limitations on the abortion decision." Those strong adjectives are conspicuously missing from the joint opinion, whose authors have for some unexplained reason now determined that a burden is "undue" if it merely imposes a "substantial" obstacle to abortion decisions. Justice O'Connor has also abandoned (again without explanation) the view she expressed in *Planned Parenthood Assn. of Kansas City, Mo., Inc. v. Ashcroft* that a medical regulation which imposes an "undue burden" could nevertheless be upheld if it "reasonably relate[s] to the preservation and protection of maternal health." In today's version, even health measures will be upheld only "*if they do not constitute an undue burden.*" Gone too is Justice O'Connor's statement that "the State possesses *compelling* interests in the protection of potential human life . . . throughout pregnancy"; instead, the State's interest in un-

born human life is stealthily downgraded to a merely
"substantial" or "profound" interest.... And "viability" is
no longer the "arbitrary" dividing line previously decried
by Justice O'Connor in *Akron I,* the Court now announces
that "the attainment of viability may continue to serve as
the critical fact." It is difficult to maintain the illusion
that we are interpreting a Constitution rather than invent-
ing one, when we amend its provisions so breezily.

.... Thus, the joint opinion would uphold the 24-hour
waiting period contained in the Pennsylvania statute's informed consent provision because "the record evidence
shows that in the vast majority of cases, a 24-hour delay
does not create any appreciable health risk." ... The requirement that a doctor provide the information pertinent
to informed consent would also be upheld because "there
is no evidence on this record that [this requirement]
would amount in practical terms to a substantial obstacle
to a woman seeking an abortion." Similarly, the joint
opinion would uphold the reporting requirements of the
Act because "there is no ... showing on the record before
us" that these requirements constitute a "substantial obstacle" to abortion decisions. But at the same time the opinion pointedly observes that these reporting requirements
may increase the costs of abortions and that "at some
point [that fact] could become a substantial obstacle."
Most significantly, the joint opinion's conclusion that the
spousal notice requirement of the Act imposes an "undue
burden" is based in large measure on the District Court's
"detailed findings of fact," which the joint opinion sets
out at great length.

I do not, of course, have any objection to the notion that,
in applying legal principles, one should relay only upon

the facts that are contained in the record or that are properly subject to judicial notice. But what is remarkable about the joint opinion's fact-intensive analysis is that it does not result in any measurable clarification of the "undue burden" standard. Rather, the approach of the joint opinion is, for the most part, simply to highlight certain facts in the record that apparently strike the three Justices as particularly significant in establishing (or refuting) the existence of an undue burden; after describing these facts, the opinion then simply announces that the provision either does or does not impose a "substantial obstacle" or an "undue burden." We do not know whether the same conclusions could have been reached on a different record, or in what respects the record would have had to differ before an opposite conclusion would have been appropriate. The inherently standardless nature of this inquiry invites the district judge to give effect to his personal preferences about abortion. By finding and relying upon the right facts, he can invalidate, it would seem, almost any abortion restriction that strikes him as "undue" - subject, of course, to the possibility of being reversed by a Circuit Court or Supreme Court that is as unconstrained in reviewing his decision as he was in making it.

To the extent I can discern *any* meaningful content in the "undue burden" standard as applied in the joint opinion, it appears to be that a State may not regulate abortion in such a way as to reduce significantly its incidence. The joint opinion repeatedly emphasizes that an important factor in the "undue burden" analysis is whether the regulation "prevent[s] a significant number of women from obtaining an abortion"; whether a "significant number of women . . . are likely to be deterred from procuring an abortion"; and whether the regulation often "deters" women from seeking abortions. We are not told, however, what forms of "deterrence" are impermissible or what degree of success in deterrence is too much to be tolerated. . . . [D]espite flowery rhetoric about the State's "substantial" and "profound" interest in "potential human life," and criticism of *Roe* for undervaluing that interest, the joint opinion permits the State to pursue that interest only so long as it is not too successful. As Justice Blackmun recognizes (with evident hope), the "undue burden" standard may ultimately require the invalidation of each provision upheld today if it can be shown, on a better record, that the State is too effectively "express[ing] a preference for childbirth over abortion." Reason finds no refuge in this jurisprudence of confusion.

"While we appreciate the weight of the arguments . . . that Roe *should be overruled, the reservations any of us may have in reaffirming the central holding of* Roe *are outweighed by the explication of individual liberty we have given combined with the force of stare decisis."*

The Court's reliance upon stare decisis can best be described as contrived. It insists upon the necessity of adhering not to all of *Roe*, but only to what it calls the "central holding." It seems to me that stare decisis ought to be applied even to the doctrine of stare decisis, and I confess never to have heard of this new, keep-what-you-want-and-throw-away-the-rest version. . . .

I am certainly not in a good position to dispute that the Court *has saved* the "central holding" of *Roe*, since to do that effectively I would have to know what the Court has saved, which in turn would require me to understand (as I do not) what the "undue burden" test means. I must confess, however, that I have always thought, and I think a lot of other people have always thought, that the arbitrary trimester framework, which the Court today discards, was quite as central to *Roe* as the arbitrary viability test, which the Court today retains. It seems particularly ungrateful to carve the trimester framework out of the core of *Roe*, since its very rigidity (in sharp contrast to the utter indeterminability of the "undue burden" test is probably the only reason the Court is able to say, in urging stare decisis, that *Roe* "has in no sense proven 'unworkable'." I suppose the Court is entitled to call a "central holding" - which is, come to think of it, perhaps one of the difficulties with this modified version of stare decisis. I thought I might note, however, that the following portions of *Roe* have not been saved:

Under *Roe*, requiring that a woman seeking an abortion be provided truthful information about abortion before giving informed written consent is unconstitutional, if the information is designed to influence her choice. Under the joint opinion's "undue burden" regime (as applied today, at least) such a requirement is constitutional.

Under *Roe*, requiring that information be provided by a doctor, rather than by nonphysician counselors, is unconstitutional Under the "undue burden" regime (as applied today, at least) it is not.

Under *Roe*, requiring a 24-hour waiting period between the time the woman gives her informed consent and the time of the abortion is unconstitutional. Under the "undue burden" regime (as applied today, at least) it is not.

Under *Roe*, requiring detailed reports that include demographic data about each woman who seeks an abortion and various information about each abortion is unconstitutional. Under the "undue burden" regime (as applied today, at least) it is not.

"Where, in the performance of its judicial duties, the Court decides a case in such a way as to resolve the sort of intensely divisive controversy reflected in Roe *. . . , its decision has a dimension that the resolution of the normal case does not carry. It is the dimension present whenever the Court's interpretation of the Constitution calls the contending sides of a national controversy to end their national division by accepting a common mandate rooted in the Constitution."*

The Court's description of the place of *Roe* in the social history of the United States is unrecognizable. Not only did *Roe* not, as the Court suggests, *resolve* the deeply divisive issue of abortion; it did more than anything else to nourish it, by elevating it to the national level where it is infinitely more difficult to resolve. National politics were not plagued by abortion protests, national abortion lobbying, or abortion marches on Congress, before *Roe v. Wade* was decided. Profound disagreement existed among our citizens over the issue - as it does over other issues, such as the death penalty - but that disagreement was being worked out at the state level. As with many other issues, the division of sentiment within each State was not as closely balanced as it was among the population of the Nation as a whole, meaning not only that more people would be satisfied with the results of state-by-state resolution, but also that those results would be more stable. Pre-*Roe*, moreover, political compromise was possible.

Roe's mandate for abortion-on-demand destroyed the compromises of the past, rendered compromise impossible for the future, and required the entire issue to be resolved uniformly, at the national level. At the same time, *Roe* created a vast new class of abortion consumers and abortion proponents by eliminating the moral opprobrium that had attached to the act. ("If the Constitution *guarantees* abortion, how can it be bad?" - not an accurate line of thought, but a natural one.) Many favor all of those developments, and it is not for me to say that they are wrong. But to portray *Roe* as the statesmanlike "settlement" of a divisive issue, a jurisprudential Peace of Westphalia that is worth preserving, is nothing less than Orwellian. *Roe* fanned into life an issue that has inflamed our national politics in general, and has obscured with its smoke the selection of Justices to this Court in particular, ever since. And by keeping us in the abortion-umpiring business, it is the perpetuation of that disruption, rather than of any pax Roeana, that the Court's new majority decrees.

"[T]o overrule under fire . . . would subvert the Court's legitimacy. . . .

"To all those who will be . . . tested by following, the Court implicitly undertakes to remain steadfast. . . . The promise of constancy, once given, binds its maker for as long as the power to stand by the decision survives and . . . the commitment [is not] obsolete. . . .

"[The American people's] belief in themselves as . . . a people [who aspire to live according to the rule of law] is not readily separable from their understanding of the Court invested with the authority to decide their constitu-

tional cases and speak before all others for their constitu-
tional ideals. If the Court's legitimacy should be under-
mined, then, so would the country be in its very ability to
see itself through its constitutional ideals."

The Imperial Judiciary lives. It is instructive to compare
this Nietzschean vision of us, unelected, life-tenured
judges - leading a Volk who will be "tested by following,"
and whose very "belief in themselves" is mystically bound
up in their "understanding" of a Court that "speak[s] before all others for their constitutional ideals" - with the
somewhat more modest role envisioned for these lawyers
by the Founders.

. . . . Or, again, to compare this ecstasy of a Supreme
Court in which there is, especially on controversial matters, no shadow of change or hint of alteration ("There is
a limit to the amount of error that can plausibly be imputed to prior courts"), with the more democratic views of a
more humble man [Abraham Lincoln]:

> "[T]he candid citizen must confess that if the policy of
> the Government upon vital questions affecting the
> whole people is to be irrevocably fixed by decisions of
> the Supreme Court, . . . the people will have ceased to
> be their own rulers, having to that extent practically
> resigned their Government into the hands of that emi-
> nent tribunal."

It is particularly difficult, in the circumstances of the
present decision, to sit still for the Court's lengthy lecture
upon the virtues of "constancy," of "remain[ing]
steadfast," and adhering to "principle." Among the five
Justices who purportedly adhere to *Roe*, at most three

agree upon the *principle* that constitutes adherence (the joint opinion's "undue burden" standard) - and that principle is inconsistent with *Roe.* To make matters worse, two of the three, in order thus to remain steadfast, had to abandon previously stated positions. . . . The only principle the Court "adheres" to, it seems to me, is the principle that the Court must be seen as standing by *Roe.* That is not a principle of law (which is what I thought the Court was talking about), but a principle of Realpolitik - and a wrong one at that.

I cannot agree with, indeed I am appalled by, the Court's suggestion that the decision whether to stand by an erroneous constitutional decision must be strongly influenced - *against* overruling, no less - by the substantial and continuing public opposition the decision has generated. The Court's judgment that any other course would "subvert the Court's legitimacy" must be another consequence of reading the error-filled history book that described the deeply divided country brought together by *Roe.* In my history book, the Court was covered with dishonor and deprived of legitimacy by *Dred Scott v. Sandford,* an erroneous (and widely opposed) opinion that it did not abandon, rather than by *West Coast Hotel Co. v. Parrish,* which produced the famous "switch in time" from the Court's erroneous (and widely opposed) constitutional opposition to the social measures of the New Deal. . . .

But whether it would "subvert the Court's legitimacy" or not, the notion that we would decide a case differently from the way we otherwise would have in order to show that we can stand firm against public disapproval is frightening. It is a bad enough idea, even in the head of someone like me, who believes that the text of the Constitution, and our traditions, say what they say and there is no fiddling with them. But when it is in the mind of a Court that believes the Constitution has an evolving meaning; that the Ninth Amendment's reference to "othe[r]" rights is not a disclaimer, but a charter for action; and that the function of this Court is to "speak before all others for [the people's] constitutional ideals" unrestrained by meaningful text or tradition - then the notion that the Court must adhere to a decision for as long as the decision faces "great opposition" and the Court is "under fire" acquires a character of almost czarist arrogance. We are offended by these marchers who descend upon us, every year on the anniversary of *Roe*, to protest our saying that the Constitution requires what our society has never thought the Constitution requires. These people who refuse to be "tested by following" must be taught a lesson. We have no Cossacks, but at least we can stubbornly refuse to abandon an erroneous opinion that we might otherwise change - to show how little they intimidate us.

Of course, as The Chief Justice points out, we have been subjected to what the Court calls "political pressure" by *both* sides of this issue. Maybe today's decision *not* to overrule *Roe* will be seen as buckling to pressure from *that* direction. ... [T]he Justices should do what is *legally* right by asking two questions: (1) Was *Roe* correctly decided? (2) Has *Roe* succeeded in producing a settled body of law? If the answer to both questions is no, *Roe* should undoubtedly be overruled.

 . . . . How upsetting it is, that so many of our citizens (good people, not lawless ones, on both sides of this abortion issue, and on various sides of other issues as well) think that we Justices should properly take into account their views, as though we were engaged not in ascertaining an objective law but in determining some kind of social consensus. The Court would profit, I think, from giving less attention to the *fact* of this distressing phenomenon, and more attention to the *cause* of it. That cause permeates today's opinion: a new mode of constitutional adjudication that relies not upon text and traditional practice to determine the law, but upon what the Court calls "reasoned judgment," which turns out to be nothing but philosophical predilection and moral intuition. . . .

[T]he American people love democracy and the American people are not fools. As long as this Court thought (and the people thought) that we Justices were doing essentially lawyers' work up here - reading text and discerning our society's traditional understanding of that text - the public pretty much left us alone. Texts and traditions are facts to study, not convictions to demonstrate about. . . . [I]f . . . our pronouncement of constitutional law rests primarily on value judgments, then a free and intelligent people's attitude towards us can be expected to be (*ought* to be) quite different. The people know that their value judgments are quite as good as those taught in any law school - maybe better. If, indeed, the "liberties" protected by the Constitution are, as the Court says, undefined and unbounded, then the people *should* demonstrate, to protest that we do not implement *their* values instead of *ours.* Not only that, but confirmation hearings for new Justices *should* deteriorate into question-and-answer sessions in which Senators go through a list of their constituents' most favored and most disfavored alleged constitutional rights, and seek the nominee's commitment to support or oppose them. Value judgments, after all, should be voted on, not dictated; and if our Constitution has somehow accidentally committed them to the Supreme Court, at least we can have a sort of plebiscite each time a new nominee to that body is put forward. Justice Blackmun not only regards this prospect with equanimity, he solicits it.

There is a poignant aspect to today's opinion. Its length, and what might be called its epic tone, suggest that its authors believe they are bringing to an end a troublesome era in the history of our Nation and of our Court....

There comes vividly to mind a portrait by Emanuel Leutz that hangs in the Harvard Law School: Roger Brooke Taney, painted in 1859, the 82d year of his life, the 24th of his Chief Justiceship, the second after his opinion in *Dred Scott.* He is all in black, sitting in a shadowed red armchair, left hand resting upon a pad of paper in his lap, right hand handing limply, almost lifelessly, beside the inner arm of the chair. He sits facing the viewer, and staring straight out. There seems to be on his face, and in his deep-set eyes, an expression of profound sadness and disillusionment. Perhaps he always looked that way, even when dwelling upon the happiest of thoughts. But those of us who know how the lustre of his great Chief Justiceship came to be eclipsed by *Dred Scott* cannot help believing that he had that case - its already apparent consequences for the Court, and its soon-to-be-played-out consequences for the Nation - burning on his mind. I expect that two years earlier he, too, had thought himself "call[ing] the contending sides of national controversy to end their national division by accepting a common mandate rooted in the Constitution."

It is no more realistic for us in this case, than it was for him in that, to think that an issue of the sort they both involved - an issue involving life and death, freedom and subjugation - can be "speedily and finally settled" by the Supreme Court, as President James Buchanan in his inaugural address said the issue of slavery in the territories would be. Quite to the contrary, by foreclosing all democratic outlet for the deep passions this issue arouses, by banishing the issue for the political forum that gives all participants, even the losers, the satisfaction of a fair hearing and an honest fight, by continuing the imposition of a rigid national rule instead of allowing for regional differences, the Court merely prolongs and intensifies the anguish.

We should get out of this area, where we have not right to be, and where we do neither ourselves nor the country any good by remaining.

BRAY v. ALEXANDRIA
WOMEN'S HEALTH CLINIC

EXCERPTS

"Even in the context of political protest, persistent, organized, premeditated lawlessness menaces in a unique way the capacity of a State to maintain order and preserve the rights of its citizens. Such actions are designed to inflame, not inform. They subvert the civility and mutual respect that are the essential preconditions for the orderly resolution of social conflict in a free society."

Justice Anthony Kennedy

"The Court ignores the obvious (and entirely constitutional) congressional intent behind [the Ku Klux Act] to protect this Nation's citizens from what amounts to the theft of their constitutional rights by organized and violent mobs across the country."

Justice John Paul Stevens

"In my opinion, [Operation Rescue]'s unlawful conspiracy to prevent the clinics from serving those women, who are targeted by [Operation Rescue] by virtue of their class characteristics, is a group-based, private deprivation of the "equal protection of the laws" within the reach of [the Ku Klux Act]."

Justice Sandra Day O'Connor

In Brief

Question:	Can the Civil Rights [Ku Klux] Act of 1871 be used to prevent abortion blockades?
Lower Court:	U.S. District Court, Eastern Virginia U.S. Court of Appeals, Fourth Circuit
Law:	Civil Rights [Ku Klux] Act of 1871
Parties:	Jayne Bray (Operation Rescue) Alexandria Women's Health Clinic
Counsel:	For Bray: Jay Allen Sekulow For Alexandria Women's Health Clinic: John H. Schafer
Arguments:	October 15, 1991; October 6, 1992
Decision:	January 13, 1993
Majority:	Chief Justice Rehnquist, Justices White, Scalia, Kennedy, Souter, Thomas
Minority:	Justices Blackmun, Stevens, O'Connor
Decision by:	Justice Scalia (p. 217)
Concurrences:	Justice Kennedy (p. 226)

Concurring in part/Dissenting in part:

	Justice Souter (p. 228)
Dissents:	Justice Stevens (p. 233) Justice O'Connor (p. 241)
Offical Text:	U.S. Reports, Vol. 506
Lower Court:	Federal Supplement, Vol. 726, p. 1483 Federal Reporter 2d, Vol. 914, p. 582

THE BRAY COURT

Chief Justice William Rehnquist
Appointed Associate Justice 1971 by Richard M. Nixon
Appointed Chief Justice 1986 by Ronald W. Reagan

Associate Justice Byron White
Appointed 1962 by John F. Kennedy

Associate Justice Harry Blackmun
Appointed 1970 by Richard M. Nixon

Associate Justice John Paul Stevens
Appointed 1975 by Gerald R. Ford

Associate Justice Sandra Day O'Connor
Appointed 1981 by Ronald W. Reagan

Associate Justice Antonin Scalia
Appointed 1986 by Ronald W. Reagan

Associate Justice Anthony Kennedy
Appointed 1988 by Ronald W. Reagan

Associate Justice David Souter
Appointed 1991 by George Bush

Associate Justice Clarence Thomas
Appointed 1992 by George Bush

BRAY v. ALEXANDRIA WOMEN'S HEALTH CLINIC

January 13, 1993

JUSTICE SCALIA: This case presents the question whether the Civil Rights [Ku Klux] Act of 1871 provides a federal cause of action against persons obstructing access to abortion clinics. Respondents [Alexandria Women's Health Clinic and others] are clinics that perform abortions, and organizations [National Organization for Women and others] that support legalized abortion and that have members who may wish to use abortion clinics. Petitioners are Operation Rescue, an unincorporated association whose members oppose abortion, and six individuals [including Jayne Bray]. Among its activities, Operation Rescue organizes antiabortion demonstrations in which participants trespass on, and obstruct general access to, the premises of abortion clinics. The individual petitioners organize and coordinate these demonstrations.

[Alexandria Women's Health Clinic] sued to enjoin [stop Operation Rescue] from conducting demonstrations at abortion clinics in the Washington, D.C. metropolitan area. Following an expedited trial, the District Court ruled that [Operation Rescue] had violated [the Ku Klux Act] by conspiring to deprive women seeking abortions of their right to interstate travel. The court also ruled for [Alexandria Women's Health Clinic] on their [pending] state-law claims of trespass and public nuisance. . . . [T]he court [stopped Operation Rescue] from trespassing on, or obstructing access to, abortion clinics in specified Virginia counties and cities in the Washington, D.C., metropolitan area. . . .

The Court of Appeals for the Fourth Circuit affirmed [agreed with the lower court], and we granted certiorari [agreed to hear the case]. The case was argued in the October 1991 Term, and pursuant to our direction, was reargued in the current Term.

Our precedents establish that in order to prove a private conspiracy in violation of the first clause of [the Ku Klux Act], a plaintiff must show, [among other things], (1) that "some racial, or perhaps otherwise class-based, invidiously discriminatory animus [lay] behind the conspirators' action," and (2) that the conspiracy "aimed at interfering with rights" that are "protected against private, as well as official, encroachment." We think neither showing has been made in the present case.

In *Griffin*, this Court held, reversing a 20-year-old precedent, that [the Ku Klux Act] reaches not only conspiracies under color of state law, but also purely private conspiracies. . . . We said that "[t]he language [of the Ku Klux Act] requiring intent to deprive of *equal* protection, or *equal* privileges and immunities, means that there must be some racial, or perhaps otherwise class-based, invidiously discriminatory animus behind the conspirators' action."

We have not yet had occasion to resolve the "perhaps"; only in *Griffin* itself have we addressed and upheld a claim under [the Ku Klux Act], and that case involved race discrimination. [Alexandria Women's Health Clinic] assert[s] that there qualifies alongside race discrimination, as an "otherwise class-based, invidiously discriminatory animus" covered by the 1871 law, opposition to abortion. Neither common sense nor our precedents support this.

To begin with, we reject the apparent conclusion of the District Court . . . that opposition to abortion constitutes discrimination against the "class" of "women seeking abortion." Whatever may be the precise meaning of a "class" for purposes of *Griffin*'s speculative extension of [the Ku Klux Act] beyond race, the term unquestionably connotes something more than a group of individuals who share a desire to engage in conduct that the [Ku Klux Act] defendant disfavors. Otherwise, innumerable . . . plaintiffs would be able to assert causes of action under [the Ku Klux Act] by simply defining the aggrieved class as those seeking to engage in the activity the defendant has interfered with. . . . "Women seeking abortion" is not a qualifying class.

[Alexandria Women's Health Clinic]'s contention, however, is that the alleged class-based discrimination is directed not at "women seeking abortion" but at women in general. We find it unnecessary to decide whether *that* is a qualifying class under [the Ku Klux Act], since the claim that [Operation Rescue]'s opposition to abortion reflects an animus against women in general must be rejected. We do not think that the "animus" requirement can be met only by maliciously motivated, as opposed to assertedly benign (though objectively invidious), discrimination against women. It does demand, however, at least a purpose that focuses upon women *by reason of their sex* - for example (to use an illustration of assertedly benign discrimination), the purpose of "saving" women *because they are women* from a combative, aggressive profession such as the practice of law. The record in this case does not in-

dicate that [Operation Rescue]'s demonstrations are motivated by a purpose (malevolent *or* benign) directed specifically at women as a class; to the contrary, the District
Court found that [Operation Rescue] define[s] their
"rescues" not with reference to women, but as physical intervention "'between abortionists and the innocent victims,'" and that "[Operation Rescue has] a deep commitment to the goals of stopping the practice of abortion and
reversing its legalization." . . . [Alexandria Women's
Health Clinic]'s contention that a class-based animus has
been established can be true only if one of two suggested
propositions is true: (1) that opposition to abortion can
reasonably be presumed to reflect a sex-based intent, or
(2) that intent is irrelevant, and a class-based animus can
be determined solely by effect.   Neither proposition is
supportable.

As to the first: Some activities may be such an irrational
object of disfavor that, if they are targeted, and if they
also happen to be engaged in exclusively or predominantly by a particular class of people, an intent to disfavor
that class can readily be presumed. A tax on wearing yar-
mulkes is a tax on Jews.   But opposition to voluntary
abortion cannot possibly be considered such an irrational
surrogate for opposition to (*or* paternalism towards) wom-
en. Whatever one thinks of abortion, it cannot be denied
that there are common and respectable reasons for opposing it, other than hatred of or condescension toward (or
indeed any view at all concerning) women as a class - as is
evident from the fact that men and women are on both
sides of the issue, just as men and women are on both
sides of [Operation Rescue]'s unlawful demonstrations.

[Alexandria Women's Health Clinic]'s case comes down, then to the proposition that intent is legally irrelevant; that since voluntary abortion is an activity engaged in only by women, to disfavor it is [in fact] to discriminate invidiously against women as a class. Our cases do not support that proposition. In *Gelduldig v. Aiello*, we rejected the claim that a state disability insurance system that denied coverage to certain disabilities resulting from pregnancy discriminated on the basis of sex in violation of the Equal Protection Clause of the Fourteenth Amendment. "While it is true," we said, "that only women can become pregnant, it does not follow that every legislative classification concerning pregnancy is a sex-based classification." We reached a similar conclusion in *Personnel Administrator of Mass. v. Feeney*, sustaining against an Equal Protection Clause challenge a Massachusetts law giving employment preference to military veterans, a class which in Massachusetts was over 98% male. "'Discriminatory purpose,'" we said, "implies more than intent as volition or intent as awareness of consequences. It implies that the decisionmaker . . . selected or reaffirmed a particular course of action at least in part 'because of,' not merely 'in spite of,' its adverse effects upon an identifiable group." The same principle applies to the "class-based, invidiously discriminatory animus" requirement of [the Ku Klux Act]. Moreover, two of our cases deal specifically with the disfavoring of abortion, and establish conclusively that it is not [in fact] sex discrimination. In *Maher v. Roe* and *Harris v. McRae*, we held that the constitutional test applicable to government abortion-funding restrictions is not the heightened-scrutiny standard that our cases demand for sex-based discrimination, but the ordinary rationality standard.

The nature of the "invidiously discriminatory animus" *Griffin* had in mind is suggested both by the language used in that phrase [according to *Webster's Second International Dictionary*] ("invidious . . . [t]ending to excite odium, ill will, or envy; likely to give offense; esp., unjustly and irritatingly discriminating,") and by the company in which the phrase is found ("there must be *some racial, or perhaps otherwise class-based*, invidiously discriminatory animus."). Whether one agrees or disagrees with the goal of preventing abortion, that goal in itself (apart from the use of unlawful means to achieve it, which is not relevant to our discussion of animus) does not remotely qualify for such harsh description, and for such derogatory association with racism. To the contrary, we have said that "a value judgment favoring childbirth over abortion" is proper and reasonable enough to be implemented by the allocation of public funds, and Congress itself has, with our approval, discriminated against abortion in its provision of financial support for medical procedures. This is not the stuff out of which a [Ku Klux Act] "invidiously discriminatory animus" is created.

. . . A [Ku Klux Act] private conspiracy "for the purpose of depriving . . . any person or class of persons of the equal protection of the laws, or of equal privileges and immunities under the laws," requires an intent to deprive persons of a right guaranteed against private impairment. No intent to deprive of such a right was established here.

. . . . Our discussion in *Carpenters* makes clear that it does not suffice for application of [the Ku Klux Act] that a protected right be incidentally affected. A conspiracy is not "for the purpose" of denying equal protection simply because it has an effect upon a protected right. The right must be "*aimed at*"; its impairment must be a conscious objective of the enterprise.... [T]he "intent to deprive of a right" requirement demands that the defendant do more than merely be aware of a deprivation of right that he causes, and more than merely accept it; he must act at least in part for the very purpose of producing it. That was not shown to be the case here, and is on its face implausible. [Operation Rescue] oppose[s] abortion, and it is irrelevant to their opposition whether the abortion is performed after interstate travel.

[Alexandria Women's Health Clinic] ha[s] failed to show a conspiracy to violate the right of interstate travel for yet another reason: [Operation Rescue]'s proposed demonstrations would not implicate that right.... As far as appears from this record, the only "actual barriers to movement" that would have resulted from [Operation Rescue]'s proposed demonstrations would have been in the immediate vicinity of the abortion clinics, restricting movement from one portion of the Commonwealth of Virginia to another. Such a purely intrastate restriction does not implicate the right of interstate travel, even if it is applied intentionally against travelers from other States, unless it is applied *discriminatorily* against them. That would not be the case here....

The other right alleged by [Alexandria Women's Health Clinic] to have been intentionally infringed is the right to abortion. The District Court declined to rule on this contention.... Whereas, unlike the right of interstate travel, the asserted right to abortion was assuredly "aimed at" by [Operation Rescue], deprivation of that federal right (whatever its contours) cannot be the object of a purely private conspiracy. In *Carpenters*, we rejected a claim

that an alleged private conspiracy to infringe First
Amendment rights violated [the Ku Klux Act]. The statute does not apply, we said, to private conspiracies that
are "aimed at a right that is by definition a right only
against state interference," but applies only to such conspiracies as are "aimed at interfering with rights . . . protected against private, as well as official, encroachment."
There are few such rights (we have hitherto recognized
only the Thirteenth Amendment right to be free from involuntary servitude, and, in the same Thirteenth Amendment context, the right of interstate travel). The right to
abortion is not among them. It would be most peculiar to
accord it that preferred position, since it is much less explicitly protected by the Constitution than, for example,
the right of free speech rejected for such status in *Carpenters*. Moreover, the right to abortion has been described in our opinions as one element of a more general
right of privacy, or of Fourteenth Amendment liberty,
and the other elements of those more general rights are
obviously *not* protected against private infringement. (A
burglar does not violate the Fourth Amendment, for example, nor does a mugger violate the Fourteenth.)
[Alexandria Women's Health Clinic's Ku Klux Act]
"deprivation" claim must fail, then, because they have
identified no right protected against private action that
has been the object of the alleged conspiracy.

. . . . Without a race- or class-based animus requirement,
the "hindrance" clause of [the Ku Klux Act] would have
been an available weapon against the mass "sit-ins" that
were conducted for purposes of promoting desegregation
in the 1960's - a wildly improbable result.

Even, moreover, if the "hindrance"-clause claim did not fail for lack of class-based animus, it would still fail unless the "hindrance" clause applies to a private conspiracy aimed at rights that are constitutionally protected only against official (as opposed to private) encroachment. . . .

[Operation Rescue] seek[s] even more. They [ask that] the injunction . . . be vacated [annulled] and the entire action dismissed. We do not agree. . . .

It may be, of course, that even though the District Court had jurisdiction over the state-law claims, judgment on those claims alone cannot support the injunction that was entered. We leave that question for consideration on remand [return to the lower court].

. . . . We construe the statute, not the views of "most members of the citizenry." By its terms, [the Ku Klux Act] covers concerted action by as few as two persons, and does not require even interstate (much less nationwide) scope. It applies no more and no less to completely local action by two part-time protesters than to nationwide action by a full-time force of thousands. And under our precedents it simply does not apply to the sort of action at issue here.

Trespassing upon private property is unlawful in all States, as is, in many States and localities, intentionally obstructing the entrance to private premises. These offenses may be prosecuted criminally under state law, and may also be the basis for state civil damages. They do not, however, give rise to a federal cause of action simply because their objective is to prevent the performance of abortions, any more than they do so (as we have held) when their objective is to stifle free speech.

The judgment of the Court of Appeals is reversed in part and vacated [annulled] in part, and the case is remanded [sent back] for further proceedings consistent with this opinion.

JUSTICE KENNEDY, concurring: In joining the opinion of the Court, I make these added observations.

The three separate dissenting opinions in this case offer differing interpretations of the statute in question, [the Ku Klux Act]. Given the difficulty of the question, this is understandable, but the dissenters' inability to agree on a single rationale confirms, in my view, the correctness of the Court's opinion. As all recognize, essential considerations of federalism are at stake here. The federal balance is a fragile one, and a false step in interpreting [the Ku Klux Act] risks making a whole catalog of ordinary state crimes a concurrent violation of a single congressional statute passed more than a century ago.

Of course, the wholesale commission of common state-law crimes creates dangers that are far from ordinary. Even in the context of political protest, persistent, organized, premeditated lawlessness menaces in a unique way the capacity of a State to maintain order and preserve the rights of its citizens. Such actions are designed to inflame, not inform. They subvert the civility and mutual respect that are the essential preconditions for the orderly resolution of social conflict in a free society. For this reason, it is important to note that another federal statute offers the possibility of powerful federal assistance for persons who

are injured or threatened by organized lawless conduct
that falls within the primary jurisdiction of the States and
their local governments.

Should state officials deem it necessary, law enforcement
assistance is authorized upon request by the State to the
Attorney General of the United States. . . . In the event of
a law enforcement emergency as to which "State and local
resources are inadequate to protect the lives and property
of citizens or to enforce the criminal law," the Attorney
General is empowered to put the full range of federal law
enforcement resources at the disposal of the State, including the resources of the United States Marshals Service,
which was presumably the principal practical advantage to
[Alexandria Women's Health Clinic] of seeking a federal
injunction under [the Ku Klux Act].

If this scheme were to be invoked, the nature and extent
of a federal response would be a determination for the
Executive. Its authority to act is less circumscribed than
our own, but I have little doubt that such extraordinary
intervention into local controversies would be ordered
only after a careful assessment of the circumstances, including the need to preserve our essential liberties and
traditions. Indeed, the statute itself explicitly directs the
Attorney General to consider "the need to avoid unnecessary Federal involvement and intervention in matters primarily of State and local concern."

I do not suggest that this statute is the only remedy available. It does illustrate, however, that Congress has provided a federal mechanism for ensuring that adequate law
enforcement resources are available to protect federally
guaranteed rights and that Congress, too, attaches great

significance to the federal decision to intervene. Thus, even if, after proceedings on remand [return to the lower court], the ultimate result is dismissal of the action, local authorities retain the right and the ability to request federal assistance, should they deem it warranted.

JUSTICE SOUTER, concurring in the judgment in part and dissenting in part: This case turns on the meaning of two clauses of [the Ku Klux Act] which render certain conspiracies civilly actionable. The first clause (the deprivation clause) covers conspiracies "for the purpose of depriving, either directly or indirectly, any person or class of persons of the equal protection of the laws, or of equal privileges and immunities under the laws"; the second (the prevention clause), conspiracies "for the purpose of preventing or hindering the constituted authorities of any State or Territory from giving or securing to all persons within such State or Territory the equal protection of the laws. . . ."

For liability in either instance the statute requires an "act in furtherance of the . . . conspiracy, whereby [a person] is injured in his person or property, or deprived of . . . any right or privilege of a citizen of the United States. . . ."

Prior cases giving the words "equal protection of the laws" in the deprivation clause an authoritative construction have limited liability under that clause by imposing two conditions not found in the terms of the text. An actionable conspiracy must have some racial or perhaps other class-based motivation, and, if it is "aimed at" the deprivation of a constitutional right, the right must be one secured not only against official infringement, but against private action as well. The Court follows these cases in applying the deprivation clause today, and to this extent I take no exception to its conclusion. I know of no reason that would exempt us from the counsel of *stare decisis* [leaving past decisions undisturbed] in adhering to this settled statutory construction, which Congress is free to change if it should think our prior reading unsound.

The meaning of the prevention clause is not thus settled. . . .

Because this Court has not previously faced a prevention clause claim, the difficult question that arises on this first occasion is whether to import the two conditions imposed on the deprivation clause as limitations on the scope of the prevention clause as well. If we do not, we will be construing the phrase "equal protection of the laws" differently in neighboring provisions of the same statute, and our interpretation will seemingly be at odds with the "natural presumption that identical words used in different parts of the same act were intended to have the same meaning." But the presumption is defeasible [subject to defeat], and in this instance giving the common phrase an independent reading is exactly what ought to be done.

This is so because the two conditions at issue almost certainly run counter to the intention of Congress, and whatever may have been the strength of this Court's reasons for construing the deprivation clause to include them, those reasons have no application to the prevention clause now before us. To extend the conditions to shorten the prevention clause's reach would, moreover, render that clause inoperative against a conspiracy to which its terms in their plain meaning clearly should apply, a conspiracy whose perpetrators plan to overwhelm available law enforcement officers, to the point of preventing them from providing a class of victims attempting to exercise a liberty guaranteed them by the Constitution with the police protection otherwise extended to all persons going about their lawful business on streets and private premises. Lest we embrace such an unintended and untoward result, we are obliged to reject any limiting constructions that *stare decisis* does not require.

The amalgam of concepts reflected in [the Ku Klux Act] witness the statute's evolution . . . from a bill that would have criminalized conspiracies "to do any act in violation of the rights, privileges, or immunities of any person. . . ," to a statute including a civil cause of action against conspirators and those who "go in disguise" to violate certain constitutional guarantees. The amendment of the original bill that concerns us occurred in the House, to calm fears that the statute's breadth would extend it to cover a vast field of traditional state jurisdiction, exceeding what some Members of Congress took to be the scope of congressional power under the Fourteenth Amendment. The principal curb placed on the statute's scope was the requirement that actionable conspiracies (not otherwise proscribed on the strength of their threats to voting rights) be motivated by a purpose to deny equal protection of the laws. The sponsor of the amendment, Representative Shellabarger, put it this way: "The object of the amendment is . . . to confine the authority of this law to the prevention of deprivations which shall attack the equality of rights of American citizens. . . ."

The effect of the equal protection requirement in thus limiting the deprivation clause has received the Court's careful attention, first in *Collins v. Hardyman*, then in a

series of more recent cases. For present purposes, *Griffin*
and *Carpenters* stand out.

. . . . I conclude that a conspiracy falls within the terms of
the prevention clause when its purpose is to hinder or prevent law enforcement authorities from giving normal police protection to women attempting to exercise the right
to abortion recognized in *Casey v. Planned Parenthood of
Southeastern Pennsylvania* and *Roe v. Wade.* My reason
for this is not a view that a State's frustration of an individual's choice to obtain an abortion would, without more,
violate equal protection, but that a classification necessarily lacks any positive relationship to a legitimate state purpose, and consequently fails rational basis scrutiny, when
it withdraws a general public benefit on account of the
exercise of a right otherwise guaranteed by the Constitution. While such a discrimination, were it wrought by the
State, could be treated as a burden on the exercise of a
right protected by a substantive due process guarantee,
and forbidden as such, the denial of generally available
civic benefits to one group solely because its members
seek what the Constitution guarantees would just as clearly be a classification for a forbidden purpose, which is to
say, independently a violation of equal protection. When
private individuals conspire for the purpose of arrogating
[seizing] and, in effect, exercising the State's power in a
way that would thus violate equal protection if so exercised by state officials, the conspiracy becomes actionable
when implemented by an act "whereby [a person] is injured in his person or property, or deprived of . . . any
right or privilege of a citizen of the United States."

. . . . The District Court found that [Operation Rescue]
conspired to cause [Alexandria Women's Health Clinic] to

cease operations by trespassing on their property and physically blocking entry into and exit from the [clinic], rendering existing and prospective patients, as well as physicians and medical staff, unable to enter the clinic to render or receive medical counseling or advice. The District Court found that [Operation Rescue]'s actions were characteristically undertaken without notice and typically overwhelmed local police officials invested with the law enforcement component of the State's police power, rendering them unable for a substantial period to give or secure the police protection otherwise extended to all persons going about their lawful business on the streets and on private premises. The victims were chosen because they would be making choices falling within the scope of recognized substantive due process protection, choices that may not be made the basis for discriminatory state classifications applied to deny state services routinely made available to all persons. The District Court found that the effects of thus replacing constituted authority with a lawless regime would create a substantial risk of physical harm, and of damage to [Alexandria Women's Health Clinic]'s property, a conclusion amply supported by the record evidence of personal assaults and tortious restrictions on lawful movement, as well as damage to property, at [Operation Rescue]'s previous demonstrations.

These facts would support a conclusion that [Operation Rescue]'s conspiracy had a "purpose of preventing or hindering the constituted authorities of [Virginia] from giving or securing to all persons within [Virginia] the equal protection of the laws," and it might be fair to read such a finding between the lines of the District Court's express conclusions. But the finding was not express, and the better course is to err on the side of seeking express clarifica-

tion. Certainly that is true here, when other Members of
the Court think it appropriate to remand [send back to
the lower court] for further proceedings. I conclude
therefore that the decision of the Court of Appeals should
be [annulled] and the case be [returned] for consideration
of purpose, and for a final determination whether implementation of this conspiracy was actionable under the
prevention clause of [the Ku Klux Act].

JUSTICE STEVENS (joined by Justice Blackmun), dissenting: After the Civil War, Congress enacted legislation
imposing on the Federal Judiciary the responsibility to
remedy both abuses of power by persons acting under col-
or of state law and lawless conduct that state courts are
neither fully competent, nor always certain, to prevent.
The Ku Klux Act of 1871 was a response to the massive,
organized lawlessness that infected our Southern States
during the post-Civil War era. When a question concerning this statute's coverage arises, it is appropriate to consider whether the controversy has a purely local character
or the kind of federal dimension that gave rise to the legislation.

Based on detailed, undisputed findings of fact, the District
Court concluded that the . . . Ku Klux Act . . . provides a
federal remedy for [Operation Rescue]'s violent concerted
activities on the public streets and private property of
law-abiding citizens. The Court of Appeals affirmed
[agreed with the lower court]. The holdings of the courts
below are supported by the text and the legislative history
of the statute and are fully consistent with this Court's
precedents. Admittedly, important questions concerning
the meaning of [the Ku Klux Act] have been left open in
our prior cases, including whether the statute covers

gender-based discrimination and whether it provides a remedy for the kind of interference with a woman's right to travel to another State to obtain an abortion revealed by this record. Like the overwhelming majority of federal judges who have spoken to the issue, I am persuaded that traditional principles of statutory construction readily provide affirmative answers to these questions.

It is unfortunate that the Court has analyzed this case as though it presented an abstract question of logical deduction rather than a question concerning the exercise and allocation of power in our federal system of government. The Court ignores the obvious (and entirely constitutional) congressional intent behind [the Ku Klux Act] to protect this Nation's citizens from what amounts to the theft of their constitutional rights by organized and violent mobs across the country.

The importance of the issue warrants a full statement of the facts found by the District Court before reaching the decisive questions in this case.

[Operation Rescue is] dedicated to a cause that they profoundly believe is far more important than mere obedience to the laws of the Commonwealth of Virginia or the police power of its cities. To achieve their goals, the individual petitioners "have agreed and combined with one another and with defendant Operation Rescue to organize, coordinate and participate in 'rescue' demonstrations at abortion clinics in various parts of the country, including the Washington Metropolitan area. The purpose of these 'rescue' demonstrations is to disrupt operations at the target clinic and indeed ultimately to cause the clinic to cease operations entirely.

The scope of [Operation Rescue]'s conspiracy is nation-wide; it far exceeds the bounds or jurisdiction of any one State. They have blockaded clinics across the country, and their activities have been enjoined [stopped] in New York, Pennsylvania, Washington, Connecticut, California, Kansas, and Nevada, as well as the District of Columbia metropolitan area. They have carried out their "rescue" operations in the District of Columbia and Maryland in defiance of federal injunctions [court orders to stop an activity].

Pursuant to their overall conspiracy, [Operation Rescue] ha[s] repeatedly engaged in "rescue" operations that violate local law and harm innocent women. [Operation Rescue] trespass[es] on clinic property and physically block[s] access to the clinic, preventing patients, as well as physicians and medical staff, from entering the clinic to render or receive medical or counseling services. . . .

To summarize briefly, the evidence establishes that [Operation Rescue] engaged in a nationwide conspiracy; to achieve their goal they repeatedly occupied public streets and trespassed on the premises of private citizens in order to prevent or hinder the constituted authorities from protecting access to abortion clinics by women, a substantial number of whom traveled in interstate commerce to reach the destinations blockaded by [Operation Rescue]. The case involves no ordinary trespass, nor anything remotely resembling the peaceful picketing of a local retailer. It presents a striking contemporary example of the kind of zealous, politically motivated, lawless conduct that led to the enactment of the Ku Klux Act in 1871 and gave it its name.

The text of the statute makes plain the reasons Congress considered a federal remedy for such conspiracies both necessary and appropriate. . . .

[Operation Rescue]'s conspiracy had both the purpose and effect of interfering with interstate travel. The number of patients who cross state lines to obtain an abortion obviously depends, to some extent, on the location of the clinic and the quality of its services. In the Washington Metropolitan area, where interstate travel is routine, 20 to 30 percent of the patients at some clinics were from out of State, while at least one clinic obtained over half its patients from other States. The District Court's conclusions in this regard bear repetition:

> "[Operation Rescue] engaged in this conspiracy for the purpose, either directly or indirectly, of depriving women seeking abortions and related medical and counselling services, of the right to travel. The right to travel includes the right to unobstructed interstate travel to obtain an abortion and other medical services. . . . Testimony at trial establishes that clinics in Northern Virginia provide medical services to . . . patients who travel from out of state. [Operation Rescue]'s activities interfere with these persons' right to unimpeded interstate travel by blocking their access to abortion clinics. . . .

The plain language of the statute is surely broad enough to cover [Operation Rescue]'s conspiracy. Their concerted activities took place on both the public "highway" and the private "premises of another." The women targeted by their blockade fit comfortably within the statutory category described as "any person or class of persons."

[Operation Rescue]'s interference with police protection of women seeking access to abortion clinics "directly or indirectly" deprived them of equal protection of the laws and of their privilege of engaging in lawful travel. Moreover, a literal reading of the second clause of the statute describes [Operation Rescue]'s proven "purpose of preventing or hindering the constituted authorities of any State or Territory" from securing "to all persons within such State or Territory the equal protection of the laws."

. . . . The terms "animus" and "invidious" are susceptible to different interpretations. The Court today announces that it could find class-based animus in [Operation Rescue]'s mob violence "only if one of two suggested propositions is true: (1) that opposition to abortion can reasonably be presumed to reflect a sex-based intent, or (2) that intent is irrelevant, and a class-based animus can be determined solely by effect."

The first proposition appears to describe a malevolent form of hatred or ill-will. When such an animus defends itself as opposition to conduct that given class engages in exclusively or predominantly, we can readily unmask it as the intent to discriminate against the class itself. . . .

The second proposition deserves more than the Court's disdain. It plausibly describes an assumption that intent lies behind the discriminatory effects from which Congress intended [the Ku Klux Act] to protect American citizens. Congress may obviously offer statutory protections against behavior that the Constitution does not forbid, including forms of discrimination that undermine [the Ku Klux Act]'s guarantee of equal treatment under the law. . . .

Both forms of class-based animus that the Court proposes are present in this case.

. . . . [The] right [of women seeking abortions] to engage in interstate travel is inseparable from the right they seek to exercise. That right, unduly burdened and frustrated by [Operation Rescue]'s conspiracy, is protected by the Federal Constitution, as we recently reaffirmed in *Planned Parenthood of Southeastern Pennsylvania v. Casey*. Almost two decades ago, the Court squarely held that the right to enter another State for the purpose of seeking abortion services available there is protected by the Privileges and Immunities Clause [of the Constitution]. A woman's right to engage in interstate travel for this purpose is either entitled to special respect because she is exercising a constitutional right, or because restrictive rules in her home State may make travel to another State imperative. Federal courts are uniquely situated to protect that right for the same reason they are well suited to protect the privileges and immunities of those who enter other States to ply their trade.

. . . . Interference with a woman's ability to visit another State to obtain an abortion is essential to [Operation Rescue]'s achievement of their ultimate goal - the complete elimination of abortion services throughout the United States. No lesser purpose can explain their multi-state "rescue" operations.

Even in a single locality, the effect of [Operation Rescue]'s blockade on interstate travel is substantial. Between 20 and 30 percent of the patients at a targeted clinic in Virginia were from out of State and over half of the patients at one of the Maryland clinics were interstate travelers. Making their destination inaccessible to women who have engaged in interstate travel for a single purpose is unquestionably a burden on that travel. That burden was not only a foreseeable and natural consequence of the blockades, but indeed was also one of the intended consequences of [Operation Rescue]'s conspiracy.

. . . . The Court has long recognized that a burden on interstate commerce may be invalid even if the same burden is imposed on local commerce. The fact that an impermissible burden is most readily identified when it discriminates against nonresidents does not justify immunizing conduct that even-handedly disrupts both local and interstate travel. . . .

Discrimination is a necessary element of the class-based animus requirement, not of the abridgement of a woman's right to engage in interstate travel. Perhaps nowhere else in its opinion does the Court reject such obvious assumptions of the authors of [the Ku Klux Act]. The Reconstruction Congress would have been startled, I think, to learn that [the Ku Klux Act] protected freed slaves and their supporters from Klan violence not covered by the Thirteenth Amendment only if the Klan members spared *local* African-Americans and abolitionists their wrath. And it would have been shocked to learn that its law offered relief from a Klan lynching of an out-of-state abolitionist only if the plaintiff could show that the Klan specifically intended to prevent his travel between the States. Yet these are the impossible requirements the Court imposes on a [Ku Klux Act] plaintiff who has shown that her right to travel has been deliberately and significantly infringed. It is difficult to know whether the Court is waiting until only a few States have abortion clinics before it finds that [Operation Rescue]'s behavior violates the right to travel, or if it believes that [Operation Rescue] could never violate that right as long as they oppose the abortion a woman seeks to obtain as well as the travel necessary to obtain it.

. . . . A conspiracy that seeks to interfere with law enforcement officers' performance of their duties entails sufficient involvement with the State to implicate the federally protected right to choose an abortion and to give rise to a cause of action under [the Ku Klux Act].

. . . . The Court concludes its analysis of [the Ku Klux Act] by suggesting that a contrary interpretation would have condemned the massive "sit-ins" that were conducted to promote desegregation in the 1960's - a "wildly improbable result." This suggestion is profoundly misguided. . . . [T]he demonstrations in the 1960's were motivated by a desire to extend the equal protection of the laws to all classes - not to impose burdens on any disadvantaged class. Those who engaged in the nonviolent "sit-ins" to which the Court refers were challenging "a political and economic system that had denied them the basic rights of dignity and equality that this country had fought a Civil War to secure." The suggestion that there is an analogy between their struggle to achieve equality and [Operation Rescue]'s concerted efforts to deny women equal access to a constitutionally protected privilege may have rhetorical appeal, but it is insupportable on the record before us, and does not justify the majority's parsimonious construction of an important federal statute.

I respectfully dissent.

JUSTICE O'CONNOR (joined by Justice Blackmun), dissenting: [Operation Rescue] act[s] in organized groups to overwhelm local police forces and physically blockade the entrances to . . . clinics with the purpose of preventing women from exercising their legal rights. [The Ku Klux Act] provides a federal remedy against private conspiracies aimed at depriving any person or class of persons of the "equal protection of the laws," or of "equal privileges and immunities under the laws." In my view, [Alexandria Women's Health Clinic]'s injuries and [Operation Rescue]'s activities fall squarely within the ambit of this statute.

The Reconstruction Congress enacted the Civil Rights Act of 1871, also known as the Ku Klux Act, to combat the chaos that paralyzed the post-War South. Section 2 of the Act extended the protection of federal courts to those who effectively were prevented from exercising their civil rights by the threat of mob violence. Although the immediate purpose of [the Ku Klux Act] was to combat animosity against blacks and their supporters, the language of the Act, like that of many Reconstruction statutes, is more expansive than the historical circumstances that inspired it. . . .

The Court's approach to Reconstruction Era civil rights statutes has been to "accord [them] a sweep as broad as [their] language." Today, the Court does just the opposite, precluding application of the statute to a situation that its language clearly covers. There is no dispute that [Operation Rescue] ha[s] "conspired" through their concerted and unlawful activities. The record shows that [Operation Rescue]'s "purpose" is "directly" to "depriv[e]" women of their ability to obtain the clinics' services, as well as "indirectly" to infringe on their constitutional privilege to travel interstate in seeking those services. The record also shows that [Operation Rescue] accomplish[es] their goals by purposefully "preventing or hindering" local law enforcement authorities from maintaining open access to the clinics. In sum, [Operation Rescue]'s activities fit precisely within the language of both clauses of [the Ku Klux Act].

Yet the Court holds otherwise, and it does so primarily on the basis of an "element" of the [Ku Klux Act] cause of action that does not appear on the face of the statute. Adhering adamantly to our choice of words in [*Griffin*], the Court holds that [Operation Rescue] did not exhibit a "class-based, invidiously discriminatory animus" against the clinics or the women they serve. I would not parse *Griffin* so finely as to focus on that phrase to the exclusion of our reasons for adopting it as an element of a [Ku Klux Act] civil action.

As the Court explained in *Griffin*, [the Ku Klux Act]'s "class-based animus" requirement is derived from the statute's legislative history. That case recounted that Section 2 of the original Civil Rights bill had proposed criminal punishment for private individuals who conspired with intent "'to do any act in violation of the rights, privileges, or immunities of another person.'" The bill was amended to placate those who believed the proposed language was too sweeping. Accordingly, the amendment narrowed the criminal provision to reach only conspiracies that deprived "any person or class of persons of the *equal* protection of the laws, or of *equal* privileges and immunities under the laws. . . ." The amendment also added a civil remedy for those harmed by such conspiracies. . . . Look-

ing to the "congressional purpose" the statute's legislative
history exhibited, the Court concluded that "there must be
some racial, or perhaps otherwise class-based, invidiously
discriminatory animus behind the conspirators' action.
The conspiracy, in other words, must aim at a deprivation
of the equal enjoyment of rights secured by the law to
all."

. . . . If women are a protected class under [the Ku Klux
Act], and I think they are, then the statute must reach
conspiracies whose motivation is directly related to characteristics unique to that class. The victims of [Operation
Rescue]'s tortious actions are linked by their ability to become pregnant and by their ability to terminate their
pregnancies, characteristics unique to the class of women.
[Operation Rescue]'s activities are directly related to those
class characteristics and therefore, I believe, are appropriately described as class based within the meaning of our
holding in *Griffin*.

[Operation Rescue] assert[s] that, even if their activities
are class based, they are not motivated by any *discriminatory* animus but only by their profound opposition to the
practice of abortion. I do not doubt the sincerity of that
opposition.   But in assessing the motivation behind
[Operation Rescue]'s actions, the sincerity of their opposition cannot surmount the manner in which they have chosen to express it.   [Operation Rescue is] free to express
their views in a variety of ways, including lobbying, counseling, and disseminating information. Instead, they have
chosen to target women seeking abortions and to prevent
them from exercising their equal rights under law. Even
without relying on the federally protected right to abortion, [Operation Rescue]'s activities infringe on a number

of state-protected interests, including the state laws that make abortion legal, and the state laws that protect against force, intimidation, and violence. It is undeniably [Operation Rescue]'s purpose to target a protected class, on account of their class characteristics, and to prevent them from the equal enjoyment of these personal and property rights under law. . . .

I cannot agree with the Court that the use of unlawful means to achieve one's goal "is not relevant to [the] discussion of animus." To the contrary, the deliberate decision to isolate members of a vulnerable group and physically prevent them from conducting legitimate activities cannot be irrelevant in assessing motivation. The clinics at issue are lawful operations; the women who seek their services do so lawfully. In my opinion, [Operation Rescue]'s unlawful conspiracy to prevent the clinics from serving those women, who are targeted by [Operation Rescue] by virtue of their class characteristics, is a group-based, private deprivation of the "equal protection of the laws" within the reach of [the Ku Klux Act].

The Court finds an absence of discriminatory animus by reference to our decisions construing the scope of the Equal Protection Clause, and reinforces its conclusion by recourse to the dictionary definition of the word "invidious." The first step would be fitting if [Alexandria Women's Health Clinic] were challenging state action; they do not. The second would be proper if the word "invidious" appeared in the statute we are construing; it does not. As noted above, *Griffin*'s requirement of "class-based, invidiously discriminatory animus" was a shorthand description of the congressional purpose behind the legislation that became [the Ku Klux Act]. Microscopic examination of the language we chose in *Griffin* should not now substitute for giving effect to Congress' intent in enacting the relevant legislative language, *i.e.*, "that any violation of the right, the *animus* and the effect of which is to strike down the citizen, to the end that he [or she] may not enjoy equality of rights as contrasted with . . . other citizens' rights, shall be within the scope of the remedies of this section."

Because [the Ku Klux Act] is a statute that was designed to address deprivations caused by *private* actors, the Court's invocation of our cases construing the reach of the Equal Protection Clause of the Fourteenth Amendment is misplaced. . . .

In today's case, I see no reason to hold a [Ku Klux Act] plaintiff to the constitutional standard of invidious discrimination that we have employed in our Fourteenth Amendment jurisprudence. . . .

I would focus not on the similarities of the two provisions, but on their differences. The Equal Protection Clause guarantees that no State shall "*deny* to any person within its jurisdiction the equal protection of the laws." In my view, [the Ku Klux Act] does not simply repeat that guarantee, but provides a complement to it: no private actor may conspire with the purpose of "*depriving* . . . any person or class of persons of the equal protection of the laws." Unlike "deny," which connotes a withholding the word "deprive" indicates an intent to prevent private actors from taking away what the State has seen fit to bestow.

The distinction in choice of words is significant in light of the interrelated objectives of the two provisions. The Fourteenth Amendment protects against state action, but it "erects no shield against merely private conduct, however discriminatory or wrongful." [The Ku Klux Act], by contrast, was "meant to reach private action." Given that difference in focus, I would not interpret "discriminatory animus" under the statute to establish the same high threshold that must be met before this Court will find that a State has engaged in invidious discrimination in violation of the Constitution. As the 42d Congress well appreciated, private actors acting in groups can be as devastating to the exercise of civil rights as hostile state actors, and they pose an even greater danger because they operate in an unregulated realm divorced from the responsibilities and checking functions of government. In recognition of that danger, I would hold that *Griffin*'s element of class-based discrimination is met whenever private conspirators target their actions at members of a protected class, by virtue of their class characteristics, and deprive them of their equal enjoyment of the rights accorded them under law.

This case is not about abortion. It most assuredly is not about "the disfavoring of abortions" by state legislatures. Rather, this case is about whether a private conspiracy to deprive members of a protected class of legally protected interests gives rise to a federal cause of action. In my view, it does. . . .

The second reason the majority offers for reversing the decision [of the court] below is that [Operation Rescue]'s activities did not intentionally deprive the clinics and their clients of a right guaranteed against private impair-

ment, a requirement that the Court previously has grafted
onto the *first* clause of [the Ku Klux Act]. I find it unnecessary to address the merits of this argument, however,
as I am content to rest my analysis solely on the basis that
[Alexandria Women's Health Clinic is] entitled to invoke
the protections of a federal court under the *second* clause
of [the Ku Klux Act]. . . [, which] address[es] conspiracies
aimed at "preventing or hindering the constituted authorities of any State or Territory from giving or securing to
all persons within such State or Territory the equal protection of the laws."

. . . . We have not previously had occasion to consider the
scope of the statute's "prevention or hindrance" provision,
but it is clear that the second clause does not require that
actionable conspiracies be "aimed at interfering with
rights" that are "protected against private, as well as official, encroachment. Rather, it covers conspiracies aimed
at obstructing local law enforcement. . . . I am satisfied
by my review of the record that the District Court made
findings that adequately support a conclusion that
[Operation Rescue]'s activities are class based and intentionally designed to impede local law enforcement from
securing "the equal protection of the laws" to the clinics
and the women they serve.

. . . . [The Ku Klux Act] . . . was intended to provide a
federal means of redress to the targets of private conspiracies seeking to accomplish their political and social goals
through unlawful means. Today the Court takes yet
another step in restricting the scope of the statute, to the
point where it now cannot be applied to a modern-day
paradigm of the situation the statute was meant to address. I respectfully dissent.

THE U.S. CONSTITUTION

THE U.S. CONSTITUTION

PREAMBLE

*We the people of the United States, in order to form a
more perfect union, establish justice, insure domestic tran-
quility, provide for the common defense, promote the general welfare, and secure the blessings of liberty to ourselves and our posterity, do ordain and establish this Constitution for the United States of America.*

ARTICLE I

Section 1. All legislative powers herein granted shall be
vested in a Congress of the United States, which shall consist of a Senate and House of Representatives.

Section 2. (1) The House of Representatives shall be composed of members chosen every second year by the people
of the several states, and the electors in each state shall
have the qualifications requisite for electors of the most
numerous branch of the State Legislature.

(2) No person shall be a Representative who shall not
have attained to the age of twenty-five years, and been
seven years a citizen of the United States, and who shall
not, when elected, be an inhabitant of that state in which
he shall be chosen.

(3) Representatives and direct taxes shall be apportioned
among the several states which may be included within
this union, according to their respective numbers, which
shall be determined by adding to the whole number of
free persons, including those bound to service for a term
of years, and excluding Indians not taxed, three-fifths of
all other persons. The actual enumeration shall be made

within three years after the first meeting of the Congress of the United States, and within every subsequent term of ten years, in such manner as they shall by law direct. The number of Representatives shall not exceed one for every thirty thousand, but each state shall have at least one Representative; and until such enumeration shall be made, the State of New Hampshire shall be entitled to choose three, Massachusetts eight, Rhode Island and Providence Plantations one, Connecticut five, New York six, New Jersey four, Pennsylvania eight, Delaware one, Maryland six, Virginia ten, North Carolina five, South Carolina five, and Georgia three.

(4) When vacancies happen in the representation from any state, the executive authority thereof shall issue writs of election to fill such vacancies.

(5) The House of Representatives shall choose their Speaker and other Officers; and shall have the sole power of impeachment.

Section 3. (1) The Senate of the United States shall be composed of two Senators from each state, chosen by the legislature thereof, for six years; and each Senator shall have one vote.

(2) Immediately after they shall be assembled in consequence of the first election, they shall be divided as equally as may be into three classes. The seats of the Senators of the first class shall be vacated at the expiration of the second year, of the second class at the expiration of the fourth year, and of the third class at the expiration of the sixth year, so that one-third may be chosen every second year; and if vacancies happen by resignation, or otherwise, during the recess of the legislature of any state, the execu-

tive thereof may make temporary appointments until the next meeting of the legislature, which shall then fill such vacancies.

(3) No person shall be a Senator who shall not have attained to the age of thirty years, and been nine years a citizen of the United States, and who shall not, when elected, be an inhabitant of that state for which he shall be chosen.

(4) The Vice President of the United States shall be President of the Senate, but shall have no vote, unless they be equally divided.

(5) The Senate shall choose their other Officers, and also a President pro tempore, in the absence of the Vice President, or when he shall exercise the Office of President of the United States.

(6) The Senate shall have the sole power to try all impeachments. When sitting for that purpose, they shall be on oath or affirmation. When the President of the United States is tried, the Chief Justice shall preside: and no person shall be convicted without the concurrence of two-thirds of the members present.

(7) Judgment in cases of impeachment shall not extend further than to removal from office, and disqualification to hold and enjoy any office of honor, trust, or profit under the United States: but the party convicted shall nevertheless be liable and subject to indictment, trial, judgment, and punishment, according to law.

Section 4. (1) The times, places and manner of holding elections for Senators and Representatives, shall be prescribed in each state by the legislature thereof; but the Congress may at any time by law make or alter such regulations, except as to the places of choosing Senators.

(2) The Congress shall assemble at least once in every year, and such meeting shall be on the first Monday in December, unless they shall by law appoint a different day.

Section 5. (1) Each House shall be the judge of the elections, returns, and qualifications of its own members, and a majority of each shall constitute a quorum to do business; but a smaller number may adjourn from day to day, and may be authorized to compel the attendance of absent members, in such manner, and under such penalties as each House may provide.

(2) Each House may determine the rules of its proceedings, punish its members for disorderly behavior, and, with the concurrence of two-thirds, expel a member.

(3) Each House shall keep a journal of its proceedings, and from time to time publish the same, excepting such parts as may in their judgment require secrecy; and the yeas and nays of the members of either House on any question shall, at the desire of one-fifth of those present, be entered on the journal.

(4) Neither House, during the Session of Congress, shall, without the consent of the other, adjourn for more than three days, nor to any other place than that in which the two Houses shall be sitting.

Section 6. (1) The Senators and Representatives shall receive a compensation for their services, to be ascertained by law, and paid out of the Treasury of the United States. They shall in all cases, except treason, felony and breach of the peace, be privileged from arrest during their attendance at the session of their respective Houses, and in going to and returning from the same; and for any speech or debate in either House, they shall not be questioned in any other place.

(2) No Senator or Representative shall, during the time for which he was elected, be appointed to any civil office under the authority of the United States, which shall have been created, or the emoluments whereof shall have been increased during such time and no person holding any office under the United States, shall be a member of either House during his continuance in office.

Section 7. (1) All bills for raising revenue shall originate in the House of Representatives; but the Senate may propose or concur with amendments as on other bills.

(2) Every bill which shall have passed the House of Representatives and the Senate, shall, before it become a law, be presented to the President of the United States; if he approve he shall sign it, but if not he shall return it, with his objections to the House in which it shall have originated, who shall enter the objections at large on their journal, and proceed to reconsider it. If after such reconsideration two-thirds of that House shall agree to pass the bill, it shall be sent together with the objections, to the other House, by which it shall likewise be reconsidered, and if approved by two-thirds of that House, it shall become a law. But in all such cases the votes of both Houses shall be determined by yeas and nays, and the names of the per-

sons voting for and against the bill shall be entered on the journal of each House respectively. If any bill shall not be returned by the President within ten days (Sundays excepted) after it shall have been presented to him, the same shall be a law, in like manner as if he had signed it, unless the Congress by their adjournment prevent its return in which case it shall not be a law.

(3) Every order, resolution, or vote, to which the concurrence of the Senate and House of Representatives may be necessary (except on a question of adjournment) shall be presented to the President of the United States; and before the same shall take effect, shall be approved by him, or being disapproved by him, shall be repassed by two-thirds of the Senate and House of Representatives, according to the rules and limitations prescribed in the case of a bill.

Section 8. (1) The Congress shall have the power to lay and collect taxes, duties, imposts and excises, to pay the debts and provide for the common defense and general welfare of the United States; but all duties, imposts and excises shall be uniform throughout the United States;

(2) To borrow money on the credit of the United States;

(3) To regulate commerce with foreign nations, and among the several states, and with the Indian Tribes;

(4) To establish an uniform Rule of Naturalization, and uniform laws on the subject of bankruptcies throughout the United States;

(5) To coin money, regulate the value thereof, and of foreign coin, and fix the standard of weights and measures;

(6) To provide for the punishment of counterfeiting the securities and current coin of the United States;

(7) To establish Post Offices and Post Roads;

(8) To promote the progress of science and useful arts, by securing for limited times to authors and inventors the exclusive right to their respective writings and discoveries;

(9) To constitute tribunals inferior to the Supreme Court;

(10) To define and punish piracies and felonies committed on the high seas, and offenses against the Law of Nations;

(11) To declare war, grant Letters of marque and reprisal, and make rules concerning captures on land and water;

(12) To raise and support armies, but no appropriation of money to that use shall be for a longer term than two years;

(13) To provide and maintain a Navy;

(14) To make rules for the government and regulation of the land and naval forces;

(15) To provide for calling forth the Militia to execute the laws of the Union, suppress insurrections and repel invasions;

(16) To provide for organizing, arming, and disciplining, the Militia, and for governing such part of them as may be employed in the service of the United States, reserving to the states respectively, the appointment of the Officers,

and the authority of training the Militia according to the discipline prescribed by Congress;

(17) To exercise exclusive legislation in all cases whatsoever, over such district (not exceeding ten miles square) as may, by cession of particular states, and the acceptance of Congress, become the Seat of the Government of the United States, and to exercise like authority over all places purchased by the consent of the legislature of the state in which the same shall be, for the erection of forts, magazines, arsenals, dockyards, and other needful buildings; - and

(18) To make all laws which shall be necessary and proper for carrying into execution the foregoing powers, and all other powers vested by this Constitution in the Government of the United States, or in any Department or Officer thereof.

Section 9. (1) The migration or importation of such persons as any of the states now existing shall think proper to admit, shall not be prohibited by the Congress prior to the year one thousand eight hundred and eight, but a tax or duty may be imposed on such importation, not exceeding ten dollars for each person.

(2) The privilege of the writ of habeas corpus shall not be suspended, unless when in cases of rebellion or invasion the public safety may require it.

(3) No bill of attainder or ex post facto law shall be passed.

(4) No capitation, or other direct, tax shall be laid, unless in proportion to the census or enumeration herein before directed to be taken.

(5) No tax or duty shall be laid on articles exported from any state.

(6) No preference shall be given by any regulation of commerce or revenue to the ports of one state over those of another: nor shall vessels bound to, or from, one state be obliged to enter, clear, or pay duties in another.

(7) No money shall be drawn from the Treasury, but in consequence of appropriations made by law; and a regular statement and account of the receipts and expenditures of all public money shall be published from time to time.

(8) No title of nobility shall be granted by the United States: and no person holding any office of profit or trust under them, shall, without the consent of the Congress, accept of any present, emolument, office, or title, of any kind whatever, from any King, Prince, or foreign State.

Section 10. (1) No state shall enter into any treaty, alliance, or confederation; grant letters of marque and reprisal; coin money; emit bills of credit; make any thing but gold and silver coin a tender in payment of debts; pass any bill of attainder, ex post facto law, or law impairing the obligation of contracts, or grant any title of nobility.

(2) No state shall, without the consent of the Congress, lay any imposts or duties on imports or exports, except what may be absolutely necessary for executing its inspection laws: and the net produce of all duties and imposts, laid by any state on imports or exports, shall be for the use of

the Treasury of the United States; and all such laws shall be subject to the revision and control of the Congress.

(3) No state shall, without the consent of Congress, lay any duty of tonnage, keep troops, or ships of war in time of peace, enter into any agreement or compact with another state, or with a foreign power, or engage in war, unless actually invaded, or in such imminent danger as will not admit of delay.

ARTICLE II

Section 1. (1) The executive power shall be vested in a President of the United States of America. He shall hold his office during the term of four years, and, together with the Vice President, chosen for the same term, be elected, as follows:

(2) Each state shall appoint, in such manner as the legislature thereof may direct, a number of electors, equal to the whole number of Senators and Representatives to which the state may be entitled in the Congress; but no Senator or Representative, or person holding an office of trust or profit under the United States, shall be appointed an Elector.

(3) The electors shall meet in their respective states, and vote by ballot for two persons, of whom one at least shall not be an inhabitant of the same state with themselves. And they shall make a list of all the persons voted for, and of the number of votes for each; which list they shall sign and certify, and transmit sealed to the Seat of the Government of the United States, directed to the President of the Senate. The President of the Senate shall, in the presence of the Senate and House of Representatives,

open all the certificates, and the votes shall then be counted. The person having the greatest number of votes shall
be the President, if such number be a majority of the
whole number of electors appointed; and if there be more
than one who have such majority, and have an equal number of votes, then the House of Representatives shall immediately choose by ballot one of them for President; and
if no person have a majority, then from the five highest
on the list the said House shall in like manner choose the
President. But in choosing the President, the votes shall
be taken by states the representation from each state having one vote; a quorum for this purpose shall consist of a
member or members from two-thirds of the states, and a
majority of all the states shall be necessary to a choice. In
every case, after the choice of the President, the person
having the greater number of votes of the electors shall
be the Vice President. But if there should remain two or
more who have equal votes, the Senate shall choose from
them by ballot the Vice President.

(4) The Congress may determine the time of choosing the
Electors, and the day on which they shall give their votes;
which day shall be the same throughout the United States.

(5) No person except a natural born citizen, or a citizen of
the United States, at the time of the adoption of this Constitution, shall be eligible to the Office of President; neither shall any person be eligible to that Office who shall
not have attained to the age of thirty-five years, and been
fourteen years a resident within the United States.

(6) In case of the removal of the President from Office,
or of his death, resignation or inability to discharge the
powers and duties of the said Office, the same shall devolve on the Vice President, and the Congress may by law

provide for the case of removal, death, resignation or inability, both of the President and Vice President, declaring
what Officer shall then act as President, and such Officer
shall act accordingly, until the disability be removed, or a
President shall be elected.

(7) The President shall, at stated times, receive for his
services, a compensation, which shall neither be increased
nor diminished during the period for which he shall have
been elected, and he shall not receive within that period
any other emolument from the United States, or any of
them.

(8) Before he enter on the execution of his office, he shall
take the following oath or affirmation: "I do solemnly
swear (or affirm) that I will faithfully execute the Office
of President of the United States, and will to the best of
my ability, preserve, protect and defend the Constitution
of the United States."

Section 2. (1) The President shall be Commander in Chief
of the Army and Navy of the United States, and of the
militia of the several states, when called into the actual
service of the United States; he may require the opinion,
in writing, of the principal Officer in each of the Executive Departments, upon any subject relating to the duties
of their respective Offices, and he shall have power to
grant reprieves and pardons for offenses against the United States, except in cases of impeachment.

(2) He shall have power, by and with the advice and consent of the Senate to make treaties, provided two-thirds of
the Senators present concur; and he shall nominate, and
by and with the advice and consent of the Senate, shall appoint Ambassadors, other public Ministers and Consuls,

Judges of the supreme Court, and all other Officers of the United States, whose appointments are not herein otherwise provided for, and which shall be established by law; but the Congress may by law vest the appointment of such inferior Officers, as they think proper, in the President alone, in the courts of law, or in the heads of departments.

(3) The President shall have power to fill up all vacancies that may happen during the recess of the Senate, by granting commissions which shall expire at the end of their next session.

Section 3. He shall from time to time give to the Congress information of the State of the Union, and recommend to their consideration such measures as he shall judge necessary and expedient; he may, on extraordinary occasions, convene both Houses, or either of them, and in case of disagreement between them, with respect to the time of adjournment, he may adjourn them to such time as he shall think proper; he shall receive Ambassadors and other public Ministers; he shall take care that the laws be faithfully executed, and shall commission all the Officers of the United States.

Section 4. The President, Vice President and all civil Officers of the United States, shall be removed from office on impeachment for, and conviction of, treason, bribery, or other high crimes and misdemeanors.

ARTICLE III

Section 1. The judicial power of the United States, shall be vested in one supreme Court, and in such inferior courts as the Congress may from time to time ordain and establish. The Judges, both of the supreme and inferior courts, shall hold their Offices during good behaviour, and shall, at stated times, receive for their services a compensation, which shall not be diminished during their continuance in office.

Section 2. (1) The judicial power shall extend to all cases, in law and equity, arising under this Constitution, the laws of the United States, and treaties made, or which shall be made, under their authority; - to all cases affecting Ambassadors, other public Ministers and Consuls; - to all cases of admiralty and maritime jurisdiction; - to controversies to which the United States shall be a party; - to controversies between two or more states; - between a state and citizens of another state; - between citizens of different states; - between citizens of the same state claiming lands under the grants of different states, and between a state, or the citizens thereof, and foreign states, citizens or subjects.

(2) In all cases affecting Ambassadors, other public Ministers and Consuls, and those in which a state shall be a party, the supreme Court shall have original jurisdiction. In all the other cases before mentioned, the supreme Court shall have appellate jurisdiction, both as to law and fact, with such exceptions, and under such regulations as the Congress shall make.

(3) The trial of all crimes, except in cases of impeachment, shall be by jury; and such trial shall be held in the state where the said crimes shall have been committed; but when not committed within any state, the trial shall be at such place or places as the Congress may by law have directed.

Section 3. (1) Treason against the United States, shall consist only in levying war against them, or, in adhering to their enemies, giving them aid and comfort. No person shall be convicted of treason unless on the testimony of two witnesses to the same overt act, or on confession in open Court.

(2) The Congress shall have power to declare the punishment of treason, but no Attainder of Treason shall work corruption of blood, or forfeiture except during the life of the person attainted.

ARTICLE IV

Section 1. Full faith and credit shall be given in each state to the public acts, records, and judicial proceedings of every other state. And the Congress may by general laws prescribe the manner in which such acts, records and proceedings shall be proved, and the effect thereof.

Section 2. (1) The citizens of each state shall be entitled to all privileges and immunities of citizens in the several states.

(2) A person charged in any state with treason, felony, or other crime, who shall flee from justice, and be found in another state, shall on demand of the executive authority of the state from which he fled, be delivered up, to be removed to the state having jurisdiction of the crime.

(3) No person held to service or labor in one state, under the laws thereof, escaping into another, shall, in consequence of any law or regulation therein, be discharged from such service or labor, but shall be delivered up on

claim of the party to whom such service or labor may be due.

Section 3. (1) New states may be admitted by the Congress into this union; but no new state shall be formed or erected within the jurisdiction of any other state; nor any state be formed by the junction of two or more states, or parts of states, without the consent of the legislatures of the states concerned as well as of the Congress.

(2) The Congress shall have power to dispose of and make all needful rules and regulations respecting the territory or other property belonging to the United States; and nothing in this Constitution shall be so construed as to prejudice any claims of the United States, or of any particular state.

Section 4. The United States shall guarantee to every state in this union a Republican form of government, and shall protect each of them against invasion; and on application of the legislature, or of the executive (when the legislature cannot be convened) against domestic violence.

ARTICLE V

The Congress, whenever two-thirds of both Houses shall deem it necessary, shall propose amendments to this Constitution, or, on the application of the legislatures of two-thirds of the several states, shall call a convention for proposing amendments, which, in either case, shall be valid to all intents and purposes, as part of this constitution, when ratified by the legislatures of three-fourths of the several states, or by conventions in three-fourths thereof, as the one or the other mode of ratification may be proposed by the Congress; provided that no amendment which may be made prior to the year one thousand eight hundred and eight shall in any manner affect the first and fourth clauses in the Ninth Section of the first Article; and that no state, without its consent, shall be deprived of its equal suffrage in the Senate.

ARTICLE VI

(1) All debts contracted and engagements entered into, before the adoption of this Constitution shall be as valid against the United States under this Constitution, as under the Confederation.

(2) This Constitution, and the laws of the United States which shall be made in pursuance thereof; and all treaties made, or which shall be made, under the authority of the United States, shall be the supreme law of the land; and the Judges in every state shall be bound thereby, any thing in the Constitution or laws of any state to the contrary notwithstanding.

(3) The Senators and Representatives before mentioned, and the Members of the several State Legislatures, and all executive and judicial Officers, both of the United States and of the several states, shall be bound by oath or affirmation, to support this Constitution; but no religious test shall ever be required as a qualification to any office or public trust under the United States.

ARTICLE VII

The ratification of the Conventions of nine states shall be sufficient for the establishment of this Constitution between the states so ratifying the same.

AMENDMENT I (1791)

Congress shall make no law respecting an establishment of religion, or prohibiting the free exercise thereof; or abridging the freedom of speech, or of the press; or the right of the people peaceably to assemble, and to petition the Government for a redress of grievances.

AMENDMENT II (1791)

A well regulated Militia, being necessary to the security of a free state, the right of the people to keep and bear arms, shall not be infringed.

AMENDMENT III (1791)

No soldier shall, in time of peace be quartered in any house, without the consent of the owner, nor in time of war, but in a manner to be prescribed by law.

AMENDMENT IV (1791)

The right of the people to be secure in their persons, houses, papers, and effects, against unreasonable searches and seizures, shall not be violated, and no warrants shall issue, but upon probable cause, supported by oath or affirmation, and particularly describing the place to be searched, and the persons or things to be seized.

AMENDMENT V (1791)

No person shall be held to answer for a capital, or otherwise infamous crime, unless on a presentment or indictment of a Grand Jury, except in cases arising in the land or naval forces, or in the Militia, when in actual service in time of war or public danger; nor shall any person be subject for the same offense to be twice put in jeopardy of life or limb; nor shall be compelled in any criminal case to be a witness against himself, nor be deprived of life, liberty, or property, without due process of law; nor shall private property be taken for public use, without just compensation.

AMENDMENT VI (1791)

In all criminal prosecutions, the accused shall enjoy the right to a speedy and public trial, by an impartial jury of the state and district wherein the crime shall have been committed, which district shall have been previously ascertained by law, and to be informed of the nature and cause of the accusation; to be confronted with the witnesses against him; to have compulsory process for obtaining witnesses in his favor, and to have the assistance of counsel for his defense.

AMENDMENT VII (1791)

In suits at common law, where the value in controversy shall exceed twenty dollars, the right of trial by jury shall be preserved, and no fact tried by jury, shall be otherwise re-examined in any court of the United States, than according to the rules of the common law.

AMENDMENT VIII (1791)

Excessive bail shall not be required, nor excessive fines imposed, nor cruel and unusual punishments inflicted.

AMENDMENT IX (1791)

The enumeration in the Constitution, of certain rights, shall not be construed to deny or disparage others retained by the people.

AMENDMENT X (1791)

The powers not delegated to the United States by the Constitution, nor prohibited by it to the States, are reserved to the States respectively, or to the people.

AMENDMENT XI (1798)

The judicial power of the United States shall not be construed to extend to any suit in law or equity, commenced or prosecuted against one of the United States by citizens of another state, or by citizens or subjects of any foreign state.

AMENDMENT XII (1804)

The Electors shall meet in their respective states and vote by ballot for President and Vice-President, one of whom, at least, shall not be an inhabitant of the same state with themselves; they shall name in their ballots the person voted for as President, and in distinct ballots the person voted for as Vice-President, and they shall make distinct lists of all persons voted for as President, and of all persons voted for as Vice-President, and of the number of votes for each, which lists they shall sign and certify, and transmit sealed to the seat of the government of the United States, directed to the President of the Senate; - the President of the Senate shall, in the presence of the Senate and House of Representatives, open all the certificates and the votes shall then be counted; - the person having the greatest number of votes for President, shall be the President, if such number be a majority of the whole number of electors appointed; and if no person have such majority, then from the persons having the highest numbers not exceeding three on the list of those voted for as President, the House of Representatives shall choose immediately, by ballot, the President. But in choosing the President, the votes shall be taken by states, the representation from each state having one vote; a quorum for this purpose shall consist of a member or members from two-thirds of the states, and a majority of all the states shall be necessary to a choice. And if the House of Representatives shall not choose a President whenever the right of choice shall devolve upon them before the fourth day of March next following, then the Vice-President shall act as President, as in the case of the death or other constitutional disability of the President. - The person having the greatest number of votes as Vice-President, shall be the Vice-President, if such number be a majority of the whole number of Electors appointed, and if no person have a majority, then from the two highest numbers on the list, the Senate shall choose the Vice-President; a quorum for the purpose shall consist of two-thirds of the whole number of Senators, and a majority of the whole number shall be necessary to a choice. But no person constitutionally ineligible to the office of President shall be eligible to that of Vice-President of the United States.

AMENDMENT XIII (1865)

Section 1. Neither slavery nor involuntary servitude, except as a punishment for crime whereof the party shall have been duly convicted, shall exist within the United States, or any place subject to their jurisdiction.

Section 2. Congress shall have power to enforce this article by appropriate legislation.

AMENDMENT XIV (1868)

Section 1. All persons born or naturalized in the United States, and subject to the jurisdiction thereof, are citizens of the United States and of the state wherein they reside. No state shall make or enforce any law which shall abridge the privileges or immunities of citizens of the United States; nor shall any state deprive any person of life, liberty, or property, without due process of law; nor deny to any person within its jurisdiction the equal protection of the laws.

Section 2. Representatives shall be apportioned among the several states according to their respective numbers, counting the whole number of persons in each State excluding Indians not taxed. But when the right to vote at any election for the choice of electors for President and Vice President of the United States, Representatives in Congress, the Executive and Judicial officers of a state, or the members of the Legislature thereof, is denied to any of the male inhabitants of such state, being twenty-one years of age, and citizens of the United States, or in any way abridged, except for participation in rebellion, or other crime, the basis of representation therein shall be reduced in the proportion which the number of such male citizens shall bear to the whole number of male citizens twenty-one years of age in such state.

Section 3. No person shall be a Senator or Representative in Congress, or elector of President and Vice President, or hold any office, civil or military, under the United States, or under any state, who having previously taken an oath, as a member of Congress, or as an officer of the United States, or as a member of any state legislature, or as an executive or judicial officer of any state, to support the Constitution of the United States, shall have engaged in insurrection or rebellion against the same, or given aid or comfort to the enemies thereof. But Congress may by a vote of two-thirds of each House, remove such disability.

Section 4. The validity of the public debt of the United States, authorized by law, including debts incurred for payment of pensions and bounties for services in suppressing insurrection or rebellion, shall not be questioned. But neither the United States nor any state shall assume or pay any debt or obligation incurred in aid of insurrection or rebellion against the United States, or any claim for the loss or emancipation of any slave; but all such debts, obligations and claims shall be held illegal and void.

Section 5. The Congress shall have power to enforce, by appropriate legislation, the provisions of this article.

AMENDMENT XV (1870)

Section 1. The right of citizens of the United States to vote shall not be denied or abridged by the United States or by any state on account of race, color, or previous condition of servitude.

Section 2. The Congress shall have power to enforce this article by appropriate legislation.

AMENDMENT XVI (1913)

The Congress shall have power to lay and collect taxes on incomes, from whatever source derived, without apportionment among the several states, and without regard to any census or enumeration.

AMENDMENT XVII (1913)

(1) The Senate of the United States shall be composed of two Senators from each state, elected by the people thereof, for six years; and each Senator shall have one vote. The electors in each State shall have the qualifications requisite for electors of the most numerous branch of the state legislatures.

(2) When vacancies happen in the representation of any state in the Senate, the executive authority of such state shall issue writs of election to fill such vacancies: *provided*, that the legislature of any state may empower the executive thereof to make temporary appointments until the people fill the vacancies by election as the legislature may direct.

(3) This amendment shall not be so construed as to affect the election or term of any Senator chosen before it becomes valid as part of the Constitution.

AMENDMENT XVIII (1919)

Section 1. After one year from the ratification of this article the manufacture, sale, or transportation of intoxicating liquors within, the importation thereof into, or the exportation thereof from the United States and all territory subject to the jurisdiction thereof for beverage purposes is hereby prohibited.

Section 2. The Congress and the several states shall have concurrent power to enforce this article by appropriate legislation.

Section 3. This article shall be inoperative unless it shall have been ratified as an amendment to the Constitution by the legislatures of the several states, as provided in the Constitution, within seven years from the date of the sub mission hereof to the states by the Congress.

AMENDMENT XIX (1920)

(1) The right of citizens of the United States to vote shall not be denied or abridged by the United States or by any state on account of sex.

(2) Congress shall have power to enforce this article by appropriate legislation.

AMENDMENT XX (1933)

Section 1. The terms of the President and Vice President shall end at noon on the 20th day of January, and the terms of Senators and Representatives at noon on the 3d day of January, of the years in which such terms would have ended if this article had not been ratified; and the terms of their successors shall then begin.

Section 2. The Congress shall assemble at least once in every year, and such meeting shall begin at noon on the 3d day of January, unless they shall by law appoint a different day.

Section 3. If, at the time fixed for the beginning of the term of the President, the President elect shall have died, the Vice President elect shall become President. If the President shall not have been chosen before the time fixed for the beginning of his term, or if the President elect shall have failed to qualify, then the Vice President elect shall act as President until a President shall have qualified; and the Congress may by law provide for the case wherein neither a President elect nor a Vice President elect shall have qualified, declaring who shall then act as President, or the manner in which one who is to act shall be selected, and such person shall act accordingly until a President or Vice President shall have qualified.

Section 4. The Congress may by law provide for the case of the death of any of the persons from whom the House of Representatives may choose a President whenever the right of choice shall have devolved upon them, and for the case of the death of any of the persons from whom the Senate may choose a Vice President whenever the right of choice shall have devolved upon them.

Section 5. Sections 1 and 2 shall take effect on the 15th day of October following the ratification of this article.

Section 6. This article shall be inoperative unless it shall have been ratified as an amendment to the Constitution by the legislatures of three-fourths of the several states within seven years from the date of its submission.

AMENDMENT XXI (1933)

Section 1. The eighteenth article of amendment to the Constitution of the United States is hereby repealed.

Section 2. The transportation or importation into any state, territory, or possession of the United States for delivery or use therein of intoxicating liquors, in violation of the laws thereof, is hereby prohibited.

Section 3. This article shall be inoperative unless it shall have been ratified as an amendment to the Constitution by conventions in the several states, as provided in the Constitution, within seven years from the date of the submission hereof to the states by the Congress.

AMENDMENT XXII (1951)

Section 1. No person shall be elected to the office of the President more than twice, and no person who has held the office of President, or acted as President, for more than two years of a term to which some other person was elected President shall be elected to the office of President more than once. But this Article shall not apply to any person holding the office of President when this Article was proposed by the Congress, and shall not prevent any person who may be holding the office of President, or acting as President, during the term within which this Article becomes operative from holding the office of President or acting as President during the remainder of such term.

Section 2. This article shall be inoperative unless it shall have been ratified as an amendment to the Constitution by the legislatures of three-fourths of the several states within seven years from the date of its submission to the states by the Congress.

AMENDMENT XXIII (1961)

Section 1. The District constituting the seat of Government of the United States shall appoint in such manner as the Congress may direct:

A number of electors of President and Vice President equal to the whole number of Senators and Representatives in Congress to which the District would be entitled if it were a state, but in no event more than the least populous state; they shall be in addition to those appointed by the states, but they shall be considered, for the purposes of the election of President and Vice President, to be electors appointed by a state; and they shall meet in the District and perform such duties as provided by the twelfth article of amendment.

Section 2. The Congress shall have power to enforce this article by appropriate legislation.

AMENDMENT XXIV (1964)

Section 1. The right of citizens of the United States to vote in any primary or other election for President or Vice President, for electors for President or Vice President, or for Senator or Representative in Congress, shall not be denied or abridged by the United States, or any state by reason of failure to pay any poll tax or other tax.

Section 2. The Congress shall have power to enforce this article by appropriate legislation.

AMENDMENT XXV (1967)

Section 1. In case of the removal of the President from office or of his death or resignation, the Vice President shall become President.

Section 2. Whenever there is a vacancy in the office of the Vice President, the President shall nominate a Vice President who shall take office upon confirmation by a majority vote of both Houses of Congress.

Section 3. Whenever the President transmits to the President pro tempore of the Senate and the Speaker of the House of Representatives his written declaration that he is unable to discharge the powers and duties of his office, and until he transmits to them a written declaration to the contrary, such powers and duties shall be discharged by the Vice President as Acting President.

Section 4. Whenever the Vice President and a majority of either the principal officers of the executive departments or of such other body as Congress may by law provide, transmit to the President pro tempore of the Senate and the Speaker of the House of Representatives their written declaration that the President is unable to discharge the powers and duties of his office, the Vice President shall immediately assume the powers and duties of the office as Acting President.

Thereafter, when the President transmits to the President pro tempore of the Senate and the Speaker of the House of Representatives his written declaration that no inability exists, he shall resume the powers and duties of his office unless the Vice President and a majority of either the principal officers of the executive department or of such other body as Congress may by law provide, transmit within four days to the President pro tempore of the Senate and the Speaker of the House of Representatives their written declaration and the President is unable to discharge the powers and duties of his office. Thereupon Congress shall decide the issue, assembling within forty-eight hours for that purpose if not in session. If the Congress, within twenty-one days after receipt of the latter written declaration, or, if Congress is not in session, within twenty-one days after Congress is required to assemble, determines by two-thirds vote of both Houses that the President is unable to discharge the power and duties of his office, the Vice President shall continue to discharge the same as Acting President; otherwise, the President shall resume the powers and duties of his office.

AMENDMENT XXVI (1971)

Section 1. The right of citizens of the United States, who are eighteen years of age or older, to vote shall not be denied or abridged by the United States or by any state on account of age.

Section 2. The Congress shall have power to enforce this article by appropriate legislation.

AMENDMENT XXVII (1992)

No law, varying the compensation for the services of the Senators and Representatives, shall take effect, until an election of Representatives shall have intervened.

BIBLIOGRAPHY

Alcorn, Randy C. *Is Rescuing Right? Breaking the Law to Save the Unborn.* Downers Grove, IL: InterVarsity Press, 1990.

Allison, Loraine. *Finding Peace After Abortion.* St. Meinrad, IN: Abbey Press, 1990.

Anderson, Richard. *Abortion Pro & Con.* Los Angeles, CA: Right to Life League, 1977.

Baird, Robert M. and Stuart E. Rosenbaum, Editors. *The Ethics of Abortion: The Continuing Debate.* Buffalo, NY: Prometheus Books, 1989.

Baker, Don. *Beyond Choice: The Abortion Story No One Is Telling.* Portland, OR: Multnomah Press, 1985.

Banks, Bill and Sue Banks. *Ministering to Abortion's Aftermath.* Kirkwood, MO: Impact Books, 1982.

Barry, Robert L. *Medical Ethics: Essays on Abortion and Euthanasia.* Billings, MT: Peter Lang Publications, 1989.

Baulieu, Etienne-Emile and Mort Rosenblum. *The "Abortion Pill": RU-486, A Woman's Choice.* New York, NY: Simon & Schuster, 1991.

Batchelor, Edward, Jr., Editor. *Abortion: The Moral Issues.* New York, NY: Pilgrim Press, 1982.

Berger, G. and W. Brenner, Editors. *Second Trimester Abortion.* Kluwer, N.V.: Kluwer Academic Publishers, 1981.

Bonavoglia, Angela, Editor. *The Choices We Made: 25 Women and Men Speak Out About Abortion.* New York, NY: Random House, 1991.

Bondesor, William B. and H. Tristram Engelhardt. *Abortion and the Status of the Fetus.* Kluwer, N.V.: Kluwer Academic Publishers, 1983.

Braun, Eric A. and LauraLee Gaudio. *Living with Your Choice: An Inner Healing for Abortion.* Sea Cliff, NY: Purelight, 1990.

Briscoe, Clarence C. *Abortion: The Emotional Issue.* Pittsburgh, PA: Dorrance Publishing Co., 1984.

Browder, Clifford. *The Wickedest Woman in New York: Madame Restelle, The Abortionist.* Hamden, CT: Archon Books, 1988.

Brown, Harold O.J. *The Bible on Abortion.* Minneapolis, MN: Free Church Publications, 1977.

Butler, J. Douglas and David F. Walbert, Editors. *Abortion, Medicine and the Law.* New York, NY: Facts on File, 1986.

Callahan, Sidney and Daniel Callahan. *Abortion: Understanding Differences.* New York, NY: Plenum Press, 1984.

Cohen, M., et al., Editors. *Rights and Wrongs of Abortion.* Princeton, NJ: Princeton University Press, 1974.

Condit, Celeste Michelle. *Decoding Abortion Rhetoric: Communicating Social Change.* Chicago: University of Illinois Press, 1990.

Connery, John. *Abortion: The Development of the Roman Catholic Perspective.* Chicago, IL: Loyola University Press, 1977.

Corsaro, Maria and Carole Korzeniowsky. *A Woman's Guide to Safe Abortion.* New York, NY: Holt, Rinehart & Winston, 1983.

Costa, Maria. *Abortion: A Reference Handbook.* Santa Barbara, CA: ABC-CLIO, 1991.

Coughlan, Michael J. *The Vatican, the Law and the Human Embryo.* Iowa City, IA: University of Iowa Press, 1990.

Cozic, Charles and Tracey Tipp, Editors. *Abortion: Opposing Viewpoints.* San Diego, CA: Greenhaven Press, 1991.

Cunningham, Paige C., et al., Editors. *Abortion and the Constitution: Reversing Roe v. Wade Through the Courts.* Washington, DC: Georgetown University Press, 1987.

Curtzinger, G. *Abortion, Person as Thing.* Mansfield, TX: Latitudes Press, 1988.

Davis, John J. *Abortion and the Christian.* Phillipsburg, NJ: Presbyterian & Reformed Publishing Co., 1984.

Devereux, George. *A Study of Abortion in Primitive Societies.* Madison, CT: International Universities Press, 1976.

Doerr, Edd and James W. Prescott, Editors. *Abortion Rights and Fetal "Personhood."* Long Beach, CA: Centerline Press, 1990.

Emmens, Carol A. *The Abortion Controversy.* New York, NY: Julian Messner, 1987.

Erdahl, Lowell O. *Pro-Life, Pro-Peace: Life Affirming Alternatives to Abortion, War, Mercy Killing, and the Death Penalty.* Minneapolis, MN: Augsburg Fortress Publishers, 1986.

Faux, Marian. *Crusaders: Voices From the Abortion Front.* Secausus, NJ: Carol Pub. Group, 1990.

Faux, Marion. *Roe v. Wade: The Story of the Landmark Supreme Court Decision That Made Abortion Legal.* New York, NY: Macmillan, 1988.

Feinberg, Joel, Editor. *The Problem of Abortion.* Belmont, CA: Wadsworth Publishing Co., 1984.

Ferraro, Barbara, and Patricia Hussey, with Jane O'Reilly. *No Turning Back: Two Nuns' Battle With the Vatican over Women's Right to Choose.* New York, NY: Poseidon Press, 1990.

Flanders, Carl N. *Abortion.* New York, NY: Facts on File, 1991.

Forelle, Helen. *If Men Got Pregnant, Abortion Would be a Sacrament.* Sioux Falls, SD: Tesseract Publications, 1991.

Fowler, Paul. *Abortion: Toward an Evangelical Consensus.* Portland, OR: Multnomah Press, 1987.

Francke, Linda Bird. *The Ambivalence of Abortion.* New York, NY: Random House, 1978.

Francome, Colin. *Abortion Freedom: A Worldwide Movement.* New York, NY: Unwin Hyman, 1984.

Gardner, Joy. *A Difficult Decision: A Compassionate Book About Abortion.* Trumansburg, NY: Crossing Press, 1986.

Garfield, Jay L. and Patricia Hennessey, Editors. *Abortion: Moral and Legal Perspectives.* Amherst, MA: University of Massachusetts Press, 1985.

Gaylor, Anne N. *Abortion is a Blessing.* New York, NY: Psychological Dimensions, 1976.

Ginsburg, Faye D. *Contested Lives: The Abortion Debate in an American Community.* Berkeley: University of California Press, 1989.

Glessner, Thomas A. *Achieving an Abortion-Free America by 2001.* Portland, OR: Multnomah Press, 1990.

Goldstein, Robert D. *Mother-Love and Abortion: A Legal Interpretation.* Berkeley, CA: University of California Press, 1988.

Grady, John L. *Abortion: Yes or No?* Rockford, IL: TAN Books Pubs., 1968.

Grenier-Sweet, Gail, Editor. *Pro-Life Feminism: Different Voices.* Lewiston, NY: Life Cycle Books, 1985.

Hall, Robert E., Editor. *Abortion in a Changing World.* NY: Columbia University Press, 1970.

Harris, Harry. *Prenatal Diagnosis and Selective Abortion.* Cambridge, MA: Harvard University Press, 1975.

Harrison, Beverly Wildung. *Our Right to Choose: Toward a New Ethic of Abortion.* Boston: Beacon Press, 1983.

Harrison, Maureen, and Steve Gilbert. *Landmark Decisions of the United States Supreme Court, Vol. I.* Beverly Hills, CA: Excellent Books, 1991.

Hern, Warren M. *Abortion Practice.* Boulder, CO: Alpenglo Graphics, 1990.

Hern, Warren M. *Abortion Services Handbook.* Durant, OK: Creative Informatics, 1978.

Hertz, Sue. *Caught in the Crossfire: A Year on Abortion's Front Line.* New York, NY: Prentice Hall, 1991.

Horan, Dennis J., Edward R. Grant and Paige C. Cunningham, Editors. *Abortion and the Constitution: Reversing Roe v. Wade Through the Courts.* Washington, DC: Georgetown University Press, 1987.

Howe, Louise K. *Moments on Maple Avenue: The Reality of Abortion.* New York, NY: Warner Books, 1986.

Ide, Arthur F. *Abortion Handbook: History, Clinical Practice and Psychology of Abortion.* Las Colinas, TX: Liberal Press, 1987.

Imber, Jonathan B. *Abortion and the Private Practice of Medicine.* New Haven, CT: Yale University Press, 1986.

Joyce, Robert and Mary R. Joyce. *Let's Be Born: The Inhumanity of Abortion.* Chicago, IL: Franciscan Herald Press, 1976.

Jung, Patricia Beattie and Thomas A. Shannon, Editors. *Abortion and Catholicism: The American Debate.* New York, NY: Crossroad, 1988.

Justus, Adalu. *Dear Mommy, Please Don't Kill Me.* Hesperia, CA: Silo Pubs., 1986.

Keemer, Edgar B. *Confessions of a Pro-Life Abortionist.* Detroit, MI: Vinco Press, 1980.

Keirse, M. and Bennebroek J. Gravenhorst, Editors. *Second Trimester Pregnancy Termination.* Kluwer, N.V.: Kluwer Academic Publishers, 1982.

Kenyon, Edwin. *The Dilemma of Abortion.* Winchester, MA: Faber & Faber, 1986.

Kerr, Fred W. *Ninety Days for Life: The Jailhouse Journal of "Operation Rescue" Internee, Fred W. Kerr.* Hannibal, MO: Hannibal Books, 1989.

Koerbel, Pam. *Does Anyone Else Feel Like I Do?* New York, NY: Doubleday, 1990.

Kogan, Barry S., Editor. *A Time to be Born and a Time to Die: The Ethics of Choice.* Hawthorne, NY: Aldine de Gruyter, 1991.

Krason, Stephen M. *Abortion: Politics, Morality, and the Constitution: A Critical Study of Roe v., Wade and Doe v. Bolton and a Basis for Change.* Lanham, MD: University Press of America, 1984.

Lader, Lawrence. *Abortion.* New York, NY: Macmillan, 1966.

Lader, Lawrence. *RU-486: The Pill That Could End the Abortion Wars and Why American Women Don't Have It.* New York, NY: Addison-Wesley, 1991.

Lee, Nancy H. *Search for an Abortionist.* Chicago: University of Chicago Press, 1969.

Legge, Jerome S., Jr. *Abortion Policy: An Evaluation of the Consequences for Maternal and Infant Health.* Albany, NY: State University of New York Press, 1985.

Luker, Kristin. *Abortion and the Politics of Motherhood.* Berkeley: University of California Press, 1984.

Luker, Kristin. *Taking Chances: Abortion and the Decision Not to Contracept.* Berkeley: University of California Press, 1975.

Lunneborg, Patricia W. *A Positive Decision*. New York, NY: Bergin & Garvey, 1992.

McCarthy, John F. *In Defense of Human Life*. Houston, TX: Lumen Christi Press, 1970.

McCartney, James J. *Unborn Persons: Pope John Paul II and the Abortion Debate*. New York, NY: Peter Lang Publishing, 1988.

McDonnell, Kathleen. *Not An Easy Choice: A Feminist Re-examines Abortion*. Boston: South End Press, 1984.

Mall, David. *In Good Conscience: Abortion and Moral Necessity*. Columbus, OH: Kairos Books, 1982.

Mannion, Michael T. *Abortion and Healing: A Cry to Be Whole*. Kansas City, MO: Sheed & Ward, 1986.

Melton, Gary B., Editor. *Adolescent Abortion: Psychological and Legal Issues*. Lincoln, NE: University of Nebraska Press, 1986.

Meyers, David W. *The Human Body and the Law*. Palo Alto: Stanford University Press, 1991.

Miley, LaVerne. *Abortion: Right or Wrong?* Nashville, TN: Randall House Publications, 1981.

Mohr, James C. *Abortion in America: The Origins and Evolution of National Policy, 1800-1900*. New York, NY: Oxford University Press, 1978.

Muldoon, Maureen, Editor. *Abortion: An Annotated Indexed Bibliography.* Lewiston, NY: Edwin Mellen Press, 1980.

Nathanson, Sue. *Soul Crisis: One Woman's Journey Through Abortion to Renewal.* New York, NY: New American Library, 1989.

National Issues Forum Staff. *The Battle Over Abortion: Seeking Common Ground in a Divided Nation.* Dubuque, IA: Kendall-Hunt Publishing Co., 1990.

Newman, Sidney H., et al., Editors. *Abortion, Obtained and Denied: Research Aproaches.* New York, NY: Population Council, 1971.

Noonan, John T., Jr. *A Private Choice: Abortion in America in the Seventies.* New York, NY: Free Press, 1979.

Norrie, Kenneth M. *Family Planning and the Law. Santa Cruz, CA: Gower Publishing Co., 1991.*

Odell, Catherine and William Odell. *The First Human Right: A Pro-Life Primer.* Huntington, IN: Our Sunday Visitor, 1983.

Paige, Connie. *The Right to Lifers: Who They Are, How They Operate, Where They Get Their Money.* New York, NY: Summit Books, 1983.

Pastuszek, Eric J. *Is the Fetus Human?* Avon, NJ: Magnificat Press, 1991.

Podell, Janet, Editor. *Abortion.* New York, NY: H.W. Wilson Co., 1990.

Powell, John. *Abortion: The Silent Holocaust.* Allen, TX: Tabor Publishing, 1981.

Reardon, David C. *Aborted Women: Silent No More.* Gaithersburg, MD: Human Life International, 1987.

Reisser, Teri K. and Paul Reisser. *Help for Post-Abortion Women.* Grand Rapids, MI: Zondervan Pub. House, 1989.

Reynolds, Brenda M. *Human Abortion: Guide for Medicine, Science and Research.* Washington, DC: ABBE Publishers Association, 1984.

Rice, Charles E. *Beyond Abortion: The Origin and Future of the Secular State.* Chicago, IL: Franciscan Herald Press, 1978.

Rodman, Hyman, et al. *The Abortion Question.* New York, NY: Columbia University Press, 1990.

Rodman, Hyman and Susan H. Lewis. *The Sexual Rights of Adolescents: Competence, Vulnerability, and Parental Control.* New York, NY: Columbia University Press, 1988.

Rosenblatt, Roger. *Life Itself: Abortion in the American Mind.* New York, NY: Random House, 1992.

Saltenberger, Ann. *Every Woman Has a Right to Know the Dangers of Legal Abortion.* Garrisonville, VA: Air-Plus Enterprises, 1983.

Sarvis, Betty and Hyman Rodman. *The Abortion Controversy.* New York, NY: Columbia University Press, 1974.

Sass, Lauren R., Editor. *Abortion: Freedom of Choice and the Right to Life.* New York, NY: Facts on File, 1978.

Scheidler, Joseph M. *Closed: 99 Ways to Stop Abortion.* Westchester, IL: Crossway Books, 1985.

Siegel, Mark A., Nancy R. Jacobs, and Patricia Von Brook, Editors. *Abortion: An Eternal Social and Moral Issue.* Wylie, TX: Information Plus, 1990.

Skolnick, Gary E. *Abortion: Index of Modern Information with Bibliography.* Washington, DC: ABBE Publishers Association, 1988.

Skowronski, Marjory. *Abortion and Alternatives.* Millbrae, CA: Les Femmes Publishers, 1977.

Sloan, Carole M. *Love, Abortion and Adoption of Carole Lovelee Williams.* Washington, DC: ABBE Publishers Association, 1988.

Sloan, Irving J. The Law Governing Abortion, Contraception and Sterilization. New York, NY: Oceana Publications, 1988.

Sloan, R. Bruce and Diana F. Horvitz. *A General Guide to Abortion.* Chicago, IL: Nelson-Hall, 1973.

Speckhard, Anne. *Psycho-Social Stress Following Abortion.* Kansas City, MO: Sheed & Ward, 1987.

Sproul, R.C. *Abortion: A Rational Look at an Emotional Issue.* Colorado Springs, CO: NavPress, 1990.

Steiner, Gilbert Y., Editor. *The Abortion Dispute and the American System.* Washington, DC: Brookings Institution, 1983.

Steinhoff, Patricia G. and Milton Diamond. *Abortion Politics: The Hawaii Experience.* Honolulu, HI: University of Hawaii Press, 1977.

Storer, Horatio R. and Franklin F. Heard. *Criminal Abortion.* Salem, NH: Ayer Co. Publishers, 1974.

Summerhill, Louise. *The Story of Birthright: The Alternative to Abortion.* Libertyville, IL: Prow Books, 1973.

Szumski, Bonnie, Editor. *Abortion: Opposing Viewpoints.* St. Paul, MN: Greenhaven Press, 1986.

Terkel, Susan Neiburg. *Abortion: Facing the Issues.* New York, NY: Watts, 1988.

Tickle, Phyllis, Editor. *Confessing Conscience: Churched Women on Abortion.* Nashville, TN: Abingdon Press, 1990.

Tooley, Michael. *Abortion and Infanticide.* New York, NY: Oxford University Press, 1986.

Tribe, Laurence H. *Abortion: The Clash of Absolutes*. New York, NY: Norton, 1990.

Wardle, Lynn D. *The Abortion Privacy Doctrine: A Compendium and Critique of Federal Abortion Cases*. Buffalo, NY: W.S. Hein & Co., 1980.

Weinberg, Roy D. *Family Planning and the Law*. Dobbs Ferry, NY: Oceana Publications, 1979.

Welton, K.B. *Abortion is Not a Sin: A New-Age Look at an Age-Old Problem*. Dana Point, CA: Pandit Press, 1988.

Wennberg, Robert. *Life in the Balance: Exploring the Abortion Controversy. Grand Rapids, MI: William B. Eerdmans Publishing Co., 1985.*

Whitney, Catherine. *Whole Life? A Balanced, Comprehensive View of Abortion From Its Historical Context to the Current Debate*. New York, NY: W. Morrow, 1991.

Wilt, Judith. *Abortion, Choice, and Contemporary Fiction: The Armageddon of the Maternal Instinct*. Chicago: University of Chicago Press, 1990.

Winden, Lori Van. *The Case Against Abortion: A Logical Argument for Life*. Ligouri, MO: Liguori Publications, 1988.

INDEX

EXCELLENT BOOKS ORDER FORM

(Please xerox this form so it will be available to other readers.)

Please send

_____ copy(ies) of ABORTION DECISIONS: THE 1970's
_____ copy(ies) of ABORTION DECISIONS: THE 1980's
_____ copy(ies) of ABORTION DECISIONS: THE 1990's
_____ copy(ies) of LANDMARK DECISIONS
_____ copy(ies) of LANDMARK DECISIONS II
_____ copy(ies) of LANDMARK DECISIONS III
_____ copy(ies) of THE ADA HANDBOOK

Name: _____

Address: _____

City: _____ State: _____ Zip: _____

Price: $15.95 for ABORTION DECISIONS: THE 1970's
$15.95 for ABORTION DECISIONS: THE 1980's
$15.95 for ABORTION DECISIONS: THE 1990's
$14.95 for LANDMARK DECISIONS
$15.95 for LANDMARK DECISIONS II
$15.95 for LANDMARK DECISIONS III
$15.95 for THE ADA HANDBOOK

Add $1 per book for shipping and handling
California residents add sales tax

OUR GUARANTEE: Any Excellent Book may be returned at
any time for any reason and a full refund will be made.

Mail your check or money order to: Excellent Books,
Post Office Box 7121, Beverly Hills, California 90212-7121
or call (310) 275-6945